101 GREAT MAIL-ORDER BUSINESSES

The Very Best (and Most Profitable!)
Mail-Order Businesses You Can Start
with Little or No Money

Tyler G. Hicks

PRIMA PUBLISHING

PRIMA PUBLISHING and its colophon, which consists of the letter P over PRIMA, are trademarks of Prima Communications, Inc.

Library of Congress Cataloging-in-Publication Data
Hicks, Tyler Gregory
    101 great mail-order businesses : the very best (and most profitable!) mail-order businesses you can start with little or no money / by Tyler G. Hicks.
        p.   cm.
    Includes index.
    ISBN 0-7615-0337-4
    1. Mail-order business.   I. Title.
HF5466.H555   1995
658.8'72—dc20   95-38504
                                                          CIP

    98 99 HH 10 9 8 7

Printed in the United States of America

HOW TO ORDER

Single copies may be ordered from Prima Publishing, P.O. Box 1260HM, Rocklin, CA 95677; telephone (916) 632-4400. Quantity discounts are also available. On your letterhead, include information concerning the intended use of the books and the number of books you wish to purchase.

WHAT THIS BOOK CAN DO FOR YOU

Do YOU WANT to have your own business that can make you rich in just a few years? A business you can run from your home (if you wish), a business that can be started for just a few dollars? If you do, this book is for *you.*

The best business in the world—in my view—is the mail-order/direct-marketing business. Why do I say this? Because:

- **You can start** in just days—or sometimes in hours
- **On little cash,** all of which can be borrowed
- **Selling** products or services you like and enjoy
- **Earning** as much as you want
- **While choosing**—and enjoying—a lifestyle that makes you happy

This book shows you exactly how to start your own mail-order/direct-marketing business.

It gives you more than 101 great mail-order businesses you can start and succeed in—on small cash. If you're a budding business person—often called an *entrepreneur* today—this book is for *you!* It shows *you:*

1. **Why the multi-billion-dollar mail-order business** is so good for you
2. **How to pick** your wealth-building product or service—easily and quickly
3. **Which printed products** can make you rich—sooner than you might think
4. **How to serve hungry people**—by mail—the gourmet food they crave while making a bundle for yourself
5. **Ways to cater to** gadget enthusiasts everywhere while you watch your trinkets pile up
6. **Conveniences you can provide** to your customers that will earn big profits for you
7. **Unusual items to sell by mail** which will help you build a lifetime business for yourself

8. **How to use catalogs to sell year round,** all over the world, the products or services you like
9. **Steps to make services** make you wealthy—quickly and easily—in today's service-starved world
10. **Ways to offer offbeat services** while you watch customers fill your mailbox or ring your order phone
11. **Where to use** proven mail-order marketing success methods to outsell the competition and keep your cash register full at all times
12. **How to run your mail-order business** profitably, keeping more of each sales dollar for yourself

No matter what your interests are—fishing, hunting, boating, flying, sports, music, art (painting, sculpture), investing, real estate, exporting, importing, licensing, etc.— there's a way for *you* to make money in mail order while enjoying your interests. Could you ask for a better deal?

And you can make your mail-order money from *any* location *you* choose. Your home, your trailer, your apartment, your boat—pick it and the money will flow in. Your customers don't care where their products or services come from so long as what they order:

- **Arrives quickly**
- **In good condition**
- **And is superior value for the money**

This book shows you exactly how to supply products, or services, that meet, and exceed, these criteria.

You can start your business on little cash. And this cash can be borrowed, obtained from a line of credit, or taken from savings. Your suppliers don't care where your funds come from, so long as you can pay for your inventory. Soon your business supports itself. Before you know it, you're drawing a regular salary from your business. In a few months you can be driving a new car, living in a better home or apartment, dining at upscale restaurants, putting money into a savings account, and taking dream vacations.

People who work for you in your mail-order business don't have to be college graduates. Neither do *you*—many mail-order millionaires (and there are plenty of them) never saw the inside of a college classroom. Some of these millionaires think that the less education you have, the better. Others believe that a good education can help you in this business. So *you* can make it big with, or without, a formal education in the world's best business!

Lack of experience is *not* a drawback in mail order. Some of the biggest successes are people who never before sold anything by mail. Yet they had a dream of making it *big* in mail order. So what did they do? They found (or developed) a product and started advertising it by mail. Today they're living a life of ease with money pouring into their mailbox and credit card merchant account every day of the week.

Being handicapped, shy, reserved, or a loner won't hurt you in mail order. Why? Because you *never* need meet your customers face-to-face. You do it all by mail, or a combination of mail and wire. To speed results you can do many of your transactions by fax, computer, and phone, if you wish. But if you don't like the computer or the telephone and its fax attachments, stick to the mail. It has been making fortunes for people for some 200 years. And it will go on doing that for the next 200 years, no matter what anyone tells you about new ways to communicate!

The Internet and cyberspace bring catalogs and ordering methods to millions more people. But the product or service will still be delivered—in most cases—by mail or courier—to your home or office. The impact of these new ways of communicating, advertising, and promoting will be to increase sales beyond the wildest dreams of mail-order professionals—which you will soon be! So your future is brighter than ever before in the history of the world's best business. And *you* will soon be part of this bright future, earning your fortune in mail order!

Almost everyone in this world enjoys receiving something nice in the mail. Kids start with birthday cards from relatives. Many of these cards have something green inside—the "nice" part of the mail for kids. Adults are just grown-up kids. They too like to receive something "nice" in the mail—be it a new sweater, an electronic gadget, a book, a newsletter, etc. And—good friend—you can't send most of these items through a wire. You must have it delivered by a human being who gets it to your door via a motor vehicle and dependable feet!

So mail order *is* here to stay. And *you* can use mail order to make *your* life better, along with the lives of your loved ones. This book shows you exactly *how* to get started, *where* to find saleable products or services, *which* ways to promote and sell, *what* to watch out for to prevent problems, *when* to sell your wares for the highest profit, and *who* to sell to to get the most revenue in your business. You can quickly become a mail-order professional using the ideas and methods in this book.

And you *always* have a friend in your author. I'm as close to you as your telephone—day and night. When you run into a mail-order problem, just pick up your phone and call me. I'll answer on the first ring and give you a fast solution to your problem. So let's start—right now—to make *you a mail-order millionaire!*

Tyler G. Hicks

CONTENTS

Other Books by Tyler G. Hicks

How to Borrow Your Way to Real Estate Riches

How to Start Your Own Business on a Shoestring and Make Up to $500,00 a Year, 3rd Edition

How to Get Rich on Other People's Money: Going from Flat Broke to Great Wealth with Creative Financing

Mail Order Success Secrets: How to Create a $1,000,000-a-Year Business Starting from Scratch

199 Great Home Businesses You Can Start (and Succeed in) for Under $1000

Mail- Order Success Secrets

CHAPTER 1

KNOW TODAY'S MULTI-BILLION MAIL-ORDER SCENE

DO YOU WANT to get into the world's greatest multi-billion dollar business—

- Quickly and easily
- Starting with little cash of your own
- Without partners or a complicated corporation?

You can! And I'm ready to show you exactly how, and where, you can get into your own mail-order business (also called direct marketing) within days after you finish this book. You might even be able to start your own mail-order business before you finish this book! What's more, I'm ready to help you—personally—one-on-one—with any questions you may have.

Why should you seek my help? What can I offer you that others in mail order don't offer? Well, my mail-order businesses have made me millions. These great businesses allow me to buy beautiful yachts, luxury cars, commodious homes, vacations on warm and sunny beaches, while making generous contributions to my college alma mater and religion I practice.

Yet I started with little cash, less know-how, and only one homemade product! The second week I was in business just $7 came in. But not too long after, more than 1,000 times that was coming in each week! So I speak from front-line-trench experience. If anything can be, or has

1

been, done in mail order/direct marketing I'm doing it, or have done it. And I love to show newcomers how to get started—quickly and easily, on little cash!

See Why Mail Order Is Such a Great Business

In recent years there have been enormous social changes around the world. These changes are making mail order/direct marketing the world's greatest business—everywhere. Here are some of the more important recent social changes:

- *More wives are working than ever* before in history, leaving less time for in-store shopping. So these women shop by mail or phone, from the comfort of their own homes, making mail-order/direct-marketing a multi-billion dollar business.
- *Mail-order firms are much more reliable* than ever before in history. So people feel comfortable and safe buying big-ticket items by mail or phone.
- *Large mail-order/direct-marketing firms today offer stylish high-quality* products and services that are competitive with any downtown department store or urban mall. Shoppers recognize and love the convenience—and safety—of shopping from home.
- *Credit cards and toll-free 800 numbers* make mail or phone shopping a breeze. And the overnight delivery services—Federal Express, Airborne, TNT, United Parcel, etc.—make it possible to call today, order what you want, and have it on your kitchen or dining room table (or in your office) by 10 A.M. tomorrow morning. People love fast, reliable delivery. Mail order/direct marketing gives expedited delivery to every customer today!
- *"The Information Superhighway"*—commercially known as Internet's World Wide Web—now offers direct marketing of thousands of products and services to computer users—enormously increasing the market for all types of offers, giving you another gigantic outlet from which to earn big money! Competing networks offer you extra outlets, too.

You—I'm sure—are experiencing one or more of these social changes in your own life. And you've probably ordered a product or service using a toll-free phone number. If you have a credit card I'm sure you've used it to order something you wanted—either by mail or phone. So you know that these social changes which have made mail order/direct mail a multi-billion dollar business are for real! And customers all over the world are waiting for the great creative products or services you're about to offer them! So let's put you into the world's greatest business— right now!

To Start, Let's Get Our Names Clear

As you've noticed, we're using two names for this great business. These are *mail order* and *direct marketing*. To be sure we're all using the same names for each moneymaking activity, here's the meaning of each term, as used today:

> *Mail order* is the business of running ads in various suitable publications to produce sales directly from the ad, or inquiries, which are followed up by advertising material which you mail or fax to your customer to make the sale.

> *Direct marketing* is the business of selling directly to a customer using the mail (called *direct mail*), the telephone (called *telemarketing*), television, or radio. *Direct marketing* is the overall name for the other methods of selling (direct mail, telemarketing, TV, radio, etc.) because it describes the process that's used—i.e. you sell directly to your customer without using a middle seller such as a store, agent, or a mall. Instead, you use ads, the mail, telephone, TV, or radio to contact your customer and sell directly to him or her.

But common usage retains the name *mail order* to cover all these ways of selling.

While the term is inaccurate in view of today's expanded ways of selling, we use the term here in its common form. But as we go along in this book showing you ways to make your fortune in this great business we'll use the terms in the way they're defined above. Then there won't be any question as to what we're talking about.

Ten Ways to Make Mail-Order Millions Today

No matter what your likes and dislikes in life are, you can make millions in mail order today, doing something you enjoy. And to me, doing what you like is important! Why? Because:

> **Making money is a boring activity**—unless you enjoy what you're doing—just try it and see!

> **When you enjoy what you're doing, you do a better job;** this shows through to your customers and they come back to spend more money with you!

> **You and your business spread good throughout the world** because your enthusiasm and joy affect the lives of everyone you meet!

Let's see—right now—how people are doing what they like while making millions in mail order today. We'll give you ten examples of real-life, ongoing mail-order businesses that keep their owners in the top-earning echelons year after year. And you—too—can do the same with a product or service you like!

1. SELLING CONTACT LENSES BY MAIL

As we all know, contact lenses are very personal. The lenses that fit your eye curvature would probably never fit mine. So if a person can get his or her lenses delivered to the front door, or a post office box, they will probably buy this way. Why? Because going to the optometrist is a nuisance. People who wear soft contact lenses—and there are about 6 million such wearers in the United States today—replace their lenses once or twice a month. How better to get your replacement lenses than by convenient mail delivery?

Several firms sell contact lenses by mail today. One firm did $52 million in sales in a recent year. Future sales projections range up to $70 million a year. That's—as the man said—a lot of contact lenses! And the number of soft lens wearers is expected to rise to 10 million in just five years. So mail-order sellers have an unbeatable situation—a rising market along with greater acceptance of mail-order sales and delivery of the product. While contact lenses may not be your favorite product, this real-life business does show you some of the potential for mail order in the future—for you and your loved ones!

2. MAIL-ORDER SALES OF COMPUTERS

All of us know about the tremendous impact computers have had on our lives (and particularly in the mail-order business). Multi-billion dollar companies are being built on mail-order sales of computers. One of these outstanding firms started in a college dormitory room. Today this firm has a full line of personal and office computers that it sells from an enormous warehouse. It has customers around the world.

When you sell computers by mail you're talking big bucks. No longer does the mail marketer talk about a $10, $20, or $30 product. With computers by mail you're talking about $1,500, $2,000 or $3,000 products. So your income from a sale is really significant. And if you make enough sales your total income can be in the multi-millions. One mail-order computer company—the one started in a dorm room now has sales in the $5-billion range! So you see, we're talking big numbers.

3. MAIL-ORDER SALES OF CHEESES

This is another specialty business that generates sales in the multi-millions every year. To succeed in such a business it's wise to locate in a cheese-producing area—such as Wisconsin. While holiday sales are big for such firms, many mail their catalog year-round. People who like cheese dine on it every month of the year.

Selling cheese by mail is a safe type of food business. Why? Because cheeses don't spoil during shipment. And most cheeses are small in size and lightweight. So you don't have any serious shipping problems. And you can use the courier services to get the cheese into the hands of your customers overnight. This pleases your customer and improves your cash flow. Could you ask for a better business?

4. MAIL-ORDER SALES OF STEAKS

This is another excellent food-by-mail business. There are millions of steak lovers around the world who will pay high prices for a lean cut of beef or any other available meat. And these slices can be frozen and shipped overnight so they can easily be slipped into a freezer on arrival.

As with cheeses, selling steaks by mail is a safe food business. Why? Because quality control is easy to maintain; products are lightweight; courier services gladly accept them for overnight shipment. Repeat sales are common. Once you get a steak enthusiast on your mailing list he or she will buy from you again and again. This cuts your marketing costs to almost zero—shooting your profits to the sky! Steak sales in the multi-millions are easily achieved if you have a reliable source of good meat.

5. MAIL-ORDER SALES OF NEWSLETTERS

Again, this is a proven way to make mail-millions today. At this writing there are nearly 5,000 for-profit newsletters published in the United States. And almost all of these earn a profit for their publisher from their early issues. Why is this? Because newsletter costs are easy to control. You can start a newsletter with just a few dollars and build its income as you expand the number of subscribers to your publication.

My own newsletter, *International Wealth Success*, is now in its thirtieth year of continuous publication, 12 times a year. It has brought in millions of dollars and is circulated throughout the world. Readers write us letters telling us about their business success using some of the ideas we suggest to them. Costing only $24 a year, you can order your subscription by sending a check or money order for this amount to IWS, Inc., POB 186, Merrick, NY 11566-0186. You'll get plenty of good ideas and financing sources every month you read this great newsletter. Figure 1-1 gives you a quick view of the typical contents of an issue of my newsletter.

My newsletter, called *IWS* for short, is a *consumer* newsletter. This means that "the man or woman in the street," reads the letter. *Business newsletters,* by comparison,

INTERNATIONAL WEALTH SUCCESS, Inc.

THE WORLD WIDE MONTHLY NEWSLETTER OF UNUSUAL BUSINESS OPPORTUNITIES FOR WEALTH BUILDERS

Twelve BIG Issues each year bring you profitable money–making ideas you can use anywhere, anytime. Here are a few ways you are shown to help you on your path to GREAT riches.

- ☛ 100%, 110%, 115% FINANCING (MONEY) SOURCES
- ☛ COMPENSATING BALANCE loan sources
- ☛ NEW WEALTH IDEAS EVERY MONTH
- ☛ MANY, many sources of BUSINESS LOANS
- ☛ Part-time MONEY-MAKING IDEAS
- ☛ MAIL-ORDER RICHES opportunities
- ☛ FINDER FEE listings of many types
- ☛ WORLDWIDE money-making ideas for YOU
- ☛ FAST–FORTUNE money-making wealth deals
- ☛ FRANCHISE RICHES ideas and METHODS
- ☛ CAPITAL AVAILABLE pages in each issue
- ☛ Monthly TY HICKS PAGE where Ty talks to YOU
- ☛ FINANCIAL BROKER OPPORTUNITIES
- ☛ CO-SIGNER LISTINGS for YOU and others
- ☛ Ways to Get Money you need for business
- ☛ UNUSUAL TECHNIQUES you can use to grow
- ☛ SECRETS that can put cash in your pocket
- ☛ Hundreds of Wealth ideas each year

See a sample page
from a recent issue
of the IWS Newsletter

* * *

**16 or more pages
each month!**

➡ ⇨ ➡ ⇨ ➡ ⇨

SUBSCRIBE TODAY— *only $24 per year brings you this up-to-date NEWSLETTER!*

ONE IDEA FROM ONE ISSUE COULD MAKE YOU WEALTHY FOREVER.

FILL IN THE COUPON BELOW: ENCLOSE YOUR CHECK OR MONEY ORDER **NOW!**
YOU'LL BE GLAD YOU DID. **MAIL TODAY!**

☎ Credit Cards Orders only: **1-516-766-5850** Operators cannot answer questions ☎

INTERNATIONAL WEALTH SUCCESS, **INC. BOX 186, MERRICK, N.Y. 11566**
Here's my $24 for a one–year subscription to the
INTERNATIONAL WEALTH SUCCESS Newsletter,
Begin my subscription with the CURRENT ISSUE!

BONUS ITEMS FOR YOU WHEN YOU SUBSCRIBE TO THE IWS NEWSLETTER

★**MAIL ORDER LENDERS LIST** shows many sources of mail-order loans for people in business

★**HOW TO BORROW YOUR WAY TO GREAT RICHES**—a 24 pg. booklet by Ty Hicks showing the how, where and why!

NAME _____

STREET _____

CITY _____ STATE _____ ZIP _____

To order by credit card please give the following information:
Card No. _____ Expiration Date _____

Home Phone # _____ Signature _____

WHEN YOU SEND US YOUR $24.00 FOR YOUR FIRST YEAR'S SUBSCRIPTION TO THE IWS NEWSLETTER, YOU can also send us 1 or more ads to run FREE in the first issue in which space is available! Send us a different ad for each month and we'll run one after the other! Do NOT run the same ad every month! It won't pull as well!

Overseas subscribers add $18 U.S. for Air Mail delivery. NO extra charge for surface mail.

HELP YOU CAN GET FROM IWS AT NO EXTRA COST! When You subscribe:

★ Talks with Ty Hicks, either in person or via phone

★ Review of Loan Packages for suggestions as to how package may be improved.

★ Review of Mail Order promotion to see what can be done to make it pull better

---

Figure 1-1. Typical newsletter order page and coupon.

are read by people in a specialized field. Thus, you'll find
newsletters for nurses, attorneys, engineers, accountants,
etc. Such newsletters are often priced much higher than
consumer newsletters. Favorite prices for business newsletters are $395 and $495 per year. With 1,000 subscribers
to such a business newsletter your annual income will be either $395,000 or $495,000 per year. Then if you sell related
materials to your subscribers—such as books or kits—your
income will be higher. With two or three such newsletters
you can easily bring in $1 million a year!

So if you like helping people with the written word,
consider starting a mail-order newsletter business. It will
help you live a dream life with lots of challenges, beautiful
vacations, and stacks of money in the bank!

6. Sell Software by Mail Order

We all know about the computer revolution that started
with mail-order sales of electronic components for computer hackers out of a garage in California. The two young
men who started the mail-order business decided to start
selling an entire computer—which they called the Apple.
The rest is history. Even IBM joined the market with its famous PC-Personal Computer.

Software developers soon offered programs for the
Apple and PC—mostly by mail. And today, well into the PC
revolution, millions of dollars of software is sold every year
by mail. Here's one real-life example of mail-order software
sales:

> **A software developer took out ads for its product line**
> in three magazines serving the business field. The developer
> spent $70,000 on ads and made sales of $4.33 million from
> the ads. Thus, they made 62 times their ad cost in sales! This is
> a spectacular ratio of sales to cost.

Now I can just hear you say—"They spent seventy-
thousand dollars on ads. I don't even have seven-thousand
dollars in the bank, Mr. Author. Get real!" Sure, I'll get real.
Suppose you spent just $700 on ads and the same ratio
held. You'd bring in $43,400 in sales. That's more than

many people make in a year. With $1,400 spent on ads you'd bring in $86,800. Now it's getting interesting, right? The point is—you *can* make money selling software by mail order—even on a tiny budget!

> **Another software developer spent $14,900 on a mailing** to 3,000 food brokerages using a compiled list. Sales totaled $282,750, or a 19 times ratio. On a mailing of 1,000 pieces they obtained 82 leads, or an 8.2% response. They converted 35.4% of these responses to sales. Again, you have an excellent return for the advertising money spent. (As an aside, a *compiled* list is one that's assembled from readily available sources, such as telephone books, membership lists, etc.)

Again, with the same ratio of sales to cost, you'd bring in $9,500 on a mailing budget of just $500. And—good friend—this $500 could be borrowed money. The person ordering from you doesn't know what paid for the mailing!

These examples show you how profitable mail-order sales of software can be. So if you're a computer "jock" you can really have fun making money selling software by mail. With almost the whole world not yet in the PC mode, you have a market of billions of people. Could you ask for anything better? Having fun while making money is the best that life can offer!

7. SELL BOOKS AND COURSES BY MAIL

All the world is trying to learn more today. And you can supply this hunger for knowledge by selling books and courses by mail. I've been doing this for some 30 years and it has made me a millionaire many times over. You—too— can do the same. It's much easier than you think.

What kinds of books and courses do I suggest you sell by mail? The best types of books and courses to sell by mail are how-to nonfiction covering topics like:

- **How to make money** in your own business
- **Where, and how,** to find a mate for a lasting love
- **How to fix** your car, house, boat, plane, etc.
- **Ways to repair** your credit while getting out of debt
- **How to get** a credit card of your choice

- **Recipes** to make mouth-watering specialty foods
- **Steps to develop** your skills in music, writing, singing, etc.
- **How to be** an income-tax return preparer
- **Earning money** repairing damaged plastics of any kind
- **How to be** a financial broker/consultant
- **Etc.**

There's almost no end to the subjects on which people will buy books and courses. You can make millions—like I have—selling books and courses you enjoy handling. For example, my specialty is books and courses on making money in a variety of what I call "paper businesses"—that is businesses in which you do not need a large factory, complicated machines, a big payroll, etc. Figure 1-2 shows a portion of our list of business books, which we sell throughout the world. Such books and courses may not turn you on. So I say:

1. **Sit down** with pencil and paper
2. **Figure out** what *you like to do*
3. **See what kinds** of books and courses are available on what you like to do
4. **Get prices** from the publishers
5. **Estimate** how many you can sell of each book or course
6. **Figure** your selling costs
7. **Compute** your profit
8. **Go ahead** if you can make money

It's that easy. And—as we move ahead in this book—I'll show you exactly how to take each of the above steps. And we'll use real-life examples of how you—too—can make your mail-order fortune selling books and courses that help people live better lives—today and tomorrow!

For the moment, let me give a real-life example of a book-selling BWB (Beginning Wealth Builder) I know of who told me:

He sold 100,000 copies of a book he wrote on how to become wealthy at a price of $10 each. All his sales were by mail order. Doing the "numbers" he brought in 100,000 × $10 = $1,000,000 from his self-published book. Yet he had never written a book before, never had sold by mail before! So you see, it CAN be done.

USEFUL BUSINESS BOOKS FOR PEOPLE SEEKING BUSINESS INFORMATION

Import/export, real estate, financing sources, manufacturers' reps, licensing, etc.

All books are 8.5 x 11 inches in size

BUSINESS CAPITAL SOURCES lists more than 1800 lenders of various types–banks, insurance companies, commercial finance firms, mortgage companies and others. 150 pages; $15.

SMALL BUSINESS INVESTMENT COMPANY DIRECTORY AND HANDBOOK lists more than 400 small business investment companies that invest in small businesses to help them prosper. Also gives tips on financial management in business. 135 pages; $15.

WORLDWIDE RICHES OPPORTUNITIES, Vol. 1. Lists more than 2500 overseas firms seeking products to import. Gives name of product(s) sought, or service(s) sought, and other important data needed by exporters and importers. 283 pages; $25.

WORLDWIDE RICHES OPPORTUNITIES, Vol 2. Lists more than 2500 overseas firms seeking products to import. (Does not duplicate Vol.1). Lists loan sources for some exporters in England. 223 pages; $25.

HOW TO PREPARE AND PROCESS EXPORT–IMPORT DOCUMENTS. Gives data and documents for exporters and importers, including licenses, declarations, free–trade zones abroad, bills of lading, custom duty rulings. 170 pages; $25.

HOW TO BORROW YOUR WAY TO REAL ESTATE RICHES using Government sources, compiled by Ty Hicks. Lists numerous mortgage loans and guidelines, loan purpose, amounts, terms, financing charge, types of structures financed, loan–value ratio, special factors. 87 pages; $15.

THE RADICAL NEW ROAD TO WEALTH by A. David Silver. Covers criteria for success, raising venture capital, steps in conceiving a new firm, the business plan, how much do you have to give up, economic justification. 123 pages; $15.

60–DAY FULLY FINANCED FORTUNE is a short BUSINESS Kit covering what the business is, how it works, naming the business, interest amortization tables, state securities agencies, typical flyer used to advertise; typical applications. 136 pages; $29.50 or $15 if you order with any $99.50 BUSINESS KIT.

CREDITS AND COLLECTION BUSINESS KIT is a 2–book kit covering fundamentals of credit business, using credits and collection methods, applications for credit, setting credit limit, Fair Credit Reporting Act, collection percentages, etc. Gives 10 small businesses in this field. 147 pages; $29.50 or $15 if you order with any $99.50 BUSINESS KIT.

MIDEAST AND NORTH AFRICAN BANKS AND FINANCIAL INSTITUTIONS lists more than 350 such organizations. Gives name, address, telephone & telex number for most. 30 pages; $15.

EXPORT MAIL ORDER. Covers deciding on products to export, finding suppliers, locating overseas firms seeking exports, form letters, listing of firms serving as export management companies, shipping orders, and more, 50 pages; $17.50.

PRODUCT EXPORT RICHES OPPORTUNITIES lists over 1,500 firms offering products for export–includes agricultural, auto, aviation, electronics, computers, energy, food, healthcare, mining, printing, robotics, etc. 219 pages; $21.50

DIRECTORY OF HIGH–DISCOUNT MERCHANDISE SOURCES lists more than 1,000 sources of products with full name, address, telephone number for items such as auto products, swings, stuffed toys, puzzles, oils and lubricants, cb radios, belt buckles, etc. 97 pages; $17.50.

CAN YOU AFFORD NOT TO BE A MILLIONAIRE? by Marc Schlechier. Covers international trade, base of operations, stationery, worksheet, starting an overseas company, metric measures, profit structure. 202 pages; $20.

HOW TO FIND HIDDEN WEALTH IN LOCAL REAL ESTATE by R.H. Jorgensen covers financial tips, self-education, how to analyze property for renovation, successful renovator is a "cheapskate," property management and getting the rents paid. 133 pages; $17.50.

HOW TO CREATE YOUR OWN REAL ESTATE FORTUNE by Jens Nielsen covers investment opportunities in real estate, leveraging, depreciation, remodeling your deal, buy and lease back, understand your financing. 117 pages; $17.50.

REAL ESTATE SECOND MORTGAGES by Ty Hicks covers second mortgages, how a 2nd mortgage finder works, naming the business, registering the firm, running ads, expanding the business, limited partnerships, etc. 100 pages; $17.50.

GUIDE TO BUSINESS AND REAL ESTATE LOAN SOURCES lists hundreds of business and real estate lenders, giving their lending data in very brief form. 201 pages; $25.

DIRECTORY OF 2,500 ACTIVE REAL-ESTATE LENDERS lists 2,500 names and addresses of direct lenders or sources of information on possible lenders for real estate. 197 pages; $25.

IDEAS FOR FINDING BUSINESS AND REAL ESTATE CAPITAL TODAY covers raising public money, real-estate financing, borrowing methods, government loan sources, venture money, etc. 62 pages; $24.50.

HOW TO BECOME WEALTHY PUBLISHING A NEWSLETTER by E. J. Mall covers who will want your newsletter, planning your newsletter, preparing the first issue, direct mail promotion, keeping the books, building your career. 102 pages; $17.50

NATIONAL DIRECTORY OF MANUFACTURERS' REPRESENTATIVES lists 6,000 mfrs reps from all over the United States both in alphabetical form and state by state, gives markets classifications by SIC. 752 pages; $28.80.

HOW TO MAKE A FORTUNE AS A LICENSING AGENT – shows the reader how to earn big fees bringing together one company wanting to license its industrial or entertainment products and another seeking to use these products. Gives examples of typical products licensed, agreements covering the licenses, plus where to find suitable items to license, etc. 66 pages; $15.00.

Enclosed is $_____. Please send me the items I've checked. (Send Check or Money Order or charge by phone–516-766-5850)

NAME _____

ADDRESS _____

CITY _____ STATE _____ ZIP _____

To order by Credit Card please include the following: Credit Card # _____ Expiration Date _____

Signature _____ Home Phone No. _____

Send order to IWS, Inc., 24 Canterbury Road, Rockville Centre, NY 11570

Figure 1-2. Book list order page for direct-mail promotion flyer.

Another BWB sells paper patterns for stuffed animals
from her home in New Mexico. Her three small children help
her pack and mail her lightweight products all over the world.
Her patterns have been so successful that she expanded into
cloth for animal bodies, stuffing materials, yarns and courses
for her customers. These, too, are light and easily mailed.
While she increases the family income and teaches her three
children the principles of business, she and her architect husband enjoy a superior life-style made possible by her extra income from her home-based mail-order business.

8. SELL CLOTHING BY MAIL

Millions of people buy clothing of all types by mail. And
this clothing can be of many different types, such as:

Work clothing—both casual and safety-based

Dress clothing—from tailored suits to tuxedos

Casual clothing of many types—for golfers, hunters, boaters,
drivers, aviators, etc.

Specialty items—shoes, sweaters, shirts, etc.

So if clothing is your interest, there's an enormous opportunity for you to make millions in mail order today.
Here's a recent example of actual clothing sales by mail:

A work-clothing seller mailed 147,053 catalogs to
prospects, on a budget of $150,000. Sales of $601,740 resulted, for a ratio of 4 times cost. Working the numbers, you
can see that the average sale was $66 with 9,117 orders, or a
6.2% response rate.

Most mail-order clothing sellers specialize in one or two
lines of clothing. Why is this? Because it's difficult—and expensive—to market a full line of clothing by mail. So if you
plan to sell clothing by mail, start with a specialty line you
like. Then you can expand from there to other lines as your
cash flow increases. The 4-to-1 ratio is a good one. Most
mail-order dealers feel that a 3-to-1 ratio is enough to make
them rich. But at 4-to-1 if you spend $500 on a mailing you
bring back 4 × $500 = $2,000 in sales! Do this every day and
you'll soon be rich!

9. "SELL" MONEY BY MAIL

Every business, and almost every individual, needs a loan at one time or another. You can "sell" money by mail to these needy businesses and individuals and make money for yourself. How? By acting as an agent for lenders offering:

- Business startup loans
- Business expansion loans
- Accounts receivable (what businesses are owed) loans
- Bridge loans to cover a shortfall between two deals
- Mortgage loans—first, second, third, etc.
- Personal loans for individuals
- Home equity loans; home refinancing
- Miscellaneous loans of all types for business and individuals

To make money in the selling of money by mail you run small classified ads in local and national publications. You will be inundated by responses. Then all you need do is separate the "bankable"—that is, lendable from the nonbankable, or nonlendable. You earn a commission from either the lender or the borrower on each loan that is made to your client. Selling money by mail is one of the simplest mail-order businesses there is. See the listings at the back of this book for several courses covering this great business. Figure 1-3 shows the contents our Financial Broker/Finder/Business Broker/Business Consultant Kit. This Kit is directed at helping a person get started "selling money."

10. RAISE FUNDS FOR GOOD CAUSES BY MAIL

Thousands of organizations need money for good causes. Typical of these causes for which you can raise money by mail include:

- Health research and improvement
- Care of disadvantaged children and adults
- Religions of many different beliefs
- Law enforcement and fire prevention organizations
- Protection against physical abuse, drunk driving, etc.

The list of fund-raising assignments you can get is almost endless. So you can pick the type of fund-raising you

How to MAKE BIG MONEY as a FINANCIAL BROKER/FINDER/BUSINESS BROKER/BUSINESS CONSULTANT

Become a FINANCIAL CONSULTANT/FINDER/BUSINESS BROKER/CONSULTANT! Some people call this the "best business anyone can get into!" Would YOU like to become a Financial Broker/Finder/Business Broker? You can! How? Read on!

If YOU like money, if YOU have ever had some type of job in business, if YOU want to help others, and if YOU like people, YOU can become a Financial Broker. All YOU need to do to start YOUR future in this great career is to use the IWS FINANCIAL BROKER/FINDER/BUSINESS CONSULTANT KIT: It shows YOU the how, where, when, and the way of this money-laden career. Here's why YOU need this great KIT. It gives YOU the ideas, methods, forms, and steps which YOU can use to get started. Here are some of the specific topics covered in detail in this great KIT!

- How to prepare your business announcement
- Developing a list of financial and business brokers
- Typical business loan application forms
- How to start your own financial broker office
- Where to locate business
- Doing business from your home
- How to get your letterhead and business cards
- How, and where, to contact money sources
- What to charge your clients for your help
- Finding clients all over the world
- 2,500 sources of business loans for you
- How to be a financial broker anywhere without needing a state or city license (this method has never been covered in print before – so far as we can determine.
- Typical financial broker/finder/business broker forms (113 pages of forms covering every aspect commonly met –from placement and processing agreements to financial statements for borrowers to commercial financing forms. You get a total of 41 forms, many of which YOU can use directly without changing a word!)
- Complete guide to becoming a highly paid business broker in your spare time
- Fees you can collect as a business broker
- Starting with NO license, NO test, NO exams
- Which industries pay the biggest fees to YOU
- How to become a highly paid business consultant (fees to $1,000 a day!)
- Kinds of problems financial brokers/finders/business brokers solve (get paid big to suggest ideas)
- Get contracts for annual consulting fee
- How to become a highly paid finder in your spare time (turn leisure into BIG cash)
- What finders do – and where •• and for what
- How much to charge for being a finder
- Typical finder–fee agreement you can use today
- How to pick a good plant site
- Taking a company public – Regulation 'A' offerings
- Terms used in the Regulation; what they mean
- How to write a selling prospectus
- Samples of forms to be used for Reg 'A'
- Irrevocable appointment of you as an agent
- Offering stock through underwriters
- Registering with the SBC for the offering
- Loan packages – how to prepare them for approval
- SBIC - Small Business Investment Companies -what they do, how you can use them
- Advertising and office mailing flier for your firm
- Typical bank letter of credit, typical surety bond for a business loan
- Plus four membership certificates in two colors suitable for framing and mounting in your office or den
- Plus much, much more to help YOU get started

Here's what some of the users say about this great FINANCIAL BROKER/FINDER/BUSINESS BROKER/CONSULTANT Kit:

"Received Financial Broker Kit yesterday morning. Using info in it, closed deal for $463,750 yesterday afternoon. Thank you. Best Regards." Tennessee.

"My financial brokerage business grossed $45,000 in first year. I am now working on starting a finance company." Virginia

"It was through your letter that I became a part-time financial broker, have been one for six months and have enjoyed several commissions!" Massachusetts

"...went out and borrowed $10,000 and bought a business brokerage representing small business opportunities. I was recently (1 year later) offered $25,000 for half of my brokerage." Pennsylvania

"My fee between two findings is $180,000." Montana

"I am underway and doing quite well. I have completed one merger deal and placed 2 loans for $75,000." Massachusetts

This great KIT contains 12 speed-Read books, a total of some 500 ages, 4 ready-to-frame membership certificates and costs only $99.50. Send your check or money order TODAY!

ABOUT THE AUTHOR

Tyler G. Hicks is the president of INTERNATIONAL WEALTH SUCCESS, INC., as well as the president of a large lending organization in New York. He is internationally recognized as the foremost expert on making money from scratch and is the best selling author of many books, including *How to Get Rich on Other People's Money, How to Start a Business on a Shoestring and Make Up to 500,000 a Year* and *How to Borrow Your Way to Real Estate Riches*. Over 2,000,000 people have read some of his books. He will provide free consultation for every buyer of this kit.

FREE CONSULTATION!

Yes, I do like money! And this sounds like the kind of business I've been looking for. Enclosed is $99.50 for the FINANCIAL BROKER/FINDER/BUSINESS BROKER/BUSINESS CONSULTANT KIT. (Air mail outside North America: add $60; there is no postage for surface – sea shipment.) I can consult with Ty Hicks as a Bonus for buying the KIT.

Name: ______________________

Street: ______________________

City: ______________________

State ______________________

Credit Card No.____________ Expiration Date________

Signature ____________ Telephone No.____________

Call (516) 766-5850 day or night to order by credit card.

SEND YOUR PAYMENT TO:

IWS, INC.
24 CANTERBURY RD.
ROCKVILLE CTR.
NY 11570

Figure 1-3. Full-page ad for self-study course sold by mail order/direct marketing.

want to do by mail. No matter what type of fund-raising you choose, you'll be paid a percentage of the money you raise. Typically this is 10%. But you can work out any acceptable deal you choose. Often, the percentage you're paid will decrease as the amount of money you raise rises.

You can aim your fund-raising at individuals. Or you can set your sights on corporations and other businesses. Much depends on the purpose for which you're raising the money. In a recent fund-raising assignment:

> **A mailing on special paper to corporations** raised over $400,000 for a camp serving handicapped people. Total cost of the mailing was in the $20,000 range. The mail-order firm's commission would likely be 10%, or some $40,000, if normal rules applied.

So you can do good while earning money for yourself in fund-raising. And—if you wish—you can combine fund-raising with other mail-order activities. Why is this? Because the same general equipment and people are used for fund-raising as for other mail-order activities. You can have the best of both worlds—if you wish! Again, you can spend much less on a mailing and still bring in big bucks for yourself. So don't let the big ad numbers frighten you. You can work with small numbers and still get rich!

Get in on Today's Billion-Dollar Mail-Order Wealth

You can now see that there's money to be made in mail order today. The 10 businesses listed above are just a fraction of the thousands in which you can make money—now, today, here! Not mentioned above are businesses that are building mail wealth for people selling:

Auto parts	Furniture, decorations
Home and garden tools	Vitamins, other health aids, etc.
Seeds, flowers, health foods	Boating, hunting, fishing equipment

Mail order is the greatest business ever invented! It can make you a millionaire—starting in your own home—faster than you think. In this great business you can:

- **Start small, and grow big, on little cash of your own** in a business that's fun to run.
- **Measure your results easily** and quickly by the size of your daily bank deposits.
- **Quickly find what works for you,** and what doesn't work, when you make a mailing or run ads.
- **Use your own creativity** to develop products that can compete head-on with some of the best firms anywhere.
- **Get data on your customers,** learning what they buy, for how much, and how often.
- **Sell day or night, holidays or weekends** without ever seeing your customer, or talking to him or her.
- **Have a steady cash flow without a job of any kind,** free of snarling, abusive bosses, with no worry—ever—of being laid off, downsized, excessed, or fired.
- **Do what some of the most profitable companies** in the world are doing—selling by mail—off your kitchen table.
- **Get out of the rat race,** off the slaughter-prone freeways, away from bosses who threaten to cut your life short with soul-crunching daily tension.

What I'm talking about is *your* freedom from money and job worries forever. That's right. Start your own mail-order business and *you* can be free forever! So let's start—right here and now—to put *you* into the world's greatest business—mail order. I'm here to help *you*, as *your* friend, day and night. Call me on the phone—I'll answer you on the first ring. And even if you need financing for your freedom business (mail order) I'm ready to help, if you're a two-year subscriber of my newsletter, described at the back of this book. If you want to visit me in my office, or have me visit you in your city, I'll do it—at your convenience!

Let's get going—good friend of mine!

CHAPTER 2

PICK YOUR WEALTH-BUILDING PRODUCT OR SERVICE

IN MAIL ORDER today you sell either a product or service. Thus, you might sell products like books, clothing, flowers, candy, food, etc. Or you might sell a service such as income-tax preparation, astrological advice, or training in auto mechanic skills.

Of the two—products or services—most Beginning Wealth Builders (BWBs) in mail order opt for products. Why is this? Because products:

- **Are easier to understand** since you can see, feel, and hold most products
- **Can be shipped easily** in one package and normally don't require any after-sale service by you, the seller
- **Can be priced more readily** than most services since a product has an inherent value based on its material and manufacturing cost
- **Are often developed by creative BWBs** who detect a need based on their knowledge of people, business, sports, or other specialty areas

Let's assume—for now—that sale of products by mail order interests you. We'll guide you through the steps of picking a winning mail-order product. Once we do this, we'll assume that you want to pick a service to sell by mail. We'll then guide you through the steps in picking a winning service to sell by mail. Either way, you'll be on your way to building great mail-order wealth in your own business.

Select a Product You Like

Getting rich has to be fun. If it isn't fun, it isn't worth the effort! Why do I say this? Because getting rich in mail order:

- **Takes time** and energy from your life
- **Is hard work**—there's no way out of the work requirement
- **Can be boring** if you don't enjoy what you're doing

When you're having fun in your work it shows through to your customers. They see that you like what you're doing. This makes them more likely to buy what you offer. So your sales increase. More money pours into your mailbox every day. You get happier, your business expands some more. And more customers come flocking to your order desk via mail, fax, or phone!

To have your business build in this delightful way, get a pencil or pen and some paper. Sit down at a table or your desk and prepare a list of headings thus:

What I Enjoy Doing Most

AT WORK	AT PLAY	AT HOME
1._____	_____	_____
2._____	_____	_____
3._____	_____	_____

List each activity as accurately as you can. Thus, a person's list might look like this after he or she finished it:

1. Running my computer	Model airplane flying	Rebuilding kitchens & bathrooms
2. Figuring break-even point for sales	Building controls for model aircraft	Drawing plans for "dream" houses
3. Talking to people about work topics	Playing pocket billiards	Sleeping as much as I can

Glance over the list above. What possible product ideas might you extract from this list? Here are some you might see:

Work-related products:

Instructions for running computers better

Book(s) on figuring break-even point for various businesses

"Play"-related products:

Model airplanes that fly

Controls for flying models

Instructions for pocket billiards

Home-related products:

Tools and/or instructions for rebuilding kitchens and bathrooms

Plans for dream houses—either from stock sets, or specially prepared for the customer at his or her request

Sleep aids—eye shades, special sheets or blankets, heaters, carbon-monoxide detectors, etc.

Assuming—for a moment—that this is your list, go through it and pick:

1. My favorite product in the list
2. My second most favored product
3. My third most favored product

Let's say your list looks like this:

1. Flying model airplanes
2. Computer instructions
3. Plans for dream houses

What kinds of products might you develop (or buy from others) that you might sell by mail order, using this list as a start? Here are a few such products:

1. Specially built flying model airplanes
2. Parts, and/or, plans for flying model airplanes

3. Computer instructions in the form of quick-to-use reports that are easily read by the computer operator while on the job

4. Stock (off-the-shelf) plans of dream houses you prepare yourself, or have others prepare for you

Let's look at each of these product possibilities, keeping in mind these important facts about mail-order products:

1. **The best-selling products** are usually those you develop yourself because you see a need for them

2. **You will earn more money** from a product you develop yourself than you will from a product you buy from a supplier who's making a profit on the sale to you

3. **The largest profit is usually made** on a product you make yourself—that is, manufacture, print, carve, etc.

Starting with the product-possibilities list above, let's put them to "the test" of practical mail-order sales:

1. Specially built flying model airplanes would take time and labor to build. Unless you want spend your time holed up in a model shop, this product really is not too attractive for mail-order sales. Further, the price you'd have to charge for each model would take it out of the normal mail-order market. If you want to build museum-grade models, then you really won't be in the mail-order business as we see it in this book. So we suggest you drop any idea that requires a large labor input, takes a long time to complete, and must carry a high price to repay the time and labor investment.

2. Parts, and/or plans for flying model airplanes have a much greater potential for mail-order sales. Why is this? Here are the reasons:

   • Parts are usually small, lightweight, easily shipped
   • Parts are often simple—you might be able to make some of these yourself, raising your profit
   • Parts can be bought at low cost from suppliers; you can mix these with your own-make parts giving you a competitive line that can sell well
   • Plans are lightweight, easily shipped, popular with modelers

- Plans can be drawn by yourself; or you can hire a drafter for a nominal fee to do the drawing
- Plans can be copied on a standard copying machine in your own home at low cost

In summary, parts and plans offer exciting mail-order possibilities for you. We'll keep them in mind as we review the other products on your list.

3. Computer instructions that are easy to read and apply have a real potential because there are millions of computers in use around the world. You can easily reach the operators of these computers with ads in computer magazines, mailings to computer owners, and bulletin-board notices on the Internet, CompuServe, Prodigy, World Wide Web, or America Online.

   And since most people are in a hurry today, you can keep your operating tips short and still charge a profit-making price for them. Could you ask for anything better? What's more, you can fax your instructions to your customers, after taking their order by credit card over the phone. This kind of delivery is in keeping with the rushed attitude most people have today. So we'll keep computer printed instructions as one of our star products for our future mail-order business.

4. Plans for dream houses are always marketable by mail order. Why? Because millions of people—the world over—are looking for their "dream" house. And the people seeking such a house usually have enough money to be able to pay for one set of plans after another.

   What's more, plans are easy to mail. You can send them flat, or rolled, depending on your customer's preference. And a good set of plans can be priced at anywhere from $25 to $500, depending on their completeness the market you're serving. Since your customers are thinking of spending at least $100,000 on their dream home, a few hundred dollars for a set of plans is a really small outlay. With this in mind, we'll keep dream-house plans as one of our potentially "hot" mail-order products in the forefront of our strategic thinking.

5. In the sleep-product world there is great attention today on alarms that can prevent us from becoming victims of

fire or, more insidiously, carbon monoxide—the odorless, colorless, and deadly gas that's a by-product of the burning of oil, gas, gasoline, and coal. Alarms are ideal mail-order products. They're lightweight, easy to ship, simple in design, and won't harm anyone.

One slight disadvantage of alarms is that you usually can't make them yourself; they're just too complex. But you *can* buy alarms at bargain prices and sell them at profit-making markups by mail, TV ads, and online shopping. People want to protect themselves and their families from deadly night and daytime fires. You can cash in on this desire—right now!

So what have we learned about selling *products* by mail order? We've learned a lot. Let's summarize what we've learned so you can apply it to the products you might want to sell by mail order, starting in the next few days:

1. **The best mail-order products** are those you develop yourself, based on a need you see for the product—either by consumers (the man or woman "in the street") or by businesses of any type.
2. **Products using lots of your time and labor are unlikely to make money** for you in mail order because you must price them at too high a level. Further, you cannot get the large volume sales that make mail-order fortunes quickly and easily.
3. **Your mail-order product must be safe to use.** Avoid products that might burn, explode, poison, or otherwise harm customers. Don't deal with any products that are illegal, prohibited, or unsafe. It isn't worth the worry and fear that are part of handling dangerous or illegal products.
4. **Seek lightweight products.** They're cheaper to ship, easier to package, and require less labor for handling. What's more, you can get a strong marketing advantage by paying for shipping. And with really lightweight products you can use Priority Mail or one of the courier services (Federal Express, United Parcel, etc.) to get your product into your customer's hands quickly and efficiently. Fast delivery makes your customer happy and less likely to return the product for a refund.

Is it worth your while to carefully qualify a product before taking it on for mail-order sales? It sure is! Take a look at these recent results in selling products by mail order/direct marketing:

363,345 moneymaking venture programs were sold in one year by a mail-order firm

91,333 astrology products were sold by another mail-order firm during one year

284,481 financial opportunity book sales were made by a third firm in two years

Just do a little mental arithmetic on these sales. Suppose that each of the products above gave the seller a profit of just $1.00. The profit would be $363,345, or $995 per day, based on a 365-day year for the first product. (Note that this is almost $1,000 a day, *every day* of the year for the moneymaking programs!) The astrology products, with a $1.00 per unit profit would give you a cash flow of $250 a day, every day of the year. And the opportunity books would give you a cash flow of $779 a day—every day—Saturday, Sunday, and holidays!

So it *is* worthwhile to carefully choose your product to build your mail-order riches. In coming chapters we'll give you more than 100 great products that can build *your* fortune quickly and easily in the world's greatest business—mail order. Figure 2-1 shows the flyer we use for our Venture Capital Millions Kit, a product that has sold widely around the world.

Choose a Service to Sell by Mail Order

Now that we know how to pick a money-making product, let's turn to services that can make *you* millions in mail order/direct marketing. Some BWBs prefer to sell a service, instead of a product. We'll start by listing a few of the services you might offer:

find VENTURE CAPITAL millions

Become an IWS VENTURE CAPITAL PROFESSIONAL and get the BIG benefits YOU can use NOW

**Nearly instant CASH FLOW to YOU!
**Start a sizeable yearly income!
**Be in business quickly--NOW!
**Fast respect from others!
**Earn by mail, by phone, or by both
**Get money for clients or yourself!
**Go from no-cash-flow to steady cas
**Use the ONE-HOUR FINANCIAL WINNER!

Become an IWS VENTURE CAPITAL PROFESSIONAL and YOU get FOUR FAST WAYS to earn big!

**Be PAID to tell if a business idea is good!
**Be PAID to have a business plan written by others!
**Be PAID to find a venture capitalist to fund the deal!
**Be PAID for a piece of the success action--for years!

Get help ALL ALONG the way--while getting paid for getting others to do the work:

YOU get PAID while we evaluate the idea for YOU!
YOU get PAID while a business plan is written by others!
YOU get PAID while we find the venture capitalist for YOU!
YOU get PAID from future company growth--NO fees to us--ever!

GET IN ON THE BIG TIME NOW! How? By sending for the newest IWS Kit--THE VENTURE CAPITAL MILLIONS ONE-HOUR FINANCIAL WINNER! This breakthrough in venture-capital funding shows YOU how to:

°Raise venture funds fast
°Earn BIG fees sooner
°Get ongoing income for years
°Work where, and when, YOU want to
°Have others do the "nitty-gritty" for YOU
°Get started in just one hour, or less
°Be a professional, respected by all in your area
°Share in the newest deals in business and real estate
°Work without the need for a license of any kind

Anyone interested in money, business or real estate can use THE VENTURE CAPITAL MILLIONS KIT! For someone just starting, it's the sure way to local "insider" deals of all kinds. And YOU can start in one hour, or less, if you want!

For brokers, finders, and business people it can be the source of NEW MONEY, much of which never has to be repaid! It can expand your world--go from small, puny deals to the BIG-TIME millions!

So send NOW for the Kit that could change your life! Or call IWS and pu your order in by credit card. Be the first in YOUR area to offer venture capital professional services for an firm needing help from YOU!

Here's $100. Send me my VENTURE CAPITAL MILLIONS KIT. If you wish, YOU can call Ty Hicks at 516-766-5850 day or night to order by credit card. Or enter your card number below and send this coupon to IWS, Inc., 24 Canterbury Rd, Rockville Centre NY 11570.

NAME__________ CARD NO.__________

ADDRESS__________ EXPIRES__________

CITY__________ STATE__________ ZIP__________

Buy this month and get Special Venture Capital List on self-adhesive labels updated every six months for one year!

Figure 2-1. Full-page ad for study program sold via mail order/direct marketing.

1. **Finding money** for businesses and individuals
2. **Helping people "cash out" of a real-estate mortgage—** that is, get cash for a piece of paper they hold
3. **Searching for, and finding, grants** for organizations or individuals
4. **Assisting companies** seeking to import or export products for profit
5. **Teaching people new skills—**such as income-tax preparation, plastic countertop repair, auto air-conditioning maintenance, etc.
6. **Raising venture capital** for businesses needing funds to start up or expand
7. **Showing people how, and where, to buy foreclosed** real-estate properties
8. **Aiding people to take any other positive step** in their lives to improve themselves, their family, their financial situation, their health, etc.

Figure 2-2 illustrates a money-finding business and Figure 2-3 shows an export-import kit.

When you sell a service you're helping people in some way. While you may provide your customers with what appears to be a product (such as reference materials) they are really buying your help. Keep this in mind when you decide to offer any type of service by mail order/direct marketing.

To choose a service you'll enjoy selling, get your pen or pencil and paper again—as we did earlier. List what services you'd like to sell. Again, you *must* like what you're thinking of selling. Services that are popular with mail-order/direct-marketing customers include:

1. **Money—**almost every business and individual needs money at one time or another in their lives. So any service that finds loans for businesses or individuals is both popular and easy to sell. People will "knock down your door" when they learn that you can get money for them!
2. **Training—**this is the age of the educated worker. With millions of people laid off, terminated, downsized, or given early retirement, there is a strong retraining movement all over the world. You can help people transfer their skills to a new career by offering them training in a field you know and enjoy.

DO YOU WANT TO USE
MEGA-MONEY METHODS?
HERE'S HOW:

Do you know that MEGA-MONEY METHODS regularly raise $50-million, $100-million, $150-million for real-estate and business deals?

Such amounts *are* available for the *right* deals. And our new kit—MEGA-MONEY METHODS—shows you how to find, work with, and profit from such deals! These are *real deals*—not dreams of some amateur who never put a deal together. Here's what this *big* kit gives you:

1. What MEGA-MONEY deals really are
2. Examples of real-life recent mega-money deals and their amounts
3. Selected active MEGA-MONEY funders—people and firms with the money
4. How to structure the MEGA-MONEY deal so it works
5. Fees you earn with MEGA-MONEY deals after funding
6. Where to get as much as 116% no-cash funding! NO CASH NEEDED!

This powerful kit is the real answer to deals from $5-million to $999-million. It puts you in command of methods used by *big money* funders who deal in multi-millions. And it gives you the names, addresses, and telephone numbers of real-life MEGA-MONEY funders—the people really doing big deals today! Written by Ty Hicks, this *big kit* shows YOU:

- ¤ Proven ways to get MEGA-MONEY loans
- ¤ Loan package methods for FAST OKs
- ¤ Full info on MEGA-MONEY lenders
- ¤ Step-by-step borrowing methods
- ¤ A turnkey business for you from your own home anywhere
- ¤ Steps to earning BIG income

Get dozens and dozens of MEGA-MONEY METHODS like these fundings:

- ¤ Long-term mortgages
- ¤ Short-term mortgages
- ¤ Private money with *no* income check, *no* credit check, *no* points
- ¤ Interest-only loans
- ¤ Interim bridge loans for real estate
- ¤ Equipment leasing to $25-million with 24-hour approval
- ¤ We-start-where-banks-stop financing
- ¤ Immediate cash for accounts receivable
- ¤ Fast closings for all types of loans
- ¤ Unlimited funds available

You can run a MEGA-MONEY METHODS business on the side while you hold a normal job or run a small business of any kind.

This is a true spare-time business that can earn you profits if you put effort into the putting through of MEGA-MONEY deals.

Order your MEGA-MONEY METHODS KIT *today* for:

- ¤ Just $100 from IWS gets you started
- ¤ Those ordering from this ad get *TWO* big bonus items: "How to Package the BIG Loan", and "Unique MEGA-MONEY Loan Source Leads".

So get started today! Send check, money order, or call day or night to order by credit card. Get into the world of BIG $!

There is no other Kit like this available anywhere! If you want to enter the world of MEGA-MONEY METHODS, this kit is for *YOU!*

Enclosed is $100.00. Send me the *MEGA-MONEY METHODS KIT now.*		
NAME		
ADDRESS		
CITY	STATE	ZIP
To order by Credit Card please include: Credit Card #		Expiration Date
SIGNATURE	PHONE #	

(Send Check or Money Order or charge by phone—516-766-5850).
Send order to IWS., Inc. 24 Canterbury Rd. Rockville Centre, NY 11570.

*Figure 2-2. Full-page flyer for grants course sold
via mail order/direct marketing.*

How to
MAKE EXPORT-IMPORT RICHES

GET STARTED IN YOUR OWN EXPORTING BUSINESS (and in importing, if YOU wish) for less than $250! Earn big fees without ever having to touch what YOU sell. As this user of our big Kit writes:

"Enclosed is a copy of my first commission check from my export business. The sale was for $32,000 and my commission was $4,269.5 . Not bad for starting with $100 capital and your 'Import-Export Kit'. They are getting ready to order two more similar machines."

YOU CAN GET SIMILAR ORDERS! How? By using our BIG "Import-Export Kit" which gives YOU:

* 5000 ways to earn big fees for selling needed products all over the world
* Easy steps to take to do the simple papers used in both importing and exporting
* Simple letters YOU can mail or fax to your overseas customers to make sales fast
* Ways to work from YOUR home without ever having to travel further than your mail box
* Get BIG repeat orders which put large fees into YOUR pocket quickly and easily
* Ways to be paid through YOUR own bank with checks that will never, never bounce!
* Quick finance sources to give YOU loans or grants to operate YOUR business
* Personal help 800-number telephone line for on-the-spot answers to YOUR questions. Or if YOU can't call, an address to write or fax to get instant answers and help

ALL THESE BENEFITS CAN BE YOURS – sooner than YOU think! YOU can bring in big fees within days after making the first contact by mail or phone. One user of this Kit is making $30,000 per month profit after ALL costs after making just one phone call! YOU might be able to do the same, once YOU have this big Kit in YOUR hands.

With this BIG Kit on hand YOU'll have 99% of what YOU need to know to get started. The other 1% YOU get by doing – while YOU're being paid to learn! Other key data YOU get in this Kit are:

* How to avoid the 12 most common mistakes of potential exporters
* Directory of Federal and State export help YOU can get free of any charge
* Sources of assistance (including financing) by state - - there's more money around for YOU than YOU ever have tought!
* Contacts for top overseas markets -- people YOU can talk to or write or fax for big sales
* Typical forms used in export-import deals all over the world
* Easy, fast ways to get paid for the work YOU do in exporting and importing
* Building YOUR export-import business to the level that gives YOU the income you desire

DON'T WASTE ANY TIME: Get into export-import NOW! YOU'll be able to get away from nasty bosses, a slave-wage pay check, and constant threats of being fired.

BE YOUR OWN BOSS IN A BUSINESS WHERE YOU WORK only a few hours a day. Bring in big chunks of money every day of the year. Go from poverty to riches in just a few hours. Why scrimp and save to get what YOU want when YOU can make millions in just a few months in an interesting and rewarding business?

SEND FOR YOUR EXPORT-IMPORT KIT TODAY! Fill out the coupon below. YOU'll get started in just hours!

ABOUT THE AUTHOR:
Tyler G. Hicks is the president of INTERNATIONAL WEALTH SUCCESS, INC. as well as the president of a large lending organisation in New York. He is internationally recognized as the foremost expert on making money from scratch and is the bestselling author of many books, including How to Get Rich on Other People's Money, How to Start a Business on a Shoestring and Make Up To $500,000 A Year and How to Borrow Your Way To Real Estate Riches. Over 2,000,000 people (worldwide) have profited from his books. He will provide free consultation for every buyer of this kit.

FREE CONSULTATION!

Here's US $99.50. Send me my EXPORT-IMPORT KIT now! (Airmail outside North America: add $60; there is no postage cost for surface - sea mail shipment)   Credit Card Orders: 516-766-5850.

Send material to: PLEASE PRINT:

Please send your payment to

Name: _____
Street: _____
City: _____
State: _____
Country: _____
Tel/Fax: _____

INTERNATIONAL WEALTH SUCCESS INC.
P.O. BOX 186
MERRICK, N. Y. 11566

Figure 2-3. Export-import kit sold via mail-order/direct-marketing methods.

3. **Help business firms** do their job better, or do a new job, such as exporting. You can help businesses of all types by supplying training—either by mail, phone, or fax. And businesses will pay you high fees for your service(s). For example, one 63-year-old BWB who reads our newsletter, *International Wealth Success,* runs an arbitration service that helps businesses settle outstanding bills for a negotiated amount. He's so busy—using the mail, phone, and fax—that he hardly has time to talk to you on the phone. Meanwhile, money pours into his business every day of the week!

4. **Raise funds** for religious organizations, social services, charities, and foundations that aim at helping lots of people in the areas of health, happiness, education, etc. Much of this fund-raising is done by mail. You can run a profitable fund-raising organization from home using little more than your local mailbox to send out requests for money and your own mailbox to receive the contributions. And while you're doing this, earning money for yourself, you'll be helping others with the money you raise. Could you ask for anything better?

CHOOSE FROM AMONG YOUR OPTIONS

Now that you know what services you might offer, choose the one(s) you'd like the most. Let's say your choices are these:

1. *Money*—you'd like to help people get loans of various types for their businesses, or for themselves.

2. *Training*—you'd like to teach people various skills so they "convert" from being a hired hand to becoming a Beginning Wealth Builder (BWB) where they will be their own boss, no longer dependent on the whims of a corporate monster that hires, and fires, at will.

Which is the better type of business for you to start? It all comes back to your previous experience and current skills. Also, you have to look at which is "the easiest sell." Here's a quick rundown of the options you should consider:

1. **Money is—in our view—the universal solvent.** Money makes the world go round. Customers will flock to you,

once they know you can raise money for them. So money is the easiest sell there is—anywhere, any time!

2. *Training*—**is a great business,** *if* you have earlier experience in *the field in which you want to train others!* You really can't train others if you haven't done the work yourself. A friend of mine sells books by mail. On a good day he sells more than 1,000 copies of various books. At an average of $7 a copy that's $7,000 a day; at $10 a copy that's $10,000 a day. He asked me: "Ty, do you think I'm qualified to run a mail-order course on how to sell books by mail?" My reply? "You sure are! With sales like that you can even teach me—if you want to!"

So analyze yourself and see which field you'd be happiest in. In our business we cross the line, selling *products that teach* the money business. Thus, our *Financial Broker/ Finder/Business Broker/Business Consultant Kit* (see the back of this book for details) has been used by many BWBs as training to get into the loan brokerage business. And some report excellent results, as the letters or phone calls cited below show:

"My financial consulting business is now entering its fourth year on a full-time basis. This is truly a great business. Last month I produced two loan packages and finished a third. One was for $146,000, another for $600,000, and the last for $2.5 million. One loan has already been granted and the other two have bank commitments pending government guarantees. I'm making four times what I was four years ago!"

"It was through the IWS Newsletter and 'Financial Broker Kit' that I became a part-time financial broker and have been one for 6 months. I have enjoyed several commissions from loans I closed. I advertise in local papers."

"I'm beginning to get started real good in my 'Financial Broker/Finder Business' and things look very promising. To this date I have made nearly a million and a quarter in loans (all by phone), and things are getting better every day."

"I recently opened my office as a financial consultant/financial broker. In the past six months I have been able to secure several loans for my clients. For the most part they have been accounts receivable (AR) loans. However, I recently sent several venture capital, commercial mortgage, and other loan packages to investors."

Here's another example of the blending of training and products. It comes from a reader of my newsletter *International Wealth Success* who told me:

> Only 11 months ago I started in the mail-order business. I decided to market a carpet cleaning course for novices who want to start a business of their own. My secret carpet cleaning formula really did a job for me because I've sold courses in the U.S., Canada, Mexico, Europe, Africa, Asia, and Australia. All this happened in less than 1 year! Many of my dealers asked for commercial carpet cleaning equipment, also. So I now handle my own name-brand equipment. Even the White House is using our machine!

This is an excellent example of how one mail-order/direct-marketing product can lead to a whole line of related items. A service—offered in the form of a product—the course in this business, led to another product—carpet cleaning equipment. Since all these items—the course, the equipment, and the cleaning formula are related, one part of the business "feeds" the other. The result? More profit and income for the Beginning Wealth Builder—BWB! You—too—can do the same in a mail-order/direct-marketing business you like!

Money is a powerful service to sell. Training is also powerful as a sales offering. What are the differences in the customers you'll serve? Here are a few:

1. *When you sell money services,* you will often deal with companies, instead of individuals. Why is this? Because companies are more likely to deal with financial consultants when seeking funds than individuals will. If you've had previous experience dealing with companies you'll be in a good position to sell money services by mail order/direct marketing.

2. *When you sell training* by mail order/direct marketing you'll deal mostly with individuals. Why? Because it is individuals who are seeking training—not companies.

So keep these facts in mind when choosing your service business to sell by mail. Would you prefer to deal with companies or individuals? As a guide remember these facts:

- **There are many more individuals** than there are companies. So your market is much larger when you sell to individuals.
- **Companies can afford to pay more** for your service than individuals. So you can price services sold to companies at a much higher level than those you sell to individuals.
- **A company check seldom bounces**—checks from individuals can be livelier than a rubber ball!
- **Sales to individuals may require more service** after the sale than sales to companies. So you may work harder for each dollar you take in selling services by mail order/direct marketing.

Now Let's Get YOU Started in Business

There you have the outlines of the pros and cons of selling money or training services. You can—of course—sell many other services by mail order/direct marketing. It all depends on your likes and dislikes, previous experience, and the market you foresee for the service(s) you plan to sell. To help *you* make *your decision,* here are a few of the helps I offer you, as a reader of my books and a subscriber to my *International Wealth Success* newsletter:

1. **I'll review—free of charge**—any product or service business proposal you may have, giving you my opinion as to whether it has a strong moneymaking potential for you.
2. **I'll consider financing your business proposal** (in the form of a loan with up to seven years to repay)—if, in my, and my staff's opinion, it has strong moneymaking potential for you. This financing would be at a low interest rate—usually 6%—depending on market conditions at the time.
3. **I'll guide you along the way**—*at no charge of any kind*—to help your business grow strong and profitable. Over the years that my firm, IWS, Inc., has been in business we've helped new firms raise money, get started in mail order, find their first export customer, buy income real estate, etc., without ever asking for, or accepting, a fee of any kind—if they were subscribers to our monthly newsletter,

International Wealth Success. This is a record of which we are very proud. We can truthfully say we've never asked for, nor received, one penny in fees for the services we've performed free of charge for our newsletter subscribers. See the back of this book for more information on subscribing to this helpful newsletter.

So let's start *you on your road to wealth* in mail order/direct marketing. You'll find it fun—and profitable. Just think how much you'll enjoy being free of cranky bosses, saying goodbye to time clocks, having financial freedom, which allows you to buy what you want, when you want it! You can move on to the next rewarding page in your life.

If you have any doubts about your future in mail order, read this quotation from the United States Department of Commerce:

MAIL ORDER AND DIRECT SELLING

Direct- and mail-order sales will continue to expand rapidly. A more affluent and older population with limited time for shopping at a retail store, will prefer to make purchases in the home. Ease of entry into direct selling should continue to offer enterprising people and companies an opportunity to provide a viable service . . .

Read this partial quote several times. It gives you valuable information on why, and how you can make your fortune in mail order/direct marketing today, namely that:

1. **Direct- and mail-order sales will continue to expand rapidly.** This means your future is very promising in mail order/direct marketing because the market is THERE, READY, and WAITING for the great products or services you plan to offer. Could you ask for anything more than a rapidly expanding market?
2. **The population prefers to buy at home.** And how does this population buy at home? By MAIL, by TELEPHONE, by INTERNET, by ONLINE. And you can sell your products or services through all these outlets to get rich in your own home business using one, or more, of the 101 great mail-order businesses in this book.
3. **A more affluent and older population**—and this population is growing all over the world. So with a growing mar-

ket you almost can't miss—if you have a product or service that's wanted, and needed, by people anywhere. Remember—the mail reaches everywhere on the globe. In our mail-order company we mail millions of items all over the world. And *the mail does go through!* Maybe once a year an item of ours is lost. But this is extremely rare. We just replace it, once the customer lets us know he or she didn't receive what we mailed. Of course, we have a mailing receipt for everything we mail. This helps us prove we did mail the item—in case there's any question about this.

4. **Ease of entry should continue to offer enterprising people and companies an opportunity** to provide a viable service. So there you have the opportunity you seek. With a growing market that prefers to buy at home your chances for mail-order/direct-marketing success are greater than ever before in history!

With the information superhighway coming into your world of mail order/direct marketing and millions of computer enthusiasts wanting to buy by using visual direct marketing the opportunities for you are enormous. Here are results of recent surveys on mail-order and television sales of sports-related items during one year:

- More than $150 million worth of exercise equipment sold by ads on television
- 29% of the above sales were for climber/steppers—those devices where you go up and down a step—usually to loud, fast music
- 24% of the sales were for cross-country ski exercise equipment
- In the same year nearly $800 million of sports equipment was sold by mail order
- Some $272 million of leisure and sports footwear was sold by mail order, also
- Another survey (of interactive electronic shoppers) shows 15 to 20 teddy bears being sold per week on the 43,000 terminals serving Wall Street traders. At $73 per teddy bear, sales reach some $1,400 per week. Yet it costs the seller only $250 per week for ads on the interactive network!

Now how can we relate superhighway ads with television ads with direct mail? All these media go directly to the buyer. There's no middle person. And what works for one media will—in general—work for others. With sales in the multi-billions through these various media there's certainly a way for you to make your fortune in this great business.

And if you ever have a question about making it big in mail order/direct marketing, give me a call on the phone. I'm as close to you as your telephone. I usually answer on the first ring. If you're a subscriber to my monthly newsletter, *International Wealth Success,* described at the back of this book, I'll be glad to try to answer every question you have.

CHAPTER 3

PRINTED PRODUCTS CAN MAKE YOU RICH—SOON

THERE'S A FAMOUS saying that goes like this: "You can never be too young, too thin, or too rich!" And the world of mail order/direct marketing of printed products proves this saying is correct. How? By the billions in sales every year of printed products covering youth, health, and wealth. Typical of these products are:

- **Books** showing people how to stay young or get rich easily and quickly
- **Newsletters** devoted to staying healthy all the days of your life or getting rich today
- **Pamphlets** on special topics in health or wealth—such as curing the common cold, making money walking dogs for a fee, etc.
- **Cardboard calculators** that help you figure your calorie intake or the interest you'll earn on an investment at various rates of return
- **Magazines** on healthy living for everyone, or for selected groups—women, men, adults, children, etc., or on the various businesses a person can enter to get rich
- **Software** (which almost always has printed backup manuals and always has printed instructions of some kind on screen) devoted to various aspects of health or wealth—for example weight control or budgeting to keep business costs in line

You can probably think of other printed products sold by mail order/direct marketing. But I think you get the idea. There are millions of printed items sold by mail every year—at hefty profits for the seller. And we want *you* to be one of those profit-making sellers—starting right now!

To show *you* how you can get started selling printed products by mail order/direct mail we'll take a look at each of the types of products above. You'll see how you can pick a winning book, newsletter, calculator, magazine, or software product that can make *you* rich in your own mail-order/direct-marketing business you can run from anywhere in the world. Let's get started—right here and now. Along the way we'll also look at other moneymaking printed products for your future wealth.

Books for the Billions—Both People and Dollars

There are some 5 billion people in the world today. And most of these people can read. So that means the market for the books you'd like to sell is almost beyond counting. To get in on this market you need take just a few simple steps. These steps are:

1. **Decide on a subject** you think needs a book written about it. Your subject could be in any field you think is neglected by current authors. Good subjects for books today include:

   Money making of all kinds

   Health for everyone

   Hobbies of all types

   Sports—both spectator and participant

   Money-saving tips for families

   Military and naval history

   Etc.

2. **Look to see if there are other books** on your chosen subject. Do this by referring to *Books in Print—Subjects,* available in any large public library. Turn to the subject of

your proposed book and see how many titles are available under that subject. If there are a lot of titles, that's a good sign. Why? Because lots of titles indicates lots of interest and lots of sales! And that's what you want. If there are only a few—or no—titles listed, this could mean that the subject is overlooked by writers, or that there's not too much interest in it. You have to decide if it's worth trying to sell a book on the subject. You'll see how to do this later in this chapter.

3. **Estimate how many copies you could sell** of the book you have in mind. The book you're planning to sell will be different from others available, otherwise it wouldn't be worth putting on the market. Its differences will—hopefully—make it sell better than any other book on its subject that's on the market today. To estimate how many copies you might sell of the book you've selected, get information (in the library, again) on the number of people in the business, hobby, or other activity the book is aimed at. Sales to 1% of this group of people should be calculable using mail order/direct marketing. For example, if there are 1 million people in the field, you should be able to sell up to $0.01 \times 1,000,000 = 10,000$ copies of the book by mail order/direct marketing.

4. **Figure your sales income** from selling the book. Thus, if your book is priced at $15.00 and you sell 10,000 copies of it, your sales income will be $10,000 \times \$15.00 = \$150,000$.

5. **Calculate if you'll make money** on the sale of the book. Your cost of sales—that is, cost of the book, advertising, postage, overhead, etc., should not be more than 70% of your income, or for this book, $0.70 \times \$150,000 = \$105,000$. So your profit would be $150,000 sales – $105,000 costs = $45,000$. With a profit of this amount on each book you can easily get rich in just a few years!

Not every book you sell by mail order/direct marketing will be a bestseller. Some books will exceed your estimates. Others will fall way below your estimated sales. What you're seeking is a good average sale that will earn you a solid profit on each title.

Don't be afraid to estimate book sales. You will find that you will get more comfortable with estimating after you've "thrown your hat," as they say, at a few titles. The worst that can happen with an estimate is that it's too high. But if you keep your costs down, even an estimate that's too high won't hurt you, or your business, that much. Now that you understand how mail sales of books works, let's get into finding product for your sales.

Now here's a key secret of estimating book sales and why you should not be afraid of making estimates of potential sales of books.

> Most books cost little to print and mail. Thus, a book that costs you $1 to print and $1.50 to ship might sell for $25.00! You'll be getting 10 times your cost for the book. So an error in your sales estimate won't be too serious because you have so much "cushion" in your sales price! Just keep this important fact in mind when making sales estimates and you'll never worry again.

How, and Where, to Find Salable Books

You are not—I'm assuming—a book author. (If you are, all that we say here will help you, too). As a nonauthor you plan to look to others than yourself for books you can sell. Where should you look for salable books? Here are excellent sources for you:

1. **Local authors** who have a special approach: recipes, hobbies, vacations, sports, health, etc. Thus, one mail-order BWB sold 29,000 copies of a health book at $14 per copy. The book reveals the health secrets of a group in the Himalayan Mountains; the group is reputed to have superior health. The book brought in $406,000 in just 6 months!

2. **Literary agents** have thousands of hungry authors who would like to have you publish their book on almost any subject you think will sell well. As publisher at *International Wealth Success* I get hundreds of book proposals each year. Most of these books are unpublishable. The ones we get from literary agents are better because the agent "shoots down" the unpublishable manuscripts before they ever arrive in our office for evaluation.

3. **Friends and business associates** are often "closet authors" who "have a book in them" that they'd love to have you

publish. Just be sure that the book is nonfiction. Why? Because its very difficult to sell fiction by mail order, unless you're set up as a book club. At the start, stick to nonfiction—it's much easier to find, publish, and sell. And the profits you'll make are much higher than with fiction! Can I say more? For example, at my firm, IWS, Inc., we've sold millions of copies of nonfiction books, bringing in millions of dollars in sales and keeping me in beautiful new yachts—my "closet" hobby, plus long cruises with successful friends in their yachts. I'm living proof that these methods do work.

4. **Publishers offering large discounts** on their books can be a ready source of published, bound books which you can easily sell. Thus, in my firm, IWS, Inc., we have an Executive Representative Plan in which you can sell our books and kits and get a 50% commission on each sale. We "drop ship"—that is, mail the books and kits out for you at no charge to you, or your customer for regular postage. This means that you have NO inventory, NO cash to pay out up front, NO shipping cost. With such a plan you can really make a hefty profit working just a few hours a week. We even supply ad sheets you can use to sell these books and kits by mail so the money comes to you first, you deduct your commission, send the order to us and we drop ship. This plan (Executive Rep) is available to 5-year subscribers to our *International Wealth Success* newsletter. Send $120 to IWS, Inc., POB 186, Merrick, NY 11566-0186 to get started.

Other publishers will sell you their books at a long discount, also. For example, Prima Publishing, the publishers of this book, have many excellent titles you can sell by mail order. And they offer you a 50% discount when you resell the books you buy from Prima. You can contact Prima Publishing at P. O. Box 1260, Rocklin, CA 95677 to get a list of the titles they have available.

When looking for publishers who can supply books to you to sell be careful of several traps for the unwary. These traps are:

1. **Publishers making their profit** selling to you and not caring whether you can, or do, resell the books at a profit to

others. These publishers are in the business of living off your dreams and don't care whether you make the profit you seek, and should earn. Such publishers are short-sighted because the more money you can make selling books, the more money they can make!

2. **"Remainder" publishers selling overstock** from other publishers. Remainder books are books that didn't sell through normal outlets—bookstores, specialty shops, etc. You can make money selling remainders by mail order. But you must get the books at a low price from the original publisher. And you must specialize in a line—such as art books, military history, health, etc. You can't—at the start—make it big in mail-order sales of books carrying a wide line of titles.

So beware of booby traps when people offer you cheap books to sell by mail order! Your "cheap" books might wind up costing you a fortune. You'll make much more money if you look for, and find, books that appeal to a specific group of people to whom you want to sell by mail order/direct marketing.

Why Mail-Order Book Sales Can Make You Rich

Books have many attractive features for you, the mail-order/direct-marketing BWB. What are these attractive features that can help make you rich—sooner than you think? Here they are—think about each feature—it's loaded with future wealth possibilities for you:

1. **Books are cheap** for you to buy, compared to other manufactured products—such as TVs, air conditioners, computers, printers, etc., that you might consider selling via mail order/direct marketing. And if you handle the printing of a book through a printer you select, your cost is even lower. Further, if you write the book you have no royalty cost!

2. **Books can be shipped at lower cost** because the Post Office offers two special rates—Fourth Class Book Rate and Library Rate. Both rates are lower than the Parcel Post rates for the same weight package. And if you have cus-

tomers in countries around the world, as my firm—IWS, Inc. does—you have a dual advantage for books. These advantages are: (1) Book shipping rate—i.e. "Books —No Commercial Value Printed Matter Rate," which is lower than other air or surface rates. (2) No customs duties are charged on books or printed matter sent anywhere in the world. Why is this? Because every country in the world encourages education and learning. So books are allowed free access across borders—without customs duties. This saves you time and money because you don't have to fill out customs declarations and pay duty, as you do with other products.

3. **Books are easy to store,** count, inventory, and ship. You can use any clean and dry area to store books. At the start you can use a garage, basement, loft, or barn to store your books. (A friend of mine uses two converted barns to store books for sale around the world. If they smell of hay, it's a clean and healthy odor, he says!)

4. **Books are simple to ship.** You can use, as we do, standard book mailing bags. Or you can use cardboard cartons for your larger orders. We do, and we find that the books are protected better by the carton. These cartons come in collapsed form and are easy to store without taking up much space. What's more, when bought in quantities of 100, or 1,000, they cost about the same as equivalent bags.

5. **Books go on selling** in good times and bad times. Why is this? Because you can read a book almost anywhere there is light—at home, on a train, on a plane, in a car when you're a passenger, etc. So people are attracted to books everywhere. And with more of the people in the world today becoming literate, book sales will rise every year. You should be in on this rise so you build your riches in an exciting and rewarding business—book sales by mail order/direct marketing!

Use Newsletters to Build Your Mail-Order Wealth

Today there are some 4,000 newsletters being published in the United States. Add the newsletters published in other parts of the world and the total is some 12,000. What do these numbers mean for you? The numbers mean that:

1. **Newsletters are popular** with thousands of readers all over the world. You can use this popularity to help build your wealth in mail order/direct marketing.
2. **Newsletters can be produced at low cost** but sold at a high price. Thus, newsletters are sold for anywhere from $12 a year to $3,000+ per year for a subscription. Yet the cost of producing your newsletter might be only pennies per issue, from a printing standpoint. So your profit on a newsletter can be extremely high.
3. **Newsletters can go on for years** with people renewing their subscriptions automatically each year. Some newsletters even have their subscribers on automatic credit card renewal, with the card charged each year for the renewal amount.
4. **Newsletters can be written for you** by people you hire. Or you can buy prewritten newsletters that are imprinted with your name and address so that the newsletter appears to be yours, and yours alone. Again, the cost is just pennies but you can collect dollars per issue!

And the beauty of newsletters is that you can sell them by mail order/direct mail all over the world. Thousands of tests by newsletter publishers show—again and again—that the best way to market and sell a newsletter is by mail order/direct mail. So the newsletter is an ideal mail-order/ direct-mail product. Notice that we say *direct mail*. Why? Because:

1. **Direct mail** works best for newsletters since in direct mail you send a letter to your prospect describing the newsletter and what benefits your reader gets from each issue.
2. **Newsletters are bought to be read**—your prospect is a reader. A letter giving the benefits of the newsletter will be welcomed by the prospect because he or she likes to read.

You can sell a newsletter on almost any subject you like. And you should pick a subject you like! Why? Because if your newsletter is successful you'll be selling issues for years and years. For instance, my newsletter, *International Wealth Success,* which is devoted to helping people get rich in their own business, has been published for—at this writing—30 years, continuously. Our newsletter has been published longer than any other opportunity newsletter in the world.

Topics you can cover in a newsletter range over the whole of human experience—in personal relations, business, real estate, etc. You name it and a newsletter can be published on it! Popular topics for newsletters include:

- **Health topics of all kinds**—personal, professional (doctors, nurses, etc.), AIDS, workplace, etc.
- **Business topics** ranging from what's new in computers to personnel benefits to good hiring practices
- **Real estate topics** for the investor who wants to buy some properties to the professional who's managing corporate real estate of all kinds
- **Government regulation topics** for people who have to deal with EPA, OSHA, Congress, FTC, SEC, etc. Washington, D.C. is an endless source of newsletter ideas
- **Hobby topics** for people into ceramics, wood carving, knitting, model building, antique collecting, etc.
- **Sports topics** for both spectators and sports participants—baseball, tennis, golf, boating, hunting, fishing, camping, surfing, scuba diving, etc.

Thus, you can publish, and sell, a newsletter on almost any topic you like—provided there are a few thousand other people in the world interested in the same subject. And you must have some way to reach your potential readers. Typical ways newsletter publishers use to reach their potential subscriber readers are:

- **Direct mail**—sending letters to potential subscribers asking them to sign up for one year or longer
- **Telephone solicitation** by a telemarketing group that sells your newsletter to people who are prospective subscribers—that is, they're interested in your subject
- **Face-to-face solicitation** at seminars, conventions, and other gatherings where people of like interests meet to discuss the subject that interests them
- **Space ads in suitable publications** that are read by the people in the field of interest. You can also run classified ads to promote your newsletter

Again, you do *not* have to write your newsletter. There are thousands of editors and writers pleading to be put on a payroll or paid a regular freelance fee. These competent editors and writers will happily write *your* newsletter the way *you* want it written!

I write and market my two newsletters, *International Wealth Success,* priced at $24 per year for 12 issues, and *Money Watch Bulletin,* priced at $95 per year for 12 issues (see Figure 3-1). While I could have someone else write these two newsletters I write them myself because it's great fun. Further, writing these two newsletters keeps me in touch with my readers. This is very rewarding because:

- **Helping people get rich** gives me hundreds of real-life stories I can use in my books and newsletters to encourage BWBs to do more for themselves.
- **Being on the "firing line"** helps me keep up to date with the problems BWBs face in starting their business, getting a loan for needed funds, finding competent employees, etc.

As my newsletters have grown in circulation with more subscribers each year, the real-life experiences of BWBs led me to offer more services to our two-year, or longer, new subscribers. These services include:

1. **Toll-free telephone hot line** where you can call day or night free of charge to have your business questions answered—quickly and in a friendly manner.
2. **Low-cost business loans** for BWBs wanting to start, buy, or expand a profitable mail-order/direct-marketing business of their own. These loans are currently offered at 6% simple interest, where allowed by local statute. A number of BWBs have used these loans over the years and every one has been repaid in full!
3. **Private meetings in my office** in New York City, or in your city, when I'm in your area. Since I travel the world over in my business, it is usually easy to get together with subscribers at their home or place of business to answer any questions you may have on starting, funding, expanding, or growing a business.
4. **Special one-on-one meetings with subscribers** to discuss, in private, their business interests and needs. There's just

Figure 3-1. Full-page ad for newsletter sold via mail order/direct marketing.

the two of us. So you need not worry about being embarrassed by others hearing questions you think may sound "stupid." To me, there's no question that's stupid. If you ask a question you must have a reason for doing so. And I respect this reason!

5. **Grants to help businesses that aid people in need.** *A grant is money that never need be repaid, if the work for which the grant was made is done.* A grant is made only for businesses which help others. For example, grants are made to help people's health, education, living standard, etc. While the business can earn a profit while helping others, it is important that as many people as possible be helped by the grant.

To get these benefits you can ask for them as soon as you subscribe to the IWS Newsletter for two years—$48. Just ask for these items when you send your check or money order to IWS, Inc., POB 186, Merrick, NY 11566-0186. We'll be glad to help you immediately.

Offering these services to our newsletter subscribers helps them do more in life. As a result they write us hundreds of letters each week. Like this one from a young lady subscriber who writes:

> "I've closed 6 loans so far. That's not many but I'm forming a network of other brokers who are interested in working with me."

Yes, newsletters are amongst the best printed products you can sell by mail order/direct marketing. I know—I've done it for many years—getting younger, better-looking, and smarter every day—as I joke to people! To prove that I know what I'm talking about I'd like to have you visit my home and boat. You'll quickly see what newsletters can do for your life—starting right now!

Start Your Own Newsletter Now

Let's say you'd like to make your mail-order fortune with a newsletter. You're a health enthusiast and you believe that a newsletter on healthful living would be well received. You check out the newsletter field in your local library and find that there is room for a practical newsletter on healthful living. You choose to call your newsletter *Living Health Today*

Looking over the competition you decide to price your newsletter at $72 per year for 12 issues—a monthly. You project you'll sell subscriptions at the following rates:

First year	1,000	$72,000
Second year	1,200	86,400
Third year	1,500	108,000

So, starting your fourth year in business you'll have 1,000 + 1,200 + 1,500 = 3,700 subscribers and an income of 3,700 × $72 = $266,400. And the interesting thing about your newsletter business is this:

1. **You do not have to write your newsletter**—there are plenty of freelance medical writers who will be happy to write your newsletter every month for a nominal fee.
2. **You do not have to print your newsletter**—there are dozens of printers who will print your newsletter every month at a modest cost.
3. **You do not have to mail your newsletter**—there are hundreds of mailing houses that will mail your newsletter every month for just a few pennies. Many printers include mailing as part of their service, including maintenance of your mailing list free of charge.
4. **You do not have to advertise and promote you newsletter**—plenty of advertising agencies will do this for you at low cost.

Your main contribution to the newsletter is its basic idea—that is, healthful living today.

All the other work can be done by others under your direction. Yet the profits will come in to you!

Who would want to read a newsletter on healthful living, you ask? Plenty of people, I say. For example:

- A newsletter covering health of the body, the mind, and the spirit has—at this writing—126,432 subscribers.
- A newsletter on natural health has 134,008 subscribers, again as of the date of this writing.

- Some of the better-known university-backed health news-letters have more than 500,000 subscribers each!

You can easily earn $500,000 a year publishing three, or more, newsletters. How can I say this? I've been publishing two newsletters for a number of years. As a member of the Newsletter Publishers Association I talk to hundreds of other publishers every year. They tell me what their income is. Further, I participate in the annual business survey made by NPA. Results are shared with participants. This survey also shows me the truth of the above earnings statement.

If you decide to publish your own newsletter I'll be happy to advise you free of charge, if you subscribe to my IWS newsletter for two years by sending $48. You can ask me any question you want and I'll be glad to give you a quick, direct answer.

Just remember—you can publish your newsletter on any subject for which there's an information need. This means the whole world of information is open to you!

Sell Small Pamphlets to Make Big Money

People like a *fast read*—that is, an important bit of information they can read quickly and easily. You can use this interest in a fast read—i.e. a short coverage of a subject—to make big money in mail order/direct marketing.

For example, a lady author writes, and sells, thousands of 3.5" × 8.5" 20-page booklets on subjects like:

- **Paperwork management**—i.e. how to control your paperwork so it doesn't control you
- **Time management**—i.e. how to control the time in your busy schedule so you get things done without having to work 24 hours a day

These 20-page pamphlets are priced at $3.95 each when sold one at a time. But when bought in quantities of thousands with your company name printed on the pamphlet the price is much less. You—too—can get into this profitable field publishing quick-read pamphlets that are of interest to most people because they deal with an important topic.

To get started as a pamphlet publisher take these easy steps starting right now. If you have any questions I'll be glad to answer them:

1. **Decide what topics you'll feature.** You won't write them—you'll hire a freelancer on a one-time fee basis to write for you.
2. **Pick your audience**—the larger the better because this means your sales potential is larger.
3. **Figure out if any companies would like to use** your pamphlets in their advertising. This is where the big-money big-sales are.
4. **Find a writer**—advertise in magazines like *Writer's Digest,* the *Writer,* etc. You'll find that authors will come flocking to you.
5. **Find a printer**—look in your local "Yellow Pages" and contact several printers for competitive estimates.
6. **Have your first pamphlet written** and printed.
7. **Contact companies to sell in bulk.** With a good topic, your sales should be easy!

Now remember this important fact:

When you sell pamphlets in bulk to companies you are selling by direct mail. You do not have to visit the company; there is no face-to-face selling. Instead of selling to individuals, you are selling to companies. And instead of selling one pamphlet at a time, you're selling thousands! Your profits can be enormous. And repeat sales can put you into the million-dollar class quickly!

So take a look at pamphlet publishing and sales as your mail-order/direct-marketing business. The results can give you great happiness and independence!

Promote Cardboard Calculators by Mail

You've seen—I'm sure—cardboard calculators that allow you to figure your weight, see the schedule for next year's football games, or figure the interest on a home mortgage loan you're thinking of taking out. These calculators—like the pamphlets mentioned above—are popular give-away items for companies.

When you sell such calculators you do almost all your promotion by direct mail to companies that might use your calculators. Or you can go to a company with a suggestion for a calculator you plan to develop. Your calculator sells by the thousands, giving you a strong cash flow from an organization whose check does not bounce!

Again, as with pamphlets you:

1. **Get someone to design** the calculators for you—you do not do this work yourself.
2. **Have a printer print the calculators**—you are not expected to do this work yourself.
3. **Sell in quantities of thousands,** instead of one calculator at a time.

The usual cardboard calculator will sell in the range of $1.00 and up for mass sales. Sold one at a time, a calculator will sell for anywhere from $3.95 to $99.95. Much depends on how useful the information on the calculator is to its users.

Don't consider selling cardboard calculators unless you enjoy working with them. While some cardboard calculators are simple in operation—such as those giving baseball, football, hockey, or basketball schedules—others can be complex. So stick with what you like in mail order—you'll make more money and have lots more fun!

Sell Magazines by Mail for Quick Profits

You can sell magazine subscriptions by mail and make money for yourself. Almost all magazines are looking for more subscribers. You can help them get additional readers while earning anywhere from one to three times the annual subscription price.

The best types of magazines to promote by mail are what people in the field call "specialty books." These are magazines that go to special interest groups—such as engineers, dentists, architects, hobbyists, etc. Such magazines tend to have smaller circulations. So they want to increase their readership. Why? Because the more readers they have, the more they can charge for a page of advertising.

To get started selling magazine subscriptions by mail, take these easy, quick, low-cost steps:

1. **Decide what types of magazines** you want to work with—they should be magazines with which you feel comfortable.
2. **Contact the magazine's circulation manager.** You'll find this person listed on the "masthead" of the magazine—the listing near the front of the publication showing the staff of the magazine.
3. **Tell the circulation manager** you want to sell subscriptions to the publication. Ask what financial arrangements they have—that is, what they pay for each subscription you get. Some magazines pay you the annual subscription fee; others will double or triple it, depending on how anxious they are for new subscriptions.
4. **Ask for the free circulation promotion material** the magazine supplies to its subscription sales people. Figure out how you can mail this and get new subscribers for the publication.
5. **Expand your field to other publications you like.** Build your mailings to prospects while you watch your income grow—every day!

Selling magazine subscriptions by mail can be fun. You work from your home and rarely have to meet anyone face-to-face. But you must like magazines to make a go of this business!

Get in on the Computer Boom—Sell Software

The personal computer (PC) boom started in a garage in California when two teenage computer enthusiasts built the first Apple computer. Their invention swept the world—including the mail-order business. Today almost everyone has a PC. And you can make money via mail order/direct marketing from this love for the PC.

There are plenty of mail-order firms selling hardware (PCs). That's a story in itself. A college student in Texas started his mail-order computer company in his dormitory room. Today—just a few years later—his company, Dell Computer, is a multi-billion dollar organization! Only in America can you see such spectacular growth, so quickly.

You—too—can market PCs by mail. But the better business—in my view—is selling software or computer programs by mail. Why? For several reasons, namely:

1. **Software is easy to inventory**—it is not bulky and resembles a book in the amount of space it takes up in your home.
2. **Most software is modestly priced**—say from $10 to about $500, meaning that mail-order sales are easy to produce.
3. **People will buy** one software program after another—this means that a happy customer will buy from you again and again.
4. **The PC market**—especially for home computers—is expanding rapidly; so, too, is your market!

You may wonder why we classify software as a printed product. The reasons are simple. All software is accompanied by some written instructions. And all software has written directions on the screen. So while software may be in disk form it is essentially a printed type product.

To see the market that's available to you with software, think of selling 10,000 copies of a $200 program. Such a sale is really a small number for a popular program. Your total income from this sale would be:

10,000 programs × $200 per program = $2,000,000

Even if you paid $100 per program you'd have $1,000,000 left for advertising, shipping, and profit. On this sale you should earn at least 20% before income taxes, or $0.2 × $1,000,000 = $200,000. So you can see that you could earn an excellent income selling software by mail order/direct marketing. For best results in marketing software by mail take these easy steps:

1. **Decide what types of software you'll start with**—you have business, entertainment, tax, and personal software as general categories.
2. **Locate software publishers**—you can do this by looking them up in computer magazines; check your local library—you'll find dozens of computer magazines there.
3. **Contact software publishers** by phone, fax, or mail; ask for their discount terms for resellers of their programs. Most publishers offer generous discounts; some will even provide camera-ready ads for your use.
4. **Assemble a listing of the software you'll sell.** It's best to have the programs related—all business, all entertainment, etc.
5. **Start running ads and making mailings** for your software. Watch the orders flow in!

You can make your fortune selling software by mail order/direct marketing. Sales of $30,000, $40,000, and $50,000 per month are not unusual for beginners in this great business. Keep in mind that every time a new PC is sold you have a new potential customer. Get to this person with a strong sales message and you have a good chance of making a sale.

While you do not need a PC to start your mail-order/direct-marketing business, you'll find that having a PC can—and does—help with:

- **Mailing list maintenance** and updating is much easier with a PC than doing it manually.
- **Database marketing**—where you keep full data on your customers—such as where the customer came from (space ad, mailing list, etc.), what the customer ordered, how the customer paid (check, money order, credit card, etc.) is much easier with a PC.
- **Routine letters to customers** concerning their order, its shipping date, refunds, etc. are much easier to produce on a PC, and you can save many hours of correspondence time.

Sell software and prosper. Get yourself a PC and expand your business quickly and easily. Software can put you into the big money in mail order faster than you think.

Why not start today—right now? I'm here to help you in every way I can.

To better understand the sales potential for you in software marketing by mail order/direct marketing, take a look at this real-life example of a computer software marketer:

> His first ad in a monthly personal computer magazine featured software, computer parts, and related items. The first day the ad ran in the magazine the firm did $75,000 in sales! Just imagine that—they sold more in one day than most families earn in one year!

Yes, the sales potential in computer software is enormous. Further, as more kids learn the computer—and almost all do in school today—the demand for software will increase—over and over. So if computers are your "bag," as they say, get into software marketing. You have a great future ahead of you.

What's more, software has many built-in advantages for the BWB—Beginning Wealth Builder. These advantages are:

1. **You can sell software from home.** The buyer does not care where the software comes from. All he/she wants is software that works right from the moment the disk is slipped into the computer.
2. **You don't have to be a software expert to sell it.** The software publisher will gladly answer any questions your customer may have about the software.
3. **Satisfied customers will buy from you—again and again.** This is a little-known secret of mail order, namely: If you can add repeat sales to your customer list your marketing costs will drop to almost zero while your profits shoot to the highest level you can imagine!
4. **Your market is increasing at an enormous rate.** For example, at this writing, one mailing-list company has 2,556,309 computer professionals and end users on just one of its lists. That's about 1% of the population of the United States! With such an enormous list you could sell every day of your life and still have gigantic potential.

And I'm here to help you every step of the way. I've been working with PCs since the day of the Apple II. When the IBM PC came along I started working on it. Today I'm into the latest laptops and desktops. Call me—I'm as close to you as your phone—tell me who you are and how you got to me. Once I know this I'll be happy to answer any software questions you may have.

For Lowest Cost Mail Order, Try Recipes

Are you a gourmet cook? Do you have secret recipes for scrumptious dishes that make a person's mouth water just thinking about them? Or do you have out-of-this-world recipes for seafood, cakes, cookies, and other delicious dishes or meals? If you do—or can get your hands on such recipes you can make yourself a lot of money!

Surprising as it may seem people love to buy unusual recipes—paying anywhere from $1 to $3 each. You'll see recipes advertised in the classified columns of the tabloid supermarket newspapers week after week. What does this mean to you? It means that the advertisers are making money from their ads. And if they can so can you—if you have, or can get, good recipes.

Keep these important facts in mind about recipes. All recipes sold one at a time:

1. **Can fit on one sheet of paper.** You can mail your recipe to your customer using just one first class stamp!
2. **Can be faxed to a customer at low cost.** Why? One page will go through a fax machine in less than one minute. So your phone charge is minimal—and it can be less than the cost of a first class stamp.
3. **You can photocopy a one-page recipe.** This means that you don't have to print it. You can lease a small photocopying machine for less than $100 a month and be in business in just days!
4. **People buy recipes from low-cost classified ads.** So you do not have to spend large amounts of money on your ads for your printed product!

If you want to sell recipes by mail order/direct marketing but you're not a gourmet of any kind then you'll have to take these easy steps:

1. **Decide what type(s) of foods you'd like to sell recipes for**—entrees, desserts, seafoods, vegetarian, etc.
2. **Locate someone who is a gourmand in your selected food** specialty—do this by advertising, attending local cooking classes, talking to people who know food.
3. **Tell the gourmet you've located that you'd like to buy recipes** from them for a one-time fee. Be frank—tell the person that you plan to resell the recipes.
4. **Study local papers and national ones** to see which ones carry classified recipe ads. Choose one or two papers for your first ads. Call or write for ad rates.
5. **Run your first ads. Keep careful track of the results.** Seek to bring in three times your ad cost—minimum. Thus, if your classified ad costs $100, seek to sell $300 (= 3 × $100) worth of recipes from the ad. If you bring in more—great! Don't tell anybody—just go on advertising and get ready to buy yourself a better car, move into a bigger home, and take longer vacations!

Yes, recipes can make you rich in mail order/direct marketing. It may take you a while to find your best ad outlets and the most salable recipes. But keep at it—your startup costs are low and it won't take you too long to make it big selling recipes!

Self-Improvement Courses Make Big Money Today

With large corporations—and medium- and small-size ones, too—downsizing, millions of people the world over are out of work. When they think of looking for a job with another large corporation their stomach revolts. They don't want any more of the fear and harassment they knew at their last large-, medium-, or small-size corporation. So a lot of these people opt for their own business.

You can help them get started while building your own business. How? With self-improvement courses of all kinds which you sell by mail order/direct marketing. I've been doing this for years and can tell you that it's a great business.

And I know almost all the other self-improvement course marketers in the world today. To a person they say "This is a great business. And it's getting better every day!" To get started in this wonderful business take these easy steps:

1. **Decide** what types of self-improvement you'll specialize in—this will help focus your efforts.
2. **Locate suppliers** of courses in your area of specialty—do this by studying the ads in the opportunity publications; you'll find them on any large newsstand and in magazine news shops.
3. **Contact the course supplier.** Ask if you can sell their courses to your customers who you'll contact by mail order/direct marketing.
4. **Negotiate a suitable commission for yourself.** The lowest commission you should accept is 40% of your selling price. Thus, if you sell a course for $100 you should keep $40 (= 0.40 × $100). If you can get a higher commission, grab it because it means more money for you!
5. **Choose how, and where, you'll promote** your self-improvement courses. Many of the people who sell my company's courses (IWS, Inc.) start with their friends, people in their place of religious worship, their place of work, and their sports centers. They often make significant sales by word of mouth, getting them off to a roaring start with little or no investment.
6. **Branch out to other forms of selling** using mail order/direct marketing in local and national outlets that appeal to your potential customers.

Self-improvement courses can be of many different types. Here are some of the more popular types you might consider selling:

1. **Personality improvement**—dealing with making oneself more popular, easier to talk to, a better public speaker, a more skilled negotiator, a better manager of people and situations.
2. **Skills improvement**—directed at better performance in business as an accountant, engineer, computer programmer, top executive, etc. Such courses are directed at people who have a job and want to move ahead in it by acquiring greater skills, or new skills which will help them perform better for their boss.
3. **Small-business skills** to help one start, and succeed in, a small business of a person's choice. Businesses popular

today include mail order, financial brokerage, export-import, real estate investing on little cash, obtaining grants for doing helpful work for groups of people, etc. This area of self-improvement is probably the hottest today because of all the lay-offs and downsizing that's hit industry in recent years. These courses help people get started in their own business—usually at home—on a small investment. My company, IWS, Inc., specializes in such courses and has prospered and grown doing so.

4. **Mechanical skills**—such as auto repair, counter-top renewal, tax-return preparation, computer maintenance, air conditioning installation and repair, etc. Such courses may require that you supply equipment to work on. This takes the course out of the realm of a printed product. But a printed manual (or video) will still be used to teach the basics.

Choose your type of course carefully. While you need not be experienced in the field you want to sell to, you must be comfortable with it! By that I mean that you should not feel ashamed, embarrassed, or guilty about selling your course or courses!

Courses have many advantages for you, as a mail-order/direct-marketing BWB. These advantages include:

1. **The sales price of the usual course** is in the $100, and up, range. This means that your unit sale is large enough to support widespread promotion activities that produce larger sales.
2. **Your buyers are sincere people** interested in getting ahead in life. So they appreciate any help you might offer in the form of personal advice on the phone or via mail or fax.
3. **People will often buy more than one course from you** when they find that your materials are useful and reliable. Your second, third, and fourth sale cost you much less. This means that your profit rises sharply.
4. **Satisfied customers will recommend others to you.** Since word of mouth is the best form of advertising, you'll find your sales rise as you produce happy buyers.
5. **Successful course sales produce an "automatic income"** for you because the more sales you make, the more customers come to you.

What steps should you take to get started in this great business? Here are the best steps to get you going on little cash in the shortest possible time:

1. **Find suitable courses** in the field of self-improvement you've chosen to work in. It's best to have more than one course to offer because then your chances of making a sale are greater.

2. **Prepare, or have a friend prepare, a leaflet describing the courses** you'll offer. This will be easy to do if your course suppliers have ads for their courses which can be photographed as is (called "camera-ready") copy.

3. **Select mailing lists to mail to.** Do this by choosing the people you think would most likely buy your courses. Good buyers include people who've bought other courses, self-improvement book buyers, newsletter subscribers, and similar people. Talk to list managers—they can give you lots of good advice on which lists might produce good sales for you. A rundown of reliable list managers is available free to subscribers to my IWS newsletter. Ask for it when you subscribe to the newsletter. Then ask each list manager for their free rate cards on lists they have available for rent. Study each rate card. It will give you valuable information about how the list was obtained—from buyers, inquiries, etc. generated by space ads, classified ads, direct mail, etc.

4. **Rent a suitable list and start mailing.** Remember: Even though the list manager may require you to rent 5,000 names, you need mail only 1,000 as a test. This way you'll save on postage. If the list produces sales of at least two-for-one—i.e. $2 for every $1 spent, consider mailing to 1,000 more names. If you bring in $3 for each $1 you spend, mail the balance of the list in your possession. It's a great list!

5. **Once you find good lists, keep mailing to them.** Remember: A large list—say 500,000 or more names that produces $3 for every $1—can be a goldmine for you! So keep looking for such lists that can make you rich. They will really pay off for you!

6. **Try space ads and classified ads.** If this is your first attempt at mail order/direct marketing, ask your list manager to recommend an advertising agency you can work

with. There are plenty of good ad agencies that will work with you at low cost and provide you with plenty of solid ideas and advice.

Sell more than one course in your catalog. While I know that some direct-mail BWBs have made it big with just one course, those that drive the biggest yachts offer several courses in their catalog. For example, in our 48-page catalog which we sell for $4, we offer courses on:

- **Financial brokerage,** finder, business consultant
- **Mail order** success methods
- **Export-import** techniques for great wealth
- **Real estate financing** sources and procedures
- **Franchising** your business idea to make big chunks of money
- **Starting millionaire** businesses you can run for yourself
- **Income real estate** techniques for beginners
- **Venture capital** methods for earning money
- **Loans-by-phone** procedures and sources (see Figure 3-2)
- **Loans by mail** systems to raise money for others and-yourself
- **Etc.**

You'll find many of these courses listed at the back of this book. To understand better what I'm talking about, assume that you're selling courses by mail at an average price of $100 per course. At the end of each week you count your income. Here's what it will be for different numbers of course sales:

No. of courses sold per week	Weekly income	Annual income*
10	$1,000	$50,000
20	2,000	100,000
30	3,000	150,000

* Based on working 50 weeks per year

So you see, with sales of only 30 courses per week, you can have an annual income of $150,000 in mail order/

Figure 3-2. Full-page ad for self-study course offered by mail order/direct marketing.

direct marketing. There are reports of people bringing in $20,000 a week selling courses. I have never seen this high an income level. But incomes of $150,000 to $250,000 a year are common among the people I know in this great business. And you can have much the same—if you market courses prepared by others for sale by yourself and other mail-order BWBs. Then maybe your readers will tell you, or write you, as these did:

> "I've acquired holdings worth 10 million rand here in South Africa reading your books and other materials. These holdings are in industrial buildings, which I rehab, and in printing and publishing. They are worth about $2.5 million U.S. with $5–$6 million buying power."

> "I bought two courses. Using the info from these publications I recently obtained a loan to start a toy distributor business, with no difficulty. The great part of all this is that I'm gaining much more than just capital to be a BWB—I'm also gaining experience and good friends."

You can sell IWS Kits and Courses as an Executive Representative of ours. To become an Executive Rep, we suggest that you be a 5-year subscriber to our newsletter. The reason we suggest this is so you can better understand our views of business and helping people succeed in their own business. To sign up quickly, send your 5-year subscription ($120) to IWS, Inc., POB 186 Merrick, NY 11566. We've had some Executive Reps who've sold $2,000 a week of our courses, giving them a commission of $1,000 a week. Of course, they worked hard to reach this level of sales. But they think the commissions they earn are worth the work!

Sell Videos by Mail to Prosper Quickly

The TV generation would rather watch a video course than read a printed course. That's why you'll find many new courses offered on videos. But even though the basic instructions are given on video, you will also have backup material in a printed book or booklet.

Friends of mine in the business tell me that there are over 3,500 how-to, motivational, instructional, and training videos on the market today. You can sell many of these by taking just a few simple steps. These steps are:

1. **Decide what field of instruction you'll specialize in.** As with other printed-type mail-order/direct-marketing products, it's best to specialize at the start. Typical fields you might consider are auto repair, boat handling and piloting, woodworking projects, home repair, wall spackling, air conditioning and heating installation and repair, etc.
2. **Look for suitable how-to videos**—do this by looking over wholesaler video catalogs. Choose the videos you think are suitable and ask for a review copy. Many wholesalers will lend you a review copy free of charge.
3. **Prepare, or have someone prepare your video ads.** Again, it's better to offer several videos instead of just one at a time.
4. **Get into the mail with your video catalog.** Do some small space ads. Watch the big bucks roll in!

You can make it big selling videos and their associated printed instructions. Just keep working at it until your name becomes known as the best video supplier in the field of your choice!

Other Printed Materials You Can Sell for a Big Profit

There are hundreds of other printed products you can sell to make big money in mail order/direct marketing. Here are a few you may want to look at for building your future wealth in this—the world's greatest business:

- **Music instructions** for beginners in a variety of different instruments
- **Travel guides** to special places for particular people—teachers, painters, musicians, etc.
- **Locksmithing** for people seeking a career in this field, which is being given a strong impetus by rising crime rates
- **Gardening, landscaping,** and vegetation sculpting for amateurs and/or professionals

- **Clothing design, tailoring,** making, repair, and restoration for people seeking information on these subjects
- **Furniture building, repair,** refurbishing in various styles and periods for the amateur and the professional
- **Health improvement, maintenance,** and care for everyone seeking a better life by being healthier
- **Sell the inquiry envelope** you get for the printed items you're promoting by mail order/direct marketing
- **Rent, or sell, mailing lists to businesses** seeking to make larger sales to specific types of prospects—opportunity seekers, computer owners, ski enthusiasts, etc.
- **Rent 900 numbers to businesses** wanting to make money from inbound calls—almost all legitimate 900 numbers sell printed products to their caller
- **Sell by mail legal kits prepared by competent legal staff** on family wills, power of attorney, living trusts, estate planning, asset protection, mortgage reduction, etc.
- **Mail diet, health, and beauty catalogs to prospects**—the catalogs do the selling for you; the company ships for you—called "drop-shipping"
- **Prepare printed tax returns on your computer** to get your customers a fast refund—there's a big shortage of talented tax preparers nationwide
- **Sell printed stationery, letterheads, envelopes,** and other items to businesses and individuals
- **Remail (drop in a mailbox) printed envelopes, letters**, and other items for people who want a different mailing address
- **Show homeowners via written materials** how to reduce their monthly mortgage payments to reduce their interest cost and the payoff time for their mortgage
- **Mail collections of advertising circulars for a fee** to selected names for a fee—your circulars can contain both small space ads and full-page display ads
- **Sell printed T-shirts for any of many special occasions,** trips, anniversaries, engagements, marriages, etc.
- **Clip, and sell, printed items about companies, individuals,** organizations, etc. who pay you for watching the press for them

You can probably think of many more printed-item businesses you can run by mail order/direct marketing that can make money for you. Great! Thinking up such businesses can make you more creative. And mail order is a creative-thinker's business!

And before we move on to our next exciting chapter let me say—again—I'm as close to you as your telephone. Do you have a mail-order/direct-marketing question? Just call me. I'll answer you on the first ring and give a you a fast response. Further, if you don't want to reveal your idea, that's fine with me. I respect you, and your ideas! Now let's see about selling food by mail order/direct marketing!

CHAPTER 4

SERVE HUNGRY PEOPLE WHAT THEY WANT

MILLIONS OF PEOPLE all over the world dream of the joy they experience when dining on good food. And many of these people prefer not to leave their home to go to a restaurant to get good food. Or there may not be any good restaurants in their area.

The solution? Order gourmet food by mail. The range of foods available by mail is astounding, including:

- **Steaks** of all kinds—from thin to thick, lean to fatty
- **Cheeses**—standard, rare, in between, domestic or imported
- **Fruits** of all kinds—oranges, apples, pears
- **Nuts** of dozens of varieties—local or foreign
- **Candies**—chocolates, hard, specialty
- **Lobsters** from the most desirable fishing grounds
- **Etc.**

These foods can be shipped to you frozen, overnight. Using any of the courier services these foods can be delivered the next day by air to any street address in the country. Outside the United States foods can be delivered by air either the next day, or the second day, depending on the country of origin and delivery.

So what does all of this mean to you—the mail-order/direct-marketing BWB? It means plenty, namely if food interests you as a product:

1. **There's a huge market** waiting for your product(s) in almost every part of the world.
2. **Food buyers are willing to pay more** for specialty items because they enjoy them during their meals.
3. **Customers who buy by mail are loyal**—they'll come back to your firm again and again to buy your products.
4. **Your products are consumed**—they can't be saved for long—this means there is constant reordering, putting more money into your pocket.

Pick the Food You'd Like to Sell by Mail

Selling oranges by mail isn't much fun if you don't like orange juice! Sure, the money may be good. But oranges do have certain characteristics—odor, feel, look. If these turn you off, sooner or later you'll turn off the business.

So pick a food *you* like and you'll be more successful in your mail-order/direct-marketing business. You'll often find that a food *you* like is a local one. Thus, if you're a Florida resident or visitor you may find that your favorite food is oranges or grapefruit. Selling either by mail order/direct marketing is a big business. Table 4-1 lists typical foods sold by mail.

Table 4-1. Some Foods and Related Products Sold by Mail Order/Direct Marketing

steaks, other meats	wines/spirits
cheeses/ dairy products	beers from large/small breweries
nuts/raisins	fish/lobsters/crabs/clams
desserts/jams/jellies	cookies/pies
fruits—fresh and preserved	candies—hard and soft
ice creams/sherbets	recipe books and collections
ovens/stoves	chef hats and clothing
special cooking utensils	pots/pans/grills
outdoor cooking devices	gift baskets

Or you may be from a foreign country and your favorite food is a national dish. Importing food from your native country and selling it by mail can make you a millionaire. Or you may skip importing and have national dishes prepared locally for sale and shipment by mail. Popular mail-order/direct-marketing foods are national dishes of:

China   Korea   Italy
Germany   Japan   France
Indonesia   Spain   India

The important point to keep in mind about selling food by mail that is often overlooked by BWBs thinking of going into the business of serving hungry people good food by mail is:

> You do NOT have to cook, prepare, peel, slice, bake, fry, boil, broil, or otherwise touch the food you sell by mail! Instead, you serve as a sales agent, bringing the food supplier and customer together. Most BWBs selling food by mail never see, taste, nor sample the food they sell! Yet they can—and do—make big money selling food to hungry people everywhere.

Find a Supplier for Your Chosen Food

Once you know the food you want to sell your next step is finding a supplier who can furnish the food you need. You want to be a mail marketer—not a grower of food! To find a food supplier for your chosen food:

1. **Find out** if there is a trade association or other group serving the food you want to sell. (Almost all foods have such a group.)
2. **To find the right trade association,** look in your public library for a directory of trade associations. The trade association you seek will probably be listed in the directory.
3. **Contact the trade association;** ask for a free list of their members. They will either mail or fax the list to you.
4. **Call, or write, selected members** of the association. Tell them you want to buy their food for resale. Ask what dis-

counts they will give you for various quantities of purchases—either pounds, units, or whatever other measure they use. This information will be supplied in writing so there's a record of it. But you can get a general idea of prices over the phone, if you wish to call.

Isolate the Food Feature(s) You Want to Promote

We all buy food based on a feature we like. This feature, or features, can vary from one person to the next. Typical features of food that turn us on include:

- **Freshness**—just picked, fully ripe, succulent
- **Frozen**—with all freshness, ripeness locked in, ready for release in your kitchen or on your dining-room table
- **Size**—large or small, but the "right" size for this fruit, vegetable, meat, etc.
- **Fast delivery**—you can have your dream food by tomorrow morning, if you so desire

Perhaps you want to promote all these features in your ads, plus others. If so, that's great. The more features you have, the more likely are you to make sales via mail order/direct marketing. Keep these facts in mind about people who buy food by mail:

1. **Your advertising words bring pictures of delight** to your customer as he or she envisions dining on the wonderful foods(s) you offer
2. **People who buy food by mail are gourmets**—even though they're buying the simplest of foods—apples, oranges, grapefruits, cheeses, steaks, etc.
3. **Speedy delivery is extremely important to food lovers**—they want to have your food on the table tomorrow—not the day after or at any later date. Gourmets demand action!
4. **The more features about your food you can promote,** the faster you will make new sales. And if your food lives up to its advertised promises, the more repeat sales you will you make. So promote as many features as you can.

Specialize Your Food Offers and Grow Fast

Successful mail order/direct marketing by food BWBs is usually done by specialists. By this we mean that people concentrate on one type of food. Thus, you'll seldom see a steak marketer who also handles fruit or cheeses. Why? Because:

By specializing you can concentrate on building the reputation of your food offerings. You become known as a "steak house," a "cheese vendor," etc. So when people think of buying by mail the food you're known for, they think of you—which is exactly what you want!

By specializing you can get better prices on the food you sell. Better (lower) prices allow you to price your food more competitively, taking market share away from other sellers in your field.

By specializing you can publish a better catalog of your foods, making it more persuasive so it generates a larger number of sales for you from each mailing. This is the key to your success as a mail-order BWB—larger sales from each mailing you make!

See What Real-Life Food Marketers Do by Mail Order

Here are eight real-life examples of mail-order/direct-marketing companies in business as of this writing. Each has unique characteristics which make it highly successful:

Tender, juicy filet mignon steaks are sold by this company in the far western part of the United States. Their regular price for six 5-ounce filet mignons is $52.00 plus $6.50 for shipping and handling. Special offers, which have an expiration date, allow you to buy up to three packages of six 1-inch thick steaks for $29.95, plus the $6.50 shipping charge. These steaks are offered for the family's enjoyment plus they are also sold for sales motivational programs to encourage salespeople to make larger sales. This dual market increases this company's sales and gets them free publicity among people likely to order steaks for their own use after having won some in a sales contest.

California pistachios direct from the farm are a specialty of a West Coast firm. Today 4 pounds of salted or unsalted pistachios sell for $20 delivered in a special introductory offer. This firm also sells almonds, candies, dried fruit, gift boxes and baskets. They have a catalog of their offerings. Their attractive wrappings make their nuts and other products most appealing to anyone who likes these foods.

A multi-food company located in a northern climate offers gourmet steaks, seafoods, smoked meats and poultry, fresh fruit, cheeses, gourmet variety cookies, natural dried fruits and nuts for both the home market and incentive programs. This company has been in business a number of years and they expanded their product line as their sales grew.

A dessert of the month club supplies three different desserts a month for $88 plus $8 shipping. Or you can get one dessert a month for $30 plus shipping. Typical desserts include pumpkin pie weighing 4 pounds, royal pecan torte, etc.

Brownies and cookies specials feature different numbers of brownies and cookies flavored with various goodies. Twelve large brownies typically sell for $27, including shipping.

Smoked fish specialties of many different kinds—salmon, mackerel, catfish, etc. Combination package $39, includes shipping.

Variety of beers from microbreweries gives you two 6-packs a month for $15 plus shipping and tax. You get to taste the output of a variety of brewmasters.

Mozzarella of many types are available from this company. All sorts of cheeses, chiles, garlics, etc. Prices range from $13 and up and do not include shipping.

Your mail-order/direct-marketing food business can grow just like these have. Note that the steak seller is a one-product company. The nut company expanded to other types of nuts, and then to candies. The multi-food company has a wide range of products that allow the firm to serve many different needs of its customers.

Starting with one food as we suggested above allows you to establish your basic market. You can then expand within this market by offering other foods as your business grows.

Expand Your Food Business as You Grow

Selling foods can make you a mail-order millionaire faster than you think. It can turn your standard aluminum mailbox to a golden hue, with hundreds of checks arriving every day. To keep up this money-laden flow of orders into your mailbox, expand to other, food-related products such as:

Gourmet recipe books—the sophisticated food buyer loves to try new recipes for meals he or she cooks, or has a chef cook. Gourmet recipe books can be sold at a high price because the food buyer loves to experiment and is willing to pay for esoteric information on food.

Special cooking utensils to enable the gourmet to turn out unusual dishes. These utensils might include special spoons, knives, ladles, pots, and pans.

Advanced stoves and ovens to enable the home gourmet to equal the professional chef's results have a big market by mail order/direct marketing. Since the gourmet reads a number of the magazines serving this field, you have a place to advertise and an audience to buy. This is an ideal mail-order/direct-marketing opportunity for you.

Stylish clothes for the gourmet cook are a rage these days. You can have these made by local people and sell them throughout the world. Aprons with "The World's Best Cook" in different languages sell by mail order/direct marketing year after year. Since they'll sell to the same people who buy your foods, you earn a larger return for your marketing dollar!

Expensive wines to top off a gourmet meal can round out your food offerings. A number of firms are marketing high-class wines to gourmets. Sales are excellent. You must get good advice on the legal aspects of selling wine from your location. You may be required to have a liquor license. Consult a competent attorney for advice before you start to offer any alcoholic beverages by mail!

Desserts and ice creams are also popular food offerings to the gourmet buyer. Again, feature the unusual and you're almost certain to be successful. Since the desert advertisement is a ride-along with your ads for other foods, your only additional cost is the printing and paper charges for your desert and/or ice-cream ads.

You now have enough ideas to get started in your mail-order/direct-marketing food business. But I'm almost sure you'll need help along the way. Here's what I offer at no cost to people who are two-year, or longer, subscribers to my newsletter, *International Wealth Success,* described at the back of this book:

1. **Free consultation** about your food idea. If you're worried that I might take your idea and run with it (which I won't because food doesn't turn me on, as a business), you can describe your idea in general terms without mentioning details and I'll react to it and give you my opinion of it.
2. **Personal meeting in New York** or in your city when I'm there to discuss (if you wish) your food business plans. I'll pay for lunch and you can order anything you wish!
3. **Information on various food trade shows** where you might sell your food products or get names of people who are interested in them. Typical such shows and the city location for each for the year of this writing (shows often change cities from year to year) are: Housewares Show, Chicago, IL; Fancy Food Show, San Diego, CA; Fiery Food Show, Albuquerque, NM; Gourmet Products Show, Las Vegas, NV. In future years these shows may be in different cities. So please do NOT write me telling me that the city has, or will, change. It is almost standard practice for shows to change their locations each year, to give local people the benefit of seeing the show close to home.
4. **Low-cost financing for promising food projects,** where allowed by local statute. These low-cost, no-points, no-advance-fee loans are for business purposes only and must be backed by some kind of marketable collateral. A borrower's personal residence is NOT accepted as collateral

because we do NOT want to be in a position of having to put a person out of his or her home in the event the business loan goes bad.

Just remember—at all times—you have a good friend in your author. Your other "friends" may leave you flat when times are bad and you need help. I never will! Readers of my books and subscribers to my newsletters are my friends for life. You can:

1. **Call me day or night** and I'll answer on the first ring. Just don't say—as so many thousands have—"I never believed it when I read it in your book or newsletter. But you really do answer your own phone." Why would I say this if I didn't do it?

2. **Ask me any questions on small business** you may have—if you're a 2-year ($48), or longer, subscriber to my IWS newsletter. You'll get fastest results if you send your check or money order to IWS, POB 186, Merrick, NY 11566-0186. You can even submit your questions with your new subscription. Or you can call (516) 766-5850 to order by credit card. After you've subscribed you'll be given my special phone number so you can call me directly, free of charge.

3. **Visit me in New York City, or I'll visit you when I'm in your area,** to discuss your business questions. Sometimes face-to-face discussion is best for getting the answers you need. If you're a 2-year, or longer subscriber, I'll answer your questions in any way you want—by mail, phone, in person, or by fax: (516) 766-5919. To clear any questions, all these services ARE available to you as soon as you become a 2-year subscriber to IWS.

Food sales by mail order/direct marketing can be your "ticket" to wealth. Just follow the suggestions in this chapter to get started. Remember: Having a basic interest in food and its many variations is a basic ingredient in the recipe for success in food mail-order/direct-marketing success today! So if food isn't your favorite subject, look elsewhere for mail-order success.

CHAPTER 5

CATER TO GADGET ENTHUSIASTS EVERYWHERE

A_{LMOST} $_{EVERYONE}$—all over the world—loves a gadget that makes his or her life simpler, more efficient, faster. And you can make this near-universal love of gadgets make you a mail-order/direct-marketing millionaire—sooner than you think!

Get Gadget Alert Today

Some people are closer to (or more alert to) gadgets than others. Why is this? Because some folks:

1. **Regularly seek ways to make their lives simpler** by using some type of device, tool, machine, or circuit they discovered in a magazine ad, mail-order catalog, TV infomercial, or by word-of-mouth (the best form of advertising) from a friend, acquaintance, or worker in a store, gas station, or shopping mall.
2. **Are mechanically or electronically curious** and can't keep their hands off any interesting gadget that promises to simplify their lives.
3. **Enjoy showing off their newest gadget to others,** hoping that their friends or relatives will think they're brilliant and full of good sense.

From all this comes a golden opportunity for you. Why? Because you can find, or develop, a gadget that can sell all over the world. Gadgets like:

- **A fast, simple potato peeler** for every kitchen—in a home, hotel, restaurant, etc.
- **A paint-mixing tool** you run off your electric hand drill.
- **A mop** containing its own water-squeezer, eliminating the need to touch the mop to squeeze it dry.
- **A paint and varnish removal tool** for your electric hand drill that works faster and surer than liquid paint and varnish removers.
- **A "key shooter"** for your auto key to get it out faster and store it more quickly and simply.
- **A credit-card holder** that allows a person with multiple credit cards (of which they are very proud) to roll the cards downwards, impressing (they think) everyone who sees the number of cards they own.
- **A high-fidelity music system** that allows you to locate speakers throughout your home without running extra wires of any kind—the music is piped through the existing electric wires in your home.
- **A radar warning monitor** (not legal in some states) that alerts you to the presence of radar-control units for regulating traffic speed.
- **A computer keyboard template** that fits over the keys, showing what commands go with which keys.
- **A notebook holder** that holds secretarial and other shorthand books in place while the user enters the data in a computer or a typewriter
- **A wrist pad** for typists entering data on a computer keyboard. The pad keeps your wrists in a relaxed and natural position for easier typing.
- **A . . . you get the idea!** I could list thousands of other gadgets used by workers of all types, sports people, hobbyists, singers, musicians, etc.

To see the potential for gadgets, take a look at just one field—personal computers for the home. In the year of this writing there were more than 30 million personal computers in American homes. The year before there were just 21 million home computers. With such rapid growth from year to year, and with such a large number of machines in place, any computer gadget has a multi-million dollar market potential for you!

What's your favorite gadget? Could you sell it to others by mail order/direct marketing and make a profit? You'll have to "work the numbers" to see.

Suppose you're not a gadget lover or user? Can you still make money in this field? Yes, you can. You might even have a more objective view of gadgets if you're not a user of them. This could be a big help in your business activities. Now let's see how you can make a million selling gadgets by mail order/direct marketing. Table 5-1 lists typical uses for gadgets which are sold by mail.

Table 5-1. Some Uses for Gadgets Which are Sold by Mail Order/Direct Marketing

HOME:	BUSINESS:	PETS:
gardening	crime prevention	feeding
cleaning	telephones	control
painting	computers	health
entertaining	production	boarding
OFFICE:	HOBBY:	ENTERTAINMENT:
computers	autos	music
word processors	boats	television
telephones	golf	movies
modems	fishing	bowling

How and Where to Find Gadgets

The best gadget of all you find in your own head! Why do I day this? Because the most profitable gadgets are those developed by people who saw a need for a gadget to perform a certain task. These people set about to make the gadget, or have someone else make it. When put on the market the gadget sells like wildfire because it answers a need felt by people.

But, we'll say, you're not a "gadget person." Instead, you enjoy finding a good gadget, using it to see that it works right, and then taking it to market to make money from it. Where can you find salable gadgets? Here are a number of good places:

1. **Explore the New Products columns** of both domestic and overseas magazines to discover new gadgets that might fit your needs.
2. **Attend product shows** such as the auto, boat, outdoor, golf, tennis, and other shows held every year around the country and the world. Such shows are a mecca for gadget lovers and collectors. You can often negotiate a nonexclusive distribution agreement with the gadget developer at such shows.
3. **Contact inventor groups**—there are hundreds of them around—and tell them what types of gadgets you're interested in. Unless your interests are offbeat, you'll be flooded with offers of "the world's greatest gadget"!
4. **Read a large-city newspaper regularly.** You'll often see articles on the newest gadget to hit the streets.

Once you hear about gadgets that interest you, take these easy steps to lock in the possibility of selling the gadgets on an exclusive basis:

1. **Contact the gadget supplier or inventor** by phone; follow up by mail or fax.
2. **Tell the gadget supplier** that you'd like to borrow one sample of the gadget for test purposes. Promise to return the gadget in good condition immediately after your testing is completed.
3. **Be ready to sign a nondisclosure agreement** if the supplier requests it. (Such an agreement states that you will not reveal details of the gadget to anyone else, nor will you take the idea behind the gadget and use it yourself to develop a competing gadget.)
4. **Test the gadget.** If it works and does what it is designed to do, decide if you can sell it at a suitable price.
5. **Make an offer to distribute the gadget** on an exclusive basis. Use the methods given later in this chapter to figure the price to pay and the selling price for the gadget.

You will probably have trouble getting an exclusive distributorship for most gadgets you find. Why is this? Because suppliers and inventors worry that you won't do a good distributing job. If they're locked into you exclusively, they may lose time and money while getting out of the agreement they have with you.

Be willing to accept a nonexclusive distributor agreement if you feel you can sell against competition. In most cases, you *can* sell against the competition and win!

How to Recognize the Sales Potential of Gadgets

Gadgets sell for two main reasons—(1) They do a job for their owner quickly and easily, saving time, expense, energy, etc., and (2) They are novel—using the gadget sets a person aside from his or her friends and/or relatives.

In any gadget one of these reasons for selling will usually be stronger than the other.

You'll also find that:

1. **Gadgets that do a good job for their owners** by saving time, expense, energy, etc. usually will have a longer, and stronger, sales history than other types of gadgets.
2. **Novelty gadgets** can have an almost instantaneous sales acceptance with enormous revenues. But—just as quickly—such gadgets can disappear from the market, never to be seen again.

Once you find what looks like a salable gadget, ask yourself several questions about the gadget. Rate it on a scale from 0 to 10 as to its salability. Thus a rating of 10 would be "Highly Salable" while a rating of 0 would be "Not Salable." The questions are:

1. Does this gadget do its job well?   *Rating*_____
2. Will this gadget last a long time in
   popularity?   *Rating*_____
3. Is the gadget affordable to its
   potential buyers?   *Rating*_____

4. Are there better gadgets for
   this task around?   *Rating_____*
5. Are there any dangers (health, legal,
   etc.) in my selling this gadget?   *Rating_____*

You should score at least 50 points on this test for a gadget to be worth spending your time and energy promoting. If you do score 50 points, or better, go on to these questions:

1. **Is this gadget practical?** Will it work every time?
2. **Can this gadget be sold** anywhere and everywhere?
3. **Would I be embarrassed** selling this gadget?
4. **Will this gadget fit well** with others I may promote at the same time?
5. **Is there any danger** of any kind selling this gadget?
6. **Does this gadget have a cachet about it?** That is, will it be fashionable for people to own, and use, this gadget? Can my promotion use this cachet as a selling feature?
7. **Is there a unique name I can use** for this gadget which will set it apart from others? Will the name define the gadget? (Often, a name will be so unique that people will refer to the name when buying the gadget. This means that your gadget will be bought, instead of those of your competitors.)
8. **Can the gadget be patented?** Or will a trade name (such as the name in Item 7) be enough to protect your interest in the gadget? (A trade name is often more important than a patent—especially where people buy the gadget using your trade name.)

Pick a Specialty Field for Your Gadgets

To make money selling gadgets by mail order/direct marketing you should specialize in a line of similar gadgets. Why? Because:

1. **Specializing makes it easier** for you to find, and rent, suitable mailing lists.
2. **Specializing gets you known** among gadget lovers; they will gladly recommend you to friends when a specialty gadget is needed—this is the best form of advertising.

3. **Specializing helps you get better prices** for your products from your suppliers, allowing you to earn a higher profit.

What kinds of gadgets can you specialize in? The answer can only come from you. Ask yourself: What kinds of gadgets would I like to sell by mail order/direct marketing? The answer to this question will point you in the right direction. Specialty gadgets you might sell include:

1. **Crime prevention gadgets**—pepper sprays, stun guns, personal alarms, anti-theft devices, etc.
2. **Telephone instruments and accessories**—there are dozens of novel phones plus the accessories used with them and standard phones for people in business and at home.
3. **Computer gadgets**—extra memory attachments, ergonomic seating, laptop carriers, etc.
4. **Auto gadgets**—the mother of gadget fields—bug screens, radiator blankets, notebook holders, large-size rearview mirrors, gas-tank locks, etc.
5. **Sports gadgets**—timers, counters, scorecards, viewers, schedules, portable listening devices, etc.
6. **Pet-gadgets**—one of the biggest fields today—pet coats, pet-actuated entrance and exit doors, feed bowls, etc.
7. **Gardening gadgets**—to help the amateur or professional gardener get more done—sooner.

The gadget field you pick should be fun to you. Why is this? Because selling gadgets can be deadly dull if you don't like what you're selling. Also, you won't be as creative if you don't like what you're selling. And—as we've said before—mail order/direct marketing is a business in which creativity can pay off in the millions of dollars in your pocket!

Once you pick your gadget field, check out the number of publications in the field and the number of Mail Order Buyer (called M.O.B. for short) lists available. For example, let's say your gadget interest is gardening. Checking gardening publications in *Standard Rate and Data—Consumer Publications*—in any large public library you'll find at least eight major gardening publications in which you can run small display ads for your gadgets.

Looking over gardening mailing lists offered by list managers you'll find some 24 lists available from just one list manager. Adding up the number of names on these lists gives a total of 9,273,000 people interested in gardening. If you could sell gadgets to just 1% of that total, you'd make 92,000+ sales. With an average price of $20 per gadget, you'd bring in $20 × 92,000 = $1,840,000! And let me say this: Selling one percent of a M.O.B. list IS possible in today's world. (A free list of list managers is available to subscribers to my IWS newsletter.)

Start Selling Your Gadgets Today

Once you find several related gadgets you're ready to start making money from them. Here are a number of easy steps that can put money into your pocket using proven mail-order/direct-marketing sales techniques:

1. **Get a few samples of each gadget** from your supplier(s). Many suppliers will provide a few samples to you free of charge. If so, grab them. If you must pay for the samples, demand a deep discount—at least 50% of the selling price.
2. **Show the samples to friends and others in the field** the gadgets serve. Watch each person's reaction. If they reach for the gadget and want to touch it, use it, or otherwise take it from you—you have a winner on your hands!
3. **Sell gadgets to all your friends who want them**. Never refuse a sale! Why? Because your customers will proudly show their gadget to friends or business associates, giving you free advertising. More sales are almost certain to result.
4. **Choose publications in which you can run free news releases** describing your new gadget. Don't be afraid of "over-selecting" outlets for your news release. The cost of each release is small. If a publication ignores your release you haven't lost much in terms of time or money.

5. **Send out your news release.** (See Chapter 11 for details on how you can get your news release written). If you follow our guidelines and include a photo or diagram of your gadget, along with its price and ordering address, you're almost certain to receive orders for it. These orders will more than pay for the gadget, plus the cost of your news release.

6. **Run small classified ads** in those publications which produce the largest number of orders from your News Release. Your ad might read thus:

   MIRACLE GARDEN TOOL allows you to trim plants in moments without damage. Free details. Write ABC Garden Associates POB 21 Anytown 12345. Or call 123-4567 day/night.

7. **Keep careful records of your ad cost** and the number of responses you receive. Remember: The more responses you get, the larger the number of sales you'll make! Consider running small space ads in the publications that give you the largest classified-ad draw if an illustration of your gadget would help people understand its use better.

8. **Expand your advertising as your sales grow.** Spend at least 10% of your sales income on future advertising during the startup phase of your business.

9. **Rent a suitable mailing list and do a test mailing.** While some experts say you must mail to at least 5,000 names for a valid test, many beginning mail-order wealth builders get by with a 1,000-name mailing for their test. If 1,000 names produce a profit, they expand the mailing to 10,000 names and watch the results. If they're profitable again, then they mail to 20,000 more names.

Gadgets can make you your mail-order/direct-marketing fortune! And you can have lots of fun while you're building your wealth. Here are a few examples of earnings reported by BWBs who sell gadgets of various kinds by mail order/direct marketing:

$40,000 in one month by a downsized mechanic who thought his working life had ended when the big company he worked for gave him a pink slip.

$90,000+ in 4 weeks using sound mail-order/direct-marketing methods to present a product to the public and sell it to them quickly.

You can get started quickly with a good gadget. If you can't think of any gadget you can develop on your own, consider importing gadgets that appeal to you. Check with overseas sources listed in *Worldwide Riches Opportunities, Vol. 1* and *2,* described at the back of this book. While importing is less profitable than developing your own gadgets, it can get you started in this great business. Look for gadgets in your area of interest and then get a few samples, as suggested above. Then follow the easy steps outlined.

If you'd like to "bounce" gadget ideas off me, give me a call. I'm as close to you as your telephone. You need not worry about me using your idea—gadgets are not my field! I deal in published items that instruct people on small business topics. I'll be glad to spend as much time with you as you need, provided you're a subscriber to one of my newsletters. Now let's move ahead to providing convenience as a way to your mail-order fortune.

CHAPTER 6

PROVIDE CONVENIENCE AND EARN BIG PROFITS

TODAY EVERYONE SEEKS greater convenience in his or her life. We all want things faster, sooner, simpler, better, etc. Why is this?—for a number of reasons, which we all recognize when we think about them, such as:

1. **Courier services**—FedEx, UPS, Express Mail, etc.—make us want faster delivery of what we order by mail, phone, or fax. We want the convenience of not having to wait the well-known "4 to 6 weeks for delivery."
2. **Credit cards** allow us to walk around in a cashless society free of a bulging wallet needed to pay for major—and minor—purchases—we have the convenience of not having to go to the bank to get cash to buy what we need. Figure 6-1 illustrates a business that satisfies this need.
3. **Cash cards** allow us to get cash at ATMs—Automatic Teller Machines—when we can't get what we want with a credit card. So we have the convenience of getting cash almost anywhere, 24 hours a day, provided we're careful when accessing the ATM.
4. **Facsimile (fax) machines** allow us to send written and illustrated messages around the world in just seconds. Thus, when one of our newsletter subscribers in Australia, Singapore, India, Africa, etc. wants a loan application from us for a business or income real estate loan, we can get the loan application to the subscriber in less than a minute (or perhaps 1 minute and 10 seconds). Again—

Figure 6-1. Example of well-prepared full-page space ad for a book.

convenience for the subscriber who doesn't have to wait weeks for an air-mailed application.

5. **Cellular phones** allow us to get calls anywhere. A good cellular phone works perfectly on the street, in your car, on your boat, in your airplane. You're never out of touch when your cellular phone is on and you're listening for its ring or waiting for its vibration.

6. **Beepers worn on the belt** allow people to tell us they want us to call when we're out of reach of a phone. Again, convenience—we don't miss important calls just because we're not next to a telephone.

7. **Credit enhancement services** help us get credit when we've had earlier problems with our personal finances. Thus, secured credit cards are available for people whose credit rating isn't strong enough for a regular unsecured credit card. And co-signer services are available to help people get loans when they cannot qualify for them because of their credit history.

8. **Searches for wanted items**—usually money but many other items might be sought—such as aircraft, specially located land, minerals, scarce industrial materials, etc. Many people's lives are so busy they don't have time to do basic searches. So they're willing to pay someone to do the search—and that could be you!

9. **Specialized advice** can solve problems quickly. You can offer this yourself if you have unique knowledge. Or you can line up—by mail—experts to give this advice to your customers—for a fee to you.

10. **Computerized handling** of personal budgets, income tax returns, letters, important dates—birthdays, anniversaries, holidays, etc.—can help people save time and avoid embarrassment while avoiding family arguments and strife (an unremembered birthday can cause bitterness that lasts for years).

Pick the Convenience You'll Offer

As with products, you must be happy with the convenience service you'll offer by mail order/direct marketing. At the start, classify your convenience into one of the following

broad categories, which show a potential customer what—
in general—they'll be getting for their money:

1. Fast delivery
2. Saving time
3. Reducing money investment
4. Improving communication between parties
5. Searching for wanted items
6. Expert advice on important topics

Let's look at a few currently offered convenience
services to see how mail-order/direct-marketing wealth
builders are serving their customers today. Here are some
typical current offers:

Mail-order grocery club   These allow people to shop by mail
for brand-name groceries which are shipped to their front
door at savings of up to 50% of the normal list price.

> CONVENIENCE FEATURES: Saves shopping time, fuel cost
> for auto, reduces cost of groceries, gets rid of searching
> the supermarket for wanted items—other people do
> this for you.

Security spray and sound devices by mail   You get a whole
range of security devices delivered to your front door without having to search stores for them or answer embarrassing
questions from clerks. This is especially attractive to women
who want reliable security devices without any hassles.

> CONVENIENCE FEATURES: Full range of personal security
> devices, which you can select in the comfort of your
> home and have delivered to you in complete privacy.
> Only you know that you're carrying a reliable personal
> security device to protect you in the event of danger.

Work-at-home plans   These allow people to find legitimate,
worthwhile work they can perform in their own home
while they care for young children, elderly relatives, or ill
people.

CONVENIENCE FEATURES: Provides a range of work-at-home offers from which a person can select one or more that appeal to them. Allows someone to "survey the field" before making a decision. Gives a "shop-at-home" benefit for a business decision.

Grants-seeking service   A service like this helps people get grants for worthwhile causes they wish to promote for the benefit of others. These services will interview the grant seeker by phone or mail and then produce a written proposal for approval by the person seeking the grant. The grants service will then distribute the approved proposal to potential grantors and report on the results.

CONVENIENCE FEATURES: Service prepares the proposal—often a stumbling block to people seeking a grant. Then the service selects potential grantors and gets the proposal into their hands. All these steps save time and energy for the person seeking a grant. Also, the service can pick those grantors it knows are most likely to make a grant for the purpose the seeker has in mind.

Money raising for business or real estate deals   These can get funds into the hands of people needing them quickly and easily while the business or real estate person is working at his or her regular duties.

CONVENIENCE FEATURES: Saves time and energy for the business or real estate person—many of whom can't get away from "turning the crank" in their business to look for the funds they need. This service helps people with language and/or social limitations (who are often excellent business proprietors) get the money they need when they couldn't do so on their own.

Sell how-to videos by mail   This market concerns people seeking education in certain skills.

CONVENIENCE FEATURES: Complete privacy to the individual seeking to improve his or her skills playing the piano, raising vegetables in a backyard garden, finding dates with attractive people, becoming more skillful at billiards or pocket pool, etc. Many people don't want anyone—relatives, their spouse, friends, etc., to know that they're trying to learn a new skill, or improve an existing skill they have. Buying by mail is the ideal way for such people—and there are millions of them around the world—to secretly, and covertly in some cases, learn a new skill. You can satisfy their desires and needs by selling them the how-to video they want!

Success Stories

To show you why mail order/direct marketing is such a powerful business and can make such an enormous difference in your life, let me tell you about two BWBs who are making a fortune in mail-order catalog sales today:

MILLION-DOLLAR HOW-TO VIDEO BUSINESS

A BWB graphics designer wanted to buy a video that would teach him how to do ballroom dance steps. He looked for weeks, seeking any how-to video that would teach him what he wanted to learn—ballroom dance steps.

His search convinced him that there was a need for a store that would sell—not rent—how-to videos on a variety of topics. Since he was at a career-changing point in his life, he prepared a business plan for a video store that would sell only how-to videos. No popular movies or shows would be carried—only videos that showed people—adults and children—how to do something.

Showing his business plan to a friend, the two joined together to open a store to sell how-to videos. Their accountant—whom they consulted about their idea—advised them not to open a store. Ignoring this advice, they opened a store in a costly downtown location. Within three years their how-to video store was grossing $1 million a year.

During these three years they sold franchises for two other retail stores and started selling by a mail-order/direct-marketing catalog. While building their business to a million-dollar level they learned several important lessons, namely: (1) Each franchise store had to invest about $150,000 to set up—that is, find the store, fix up its interior, buy inventory, etc. (2) Startup time for each franchise store was many months—during which there was no income from the store. (3) Their mail-order catalog sales began to boom while they were franchising retail outlets. (4) Their market seemed to want to buy by mail, instead of going into a retail outlet to buy a how-to video.

Result? These two highly successful BWBs decided to sell catalog franchises to sellers in the United States and overseas. Their catalog now has (at this writing) some 3,000 how-to video titles in it. Their records show that the average customer in one of their stores spends about $70 at the retail level. But when ordering from the catalog the average customer spends about $90 on how-to videos! This shows that mail-order/direct-marketing is more powerful than retailing for how-to videos.

Now these two smart BWBs are finding that corporations are buying how-to videos for computer training of their personnel. It's much cheaper for a firm to buy one (or a few) how-to videos that their people can use on-site, as opposed to sending the same people to an external training program. What's more, an employee can use the how-to video over and over again at no extra cost. Once an external training program is over the attendee can't go back to the instructor for reinforcement or clarification of a point that's not understood.

So a business that started off as an expensive retail concept— and succeeded at the retail level—soon found that mail order/direct marketing was the better way to go. Why? **BECAUSE MAIL ORDER/DIRECT MARKETING OFFERS CONVENIENCE, SPEED, AND PRIVACY, WHICH PEOPLE ARE HAPPY TO PAY FOR!** That is the whole focus of this chapter.

This shows you the potential in just this one business— sometimes called special interest videos instead of how-to videos—some people say videos are a $17-billion business! That's a BIG business! But let's take a quick look at several other convenience businesses to see how they market their products to their customers.

SPECIALIZED TENNIS APPAREL AND GIFTS

Tennis players—particularly women—are interested in dressing properly and well. One catalog mail-order/direct-marketing firm doing some $500,000 a year in sales has the following unique convenience features: (1) They design their tennis outfits exclusively for their customers; (2) Styles are unique—the firm's customers could spend weeks looking for similar styles and never find them in any retail stores; (3) The firm's mail-order catalog is helpful and informative—it features apparel and tennis gift items that are unique in this field; if a customer wants tennis clothing or a gift that's unique they have to get it from this firm because it's the only place in the whole world they can get it!

CONVENIENCE FEATURES: Unique, one-of-a-kind tennis outfits and gifts delivered quickly with the assurance you won't see yourself on the court in someone else's clothing!

GIFTS FOR FIREFIGHTERS AND DALMATIANS

This mail-order/direct-marketing firm specializes in gifts unique to firefighters and their spotted dalmatian pets—sometimes called "fire dogs." Annual sales are in the $300,000 range. They mail their catalog to lists of buyers and to people who leave their name at the booth the firm rents at firefighting conventions each year. Their mail-order catalog is a slip size that easily fits a firefighter's pocket. Giving product information, some historical background where suitable, the catalog is fun to read and use. Most firefighters save each copy of their catalog until the next new one arrives. This produces great sales from each edition of the catalog.

CONVENIENCE FEATURES: Carefully selected unique gifts for firefighters and their pet dogs presented in an interesting and factual way in an easy-to-use handy catalog. Regular mailings keep the firefighter alert to new gifts for people in this unique and needed profession, along with their spotted pets.

STYLISH NURSES UNIFORMS BY MAIL

There are dozens of retail stores selling nurses uniforms. But many focus on price—not style and quality. One mail-order/direct-marketing firm sells nurses uniforms from a catalog and does multi-millions in sales each year. The catalog features brand-name uniforms known for their superior style and quality. A busy nurse can order by credit card and have her (or his) new uniform delivered the next day if they're in a rush. If time is not too critical, they can have the new uniform in three or four days. Size directions in the catalog tell the nurse exactly how to judge which size will be best for them. And if the fit isn't right, a quick exchange is made.

CONVENIENCE FEATURES: Fast delivery of high-quality name-brand uniforms that are the latest style. Complete size and quality satisfaction guaranteed.

DISCOUNTED DESIGNER JEWELRY BY MAIL

Do you want an expensive watch at up to 50% off the retail list price? You can get it by mail with names such as Cartier, Rolex, etc. on your watch. This mail-order/direct-marketing firm does some $8 million a year in business by mail. Its customers are typically 35 years of age, or older, with an income of over $100,000 a year. The average order is about $2,000! Compare that to average orders under $100, which some mail-order firms report. Payment for this jewelry firm's products is by check, money order, or wire transfer. Credit cards are not accepted by the firm because the fee on this size order would be significant. The firm does not believe that it loses sales because of its unwillingness to accept credit cards. Instead, it believes that this feature of its business attracts customers to it! In mail order/direct marketing you never know what will work until you try it.

Use Convenience Features to Ease Ordering from Your Firm

When you're selling convenience you should make it easy for your customers to order from you in a convenient way. While this may sound obvious, many BWB mail-order dealers overlook this important aspect of their business. Table 6-1 lists important convenience features you can offer your customers.

Fortunately, technology is making convenience more convenient every day for you! How? By all the great ways people can order from you and the services you can offer your customers. Here are convenience features you must

Table 6-1. Convenience Features Offered by
            Direct Marketers Today

1. **Toll-free order number**—usually an 800 number—for fast ordering by customers

2. **Credit-card facility** to accept credit-card charges by phone or mail from customers

3. **Courier overnight shipping** for customers seeking, or needing, fast delivery

4. **Fax ordering capability** so customers can fax their orders to you any time

5. **Telephone help line** to answer customer questions or give advice by phone

6. **Printed returns policy** so customers know how, when, and where to return items

7. **Extra telephone numbers** for easy access to your company and its people

8. **Named people** for customers to contact when they have questions or need help

9. **List of business organizations** your firm belongs to or supports in its field

10. **Longer business hours** so people can reach you day and night to place orders

---

offer your customer today if you want to make millions in mail order/direct marketing:

- **A toll-free 800 number** for ordering from your company quickly and easily—conveniently!
- **Accept credit cards**—Mastercard, VISA, American Express, Discover, Diner's, etc. for your orders.
- **Ship via any of the courier services**—Federal Express, United Parcel, Express Mail, TNT, Airborne, etc.—at the customer's expense.
- **Have a telephone help line** where buyers can call you to get personal help or guidance with the purchases they're thinking of making, or have already made.

- **Use a fax machine to take orders** from people who are too busy to call you on the phone, or who don't like to use the phone, or who love to use gadgets.
- **Easy return of items** that are the wrong size, color, cut, etc. You make friends when you exchange—without question or hassle—items the customer finds unsuitable.
- **Clearly defined refund policy** which makes your customer feel safe in ordering from you because he or she knows their money will be refunded in the event they don't like what they ordered from your firm.

Use these convenience tools in any mail-order/direct-marketing business and you'll see your business boom. Why? Because today's mail-order buyer *expects* you to offer these conveniences. Further, offering conveniences such as those listed above:

1. **Increases your credibility** in the marketplace—and let me tell you that there are millions of people out there who are suspicious, doubting, unbelieving, distrustful, cynical, and ready to call you a crook, rip-off, scam, and other similar names. So any way you can increase your credibility in the market will help your sales. But don't worry about such disbelievers—most of them are troubled, unhappy, envious people who want to vent their frustrations on someone and they pick you!
2. **Can increase your sales enormously** because the fact that you have the convenience—such as accepting credit-card charges—shows that your firm is customer oriented—i.e. you want to help your customer get through his or her life in an easier way.
3. **Puts your firm in the mainstream of today**—you're "just like the big, dependable, trustworthy firms" that are safe to do business with. Presto—the good reputation of the "big guys" rubs off on you—the little guy or gal—to *your* benefit and increased cash flow!

How To Set Up Your Convenience Features

Seven convenience features are listed following. You can set these up easily for any mail-order/direct-marketing firm.

And if you have trouble with any of them I'm always here—as close as your telephone—to help you in every way I can to set up these features for your business. To get you started fast, here are the easy steps you take:

1. **Toll-free 800-number service:** Call your local phone company. The company will probably have two, or more, 800-number options for you. Start with the cheapest offer and then move on to fuller service as your call volume rises. If your local phone company doesn't offer 800-number service you can use one of the answering services that include toll-free lines. Look in your local phone book under "Answering Services—Telephone" and call them. If no such services are listed, call me (as a subscriber to my newsletter and I'll give you three national services free of charge).

2. **Get a Merchant Account to accept credit cards** for your business. Do this by applying at your commercial bank. If they turn you down, get a copy of my "Merchant Account" Kit—see Figure 6-2 to learn how you can get your Merchant Account. I've helped dozens of people get their Merchant Account quickly and easily.

3. **Get a courier service(s) account number.** This is easy—just call FedEx, UPS, etc. and apply for your account number. You may be able to get it over the phone. If not, ask that an application be sent to you. Fill it out and send it back. You're in business!

4. **Set up a telephone help line.** At the start this will be YOU, answering your own phone when customers call to ask questions. As your business grows you can hire a person to do this work for you, freeing you for more creative tasks—such as finding new products to sell.

5. **Get access to fax services.** You can use a local quick-print shop to accept your faxes at the start. Once you begin to get a strong flow of orders, buy your own fax machine. Today you can get a good fax machine that operates in the tele/fax mode for just a few hundred dollars. After your business builds you can get a separate fax line for your orders for just a few dollars a month. This will free your regular telephone line.

6. **Write out your shipping policy.** If you don't know what to write, read the shipping policies of several mail-order firms. Then pattern yours after theirs. This way you'll be

HOW, AND WHERE, TO GET A MERCHANT ACCOUNT FOR YOUR BUSINESS

TO ACCEPT ALL MAJOR CREDIT CARDS FOR SALES

Do you want to make sales by credit card in your business? Are your customers offering to pay for your products or services by credit card?

If you answer YES to either question, then you need a MERCHANT ACCOUNT for your business so you can accept credit card payments.

Have you tried to get a MERCHANT ACCOUNT and been turned down? If you have you know the feeling of rejection the

turndown gave you. But don't worry, there's plenty of hope for you!

Ty Hicks, well-known business author, shows you exactly how, and where you can get a MERCHANT ACCOUNT TODAY. Better yet, you have unlimited free consulting time with Ty by phone or in person to answer any questions you may have about getting your MERCHANT ACCOUNT.

Here's what you get in this helpful, practical kit:

Why Get a Merchant Account?	Filled-Out Telephone Order Form for Credit Card Sales
How to Get a Merchant Account Today	Equipment Lease Agreement for Printer and Terminal
Getting a Merchant Account Directly from a Bank	Using an Independent Sales Organization (ISO)
Reasons Why Banks Reject Merchant Account Applications	Working with an ISO to Get Your Merchant Account
How to Get Your Merchant Account at a Smaller Bank	How to Protect Your ISO Dealings
What You'll Do to Get A Bank Merchant Account	How to Deal with a Typical ISO When Getting Your Account
Where to Apply for Your Merchant Account	Practical Tips on Working with ISOs Anywhere
Using Sample Applications to Improve Your Approval Chances	Typical ISO Agreements You'l Fill Out and Sign
Equipment You'll Use With Your Merchant Account Today	Appointment Agreement for An ISO
How to Key in a Card Charge on Your Merchant Account	ISO Agreement to Procure a Merchant Account
Telephone Procedures for Merchant Account Charges	Merchant Cover Sheet for An ISO
Saving Money on Your Terminal and Printer Equipment	Merchant Authorization for An ISO
Typical Merchant Account Application Used Today	ISO Client Application
Filled-Out Merchant Account Application	Equipment Sales Agreement for a Merchant Account
Resolutions to Open a Deposit Account for Your Merchant Status	Sample Bank Credit Card Service Rates
Equipment Purchase Agreement for Your Merchant Account	Equipment Purchase Agreement for a Merchant Account
Merchant Account Terminal of the Type Used Today	Use a Credit Card Processor to Handle Your Orders
Some of the Credit Cards You'll be Accepting in Your Business	Use An Answering Service to Handle Your Credit Card Orders
Printer Used with Credit Card Sales—One of Many Types Available	Answering Service Application Form
Typical Credit Card Sales Slip You'll Use as a Payment	Typical Answering Service Fees
Mail Order Coupon for Use with Credit Card Sales	Buy, or Merge, with a Firm Having a Merchant Account
Telephone Order Form for Credit Card Sales in any Business	

NOTE: Because you may get a Merchant Account from just one phone number in this kit, it is sold with the understanding that there will be no refunds made; each sale is final.

Enclosed is $100.00. Send me the *MERCHANT ACCOUNT KIT.*		
NAME		
ADDRESS		
CITY	STATE	ZIP
To order by Credit Card please include: Credit Card #		Expiration Date
SIGNATURE	PHONE #	

(Send Check or Money Order or charge by phone—516-766-5850).
Send order to IWS., Inc. 24 Canterbury Rd. Rockville Centre. NY 11570.

Figure 6-2. Full-page ad for data kit to help buyers get a credit-card merchant account.

firms. Then pattern yours after theirs. This way you'll be certain to be "following the leader"!

7. **Think through, and write, a returns policy.** Again, look over the returns policies of several large firms and pattern yours after theirs. Just be sure to follow your policy when a customer demands an instant refund. By making a quick refund you'll stay out of trouble with the various regulatory agencies governing mail order/direct marketing today.

Take these seven steps for ANY mail-order/direct-marketing business and you'll be on your way to millions in mail order. How can I say this? Because I've done it myself—many times over. And many of my mail-order "students" who've read my books and subscribed to my newsletters have done the same. If they can, so can YOU!

Offer Convenience and Your Wealth Is Assured

All the world seeks convenience! Offer it to the world and your wealth will pour in through your mailbox, fax machine, and telephone in the greatest business on earth—mail order/direct marketing. Let me give you one more real-life example before we move on to our next wealth-building, mail-order/direct-marketing business.

A reader attended a new-products show in his city and found a burglar alarm that the buyer could install himself or herself. Operating on the infrared principle, this alarm can have up to four stations. It comes with a video showing the buyer how to install the alarm in just 30 minutes. Priced at $250 the alarm costs just 25% of a $1,000 contractor-installed system, yet it does just as good a job. This reader got mail-order/direct-marketing sales rights for the alarm. He pays $150 for the alarm and has a $100 markup on it. Selling by mail order/direct marketing, he has sold some 2,000 units in just a short time. With millions of homes, boats, trailers, factories, and similar buildings needing crime protection, this BWB sees a bright future for himself and his product!

To be sure you don't overlook how you can offer convenience to your customers, think about these ways to help your customers:

Shopping—help your customers save time, energy, fuel, frustration, money by offering them products delivered to their front door quickly.

Services—deliver in-home or in-office service by mail or fax to allow your customer to select what serves him or her best. Types of services you can offer include insurance, investment advice, resumes of potential employees, etc.

Education—teach people needed skills or hobbies via video, books, kits, fax, telephone. Select the "hot" subjects—such as we at IWS have (money and success) and people from all over the world will beat a path to your door via mail/phone/fax to buy what you offer!

You are now ready to make your mail millions offering convenience to your customers.

And I'm ready—here and now—to help YOU every step of the way. Call me—visit me—fax me—I'll answer you quickly and completely—especially if you're a subscriber to one of my newsletters or a buyer of one of my convenience kits! This ease of communication is one of my convenience features that has built my IWS firm into a world leader in mail order/direct marketing.

CHAPTER 7

SELL THE UNUSUAL BY MAIL

THINK ABOUT THE last time you bought something by mail order/direct marketing. Was what you bought an unusual item or service? Chances are that it WAS. Why do I say this? Because for more than 200 years mail order/direct marketing has prospered by:

- **Selling unusual products** that you can't find in the corner store
- **Delivering the ordered product** to your front door or post office box quickly
- **Giving you privacy of choice** in what you buy, use, read, or play with in your home or business

From the earliest days of mail order/direct marketing, people have bought the unusual. The famous "plain brown wrapper" aspect of mail order concealed what a person bought from the prying eyes of neighbors. Even if what they bought wasn't unusual or personal, mail order/direct marketing gave them privacy. And—of course—if what they bought *was* unusual—the plain brown wrapper protected them from inquisitive folks in the neighborhood—and even from the mail carrier! So the unusual *has* been with us since mail order/direct marketing began.

Decide on the Unusual Items or Services You'll Sell

Unusual items or services are those not regularly offered by mail-order/direct-marketing firms. Thus, you'll find that clothing, food, self-improvement books, electronic equipment, and similar items are regularly offered by mail-order/direct-marketing firms. Unusual items not regularly offered are among those you might consider. Here are a number to help stimulate your imagination so you come up with *your* unique offerings:

- **Astrology products**—such as charts, books, personal forecasts and predictions
- **Gambling products** and/or instructions for people who want to excel at poker, blackjack, craps, and similar gambling pursuits
- **Ostrich raising** and feather, chick, or egg sales for people who want to earn money in this field of farming
- **Hypnotism instruction and practice** for novices and those interested in developing hypnotic skills
- **Romance**—how, and where, to meet men and/or women and charm them for a lasting relationship
- **Diet secrets** not available in any of the standard sources—books, exercise clubs, etc.
- **Body flattening or buildup** for any of the key body parts of interest to men and women
- **Getting money from the U. S. Government** for any of thousands of useful purposes
- **New Age books, cards, devices** covering the mixture of religion, mysticism, self-help, and other potions that make up the New Age movement
- **Horse or dog racing handicapping,** winning formulas, and other systems for beating the odds
- **Home tests** for a variety of conditions—pregnancy, AIDS, diabetes, etc.

You can probably think of many more unusual items that are—or might be—sold by mail. In giving you the above list I'm *not* recommending them as items or services *you* might sell. I'm just giving you a rundown on a few of the unusual items currently on the market.

To pick the unusual items or services you want to sell by mail order/direct marketing get out your pencil and paper. List:

1. **Unusual items or services** that interest you, or your family and friends
2. **Current fads in your area** that are unusual or might appeal to a larger group of people
3. **Products or services developed by yourself** or friends that might be marketed as unusual

The best items or services fitting the unusual category are those you develop yourself. Many of my readers have been outstanding successes in the field of the unusual. Printed products—when based on a new development—can be enormous and quick wealth builders. Here are a few of the printed products that are making big money for mail-order/direct-marketing BWBs today:

- **How to Make a Million in 900-Number Marketing**—sold at $200 a copy, this book is keeping one BWB in yachts and expensive cars with long vacations to enjoy both
- **How, and Where, to Find, and Get, Hard Money Real Estate Loans**—a course selling for $100 that combines an instruction manual plus audiotapes
- **How to Get SBA Loans**—a video course with a manual showing readers how, and where, to get government loans
- **How to Get Rich in Mail Order**—my Kit (see Figure 7-1), which shows you how to make millions in mail order/direct marketing, as I have, starting with little cash of your own

These printed items won't be found in the usual bookstore. Why? Because they're unusual—the average bookstore doesn't have much demand for them. So they're marketed by mail-order BWBs who are willing to find, and sell to, interested customers.

If you have an unusual printed-product idea, consider taking it to market. If you want, you can call me on the phone and I'll be glad to talk to you about it—without you revealing to me the specific details of your unusual printed product. My thoughts might help you. Further, I guarantee that I will NOT use your idea. I'm just too busy with my own ideas!

DO YOU SINCERELY WANT TO
MAKE A MILLION IN MAIL ORDER?

Today YOU have a golden opportunity to make millions in mail order! There never was a better time to make BIG money in this easy, laid-back way!

Thousands of money-making opportunities exist today for the mail-order beginner. Get rich without ever going to work! Cash in on the double-income family that has plenty of money to spend but no time to spend it! So they shop by mail — sending you buckets of cash every day!

Order your money-in-the-bank, good-as-gold 'Mail Order Riches Success Kit' today and start:

* Seeing your mailbox stuffed with big, big cash orders every day
* Going to the bank every day to deposit money — not to take it out
* Building business-at-home riches free of cranky, surly bosses
* Racking up easy, ovenight profits in the world's best business!

This BIG, opportunity-of-a-life Kit will deliver sizzling sales of any item YOU want to sell by mail order. You'll have a top-dollar income because the author of the Kit, Ty Hicks, has made millions in mail order himself. He shows YOU exactly:

* How to start your mail-order business at home in just hours
* Where to find products that will deliver megabucks to your wallet
* Dozens of ways to bring money into YOUR business in just a few days
* How to find low-cost (and no-cost) mailing lists to use
* Secret ways to get the people to buy from you again and again
* Where to meet with Ty Hicks free of charge or how to call him on the phone!

This BIG Kit helps YOU move ahead with little or no effort. You owe it to yourself to advance great wealth! To go for it ... to live your dreams in your own golden-opportunity business!

What's more, Ty Hicks is as close to you as your phone to help YOU unleash your greatest creative skills -- which we all have. Then you may tell us, as the readers did, who bought the kit from us:

"I ordered your Kit 2 months ago. I've already made $16,400 from it and project an income of over $100,000 in the next to months. Thanks for the time you spent with me on the phone — you've been wonderful."

"I raised $200,000 from a 20,000 mailing in just a few weeks. Thanks for your help!"

"Not long ago I was working my head off at two jobs and not enjoying either. Now I make more money and work at home when I feel like it."

So send for the BIG 'Mail Order Richess Success Kit' which is guaranteed to give YOU the info YOU need to start your own riches-building mail-order business that can deliver millions to YOUR mailbox!

Priced at only $99.50, Ty Hicks tells thousands of his happy buyers: "This Kit gives YOU 99% of what YOU need to know to get started in mail order today. The other 1% you learn by doing -- while you bring in the big bucks!"

To order, use the coupon below. Make a jumbo income from the wealth methods this BIG kit gives YOU! Once you have YOUR kit Ty Hicks will help you:

* Pick money-making products or services to earn YOUR millions
* Reach your income goals quickly and easily in your own business
* Get any financing YOU may need to-start making YOUR millions!

ABOUT THE AUTHOR
Tyler G. Hicks is the president of INTERNATIONAL WEALTH SUCCESS, INC. as well as the president of a large lending organisation in New York. He is internationally recognized as the foremost expert on making money from scratch and is the bestselling author of many books, including How to Get Rich on Other People's Money, How to start a Business on a Shoestring and Make Up To $500,000 a year and How to Borrow Your Way To Real Estate Riches. Over 2,000,000 people (worldwide) have profited from his books.

FREE CONSULTATION!

Future Mail Order Millionaire Response Coupon

Here's US$100. Please send me my MAIL ORDER SUCCESS KIT now. Airmail outside North America: add US$60.

Send material to: PLEASE PRINT:

Please send your payment to

Name: _____
Street: _____
City: _____
State: _____
Country: _____
Tel/Fax: _____

INTERNATIONAL WEALTH SUCCESS INC.
P.O. BOX 186
MERRICK, N. Y. 11566

To order by credit card call 516-766-5850

Figure 7-1. Mail-order self-study course
marketed by mail order.

Figure Out If You Can Sell Your Unusual Item

You can come up with the most unusual product in the world. But if you can't sell it you might as well forget the item. How do you determine if you can sell your unusual item or service?

That's easy. Just take a look at the mailing lists that are available for rent. For example, mailing lists available at this writing include:

50,000 monthly hotline names for people interested in astrology products—newsletters, horoscopes, psychic readings, 900 numbers, etc. And there are 50,000 members of an astrology club. With numbers like these you can make money with a good product or service you offer to these prospects! (A *hotline name* is that of a recent buyer or inquirer about a given product or service.)

New age lists from just one mailing-list house have 450,000 names of 900-number callers; 40,000 monthly hotline names; 120,000 last 12-month multi-callers—i.e. more than one phone call for information.

Opportunity seekers—people seeking ways to make money in their own business—really rack up large numbers. For example, one mailing-list house offers 100,000 monthly hotline names for rent. Again, with numbers like these, your unusual product or service has real potential. Another mailing-list house offers a 92,500-name opportunity seekers list—a good number to start with when offering such products or services.

People rejected for credit by banks and other financial institutions can be a lucrative source of sales for you. One list house offers 1.3 million people who are called rejectees, credit seekers, or denials. You can offer them secured credit cards, credit repair, or creative finance, states Act One Mailing List Services, the firm managing this list.

Computer owners spending some $50 on electronic books are available in large numbers. Thus, one mailing-list house offers some 64,000 names of such people who bought books on free travel and exporting.

The above lists are just a few examples of your market potential. To summarize the basic idea here you can say:

> If there are mailing lists with a count of 100,000, or more, available for rent, your unusual product or service has a chance of earning you a fortune. In general, the more names available for rent, the larger your potential market for your product or service.

With the growing popularity of Cyberspace via the Internet Shopping Network (ISN) the numbers go far beyond those for mailing lists. Home Shopping Network (HSN), which owns ISN has—at this writing—some 100,000 "hits," or accesses, per day! You, the seller of the product or service, will pay ISN a commission from 10% to 50% of your product or service sales price.

In Cyberspace your customers can order by credit card in complete safety. And your customers can be worldwide because PCs anywhere can access the Internet. You may find that the sales of your unusual product or service are stronger outside your own country than inside it. But who cares—so long as the money reaches your bank!

What's more, in Cyberspace you can make instantaneous changes in your products or offer. It takes a lot longer to make such changes in a printed catalog.

So—if there's a world of prospects for your item or service—you can safely assume that it's worth spending money to promote your offering. You can promote by mail, telephone, TV, Internet, fax (when the information is requested by the prospect), or radio. Truly, it's a big world in which *YOU can make BIG money!*

Unusual Services That Can Make Money For You

Services can make you a mail-order millionaire sooner than you think! Why is this? Because people will gladly send you money for an unusual service that they believe is valuable. One of the best examples of this occurred recently:

A police officer involved in an arrest was charged with a crime and sentenced to jail. Once in prison his pay stopped and he had no income of any kind to pay for the care of his wife and children. From his jail cell, with the help of knowledgeable mail-order pros, he made mailings that raised about $5 million to pay for his legal expenses and for the care and feeding of his family. The net to him, after all money-raising expenses, was over $1 million!

This real-life example shows that YOU CAN RAISE MONEY with an unusual service that attracts people. Other unusual services you might consider include:

Dating services in which you introduce—by mail, fax, or 900 number—people seeking to meet others. These services are the modern version of the lonely hearts clubs which have made money for mail-order/direct-marketing BWBs for more than 100 years.

Loans by mail—where you help people get business, real estate, or personal loans without having to show up at a lender's office for an interview. You receive a commission from the borrower on each loan you get for him or her. This is a great mail-order/direct-marketing business you can run from your own home. (See Figure 7-2 for more data.)

Loans by phone—where you help people get business, real estate, or personal loans, using the phone to learn if the lender would be interested in the particular loan. You can also get loans for yourself this way. As with loans by mail, you earn a fee for each loan you get for a client.

Consulting by mail—where you help people with a variety of problems—business, personal, marital, etc.—by mail and/or phone, depending on how you want to work with them. One of my readers in the Southwest runs a successful personal advice consulting business by mail. Her clients send her details of their problem(s) and she responds by mail. For faster service, she also faxes questions and responses. While her fee per question is low ($3), she gets lots of questions every day!

Autographs by mail—where you sell autographs of famous sports people—baseball, football, basketball, hockey, etc.—by mail. Since sports figures are so popular today, their auto-

How to Get Rich in MAIL ORDER CA$H LOAN DOLLARS.

°Overcome BAD CREDIT for yourself and others!

°Get CASH in a flash--maybe one day, or less!

°Find an "Angel" for your cash needs!

°Develop signature-loan MONEY POWER!

°Rate YOUR loan chances in minutes!

°Wipe out ALL DEBTS with just one loan!

°Deal by mail--NO interviews; NO pain!

°Get liquid assets for any personal need!

°Get INTEREST-ONLY mail-order loans!

°Be the "fastest loan broker" around!

°Get DOZENS of different kinds of loans!

°Be a MAIL-ORDER UNSECURED SIGNATURE LOAN wheeler-dealer!

°Make friends with money lenders forever!

°Get MAIL-ORDER LOAN convenience, speed, efficiency, confidentialty!

°Earn BIG FEES helping others get quick unsecured signature loans!

°Know who's lending for what use!

°Laugh "all the way to the bank" NOW!

°Deal by mail and avoid face-to-face hassles and arguments!

GET UNSECURED PERSONAL SIGNATURE LOANS FOR YOUR CLIENTS OR YOURSELF using the IWS MAIL-ORDER LOAN SUCCESS SYSTEM--the fastest way to get a signature loan today! Learn how to deal with lenders--prepare winning loan applications--help yourself or others to the BILLIONS available for unsecured loans! Build your own, or your client's loan rating fast! It's ALL here--plus much, much more in this NEW powerful SYSTEM!

Written by Ty Hicks, a man who has supervised the lending of some $50-million in all types of unsecured signature loans, this SYSTEM is just what's needed to get people the money they seek! And YOU can use the SYSTEM for your clients, or for yourself. It works, works, works for YOU! And it works for anyone you're helping get a loan. The SYSTEM gives you thousands of lenders to contact--shows YOU how to build your own list of willing and interested lenders! Send your check or money order for your SYSTEM today! Get loans SOON!

THIS IS THE ORDER BLANK

Here's $100. Send me my MAIL-ORDER LOAN SUCCESS SYSTEM. If you wish, you can call Ty Hicks with your credit-card (Master or Visa) order at 516-766-5850 9am to 10 pm. Have your credit card ready? Ask Ty any questions you may have!

NAME________________________ Apt/Suite #_____

ADDRESS________________ CITY__________ STATE_____ ZIP________

Send check or money order to: IWS, Inc., 24 Canterbury Rd, Rockville Centre NY 11570

Figure 7-2. Full-page ad for kit to help people get loans by mail.

graphs are valuable to collectors. Close to 7,000 names of buyers are available from just one mailing-list house. And once you make one autograph sale you can make many others because a hunger sets in to get every autograph possible. Other sales possibilities include World Series, Superbowl, Stanley Cup, etc. participants, rookie of the year, etc.

Military display model supplier—where you sell nostalgia models of ships and aircraft to former military (or active) personnel. You don't build the models; instead you have model builders do this in their own home or shop where they pay their own overhead—rent, light, heat, etc. One such supplier proudly advertises "We are a 'Mail-Order Only' Company—no store." Further, this firm says "No Credit Cards."

There are other unusual services you can sell by mail. I'm sure you can think of at least a dozen or so. The main point is to have an unusual service to offer that will give you a niche that sets you apart from the other mail-order/ direct-marketing sellers. With a niche position you almost can't lose in the world's best business!

Pricing Your Unusual Product or Service

When you have an unusual product or service to offer you have greater pricing flexibility than when your item or service is run-of-the-mill. Why is this? Because the unusual product or service:

- **Cannot be obtained in the usual corner store**—so you don't have to worry about local competition
- **Will often be one-of-a-kind,** or close to this type of rare product or service
- **Will have to be searched out by the buyer;** he, or she, feels a sense of victory when they finally find the product or service you offer because they've looked so long for it
- **May be uniquely yours,** making you special, different, a "rare bird," etc.

These—and other features—of the unusual product or service allow you to price it at a level where you can earn a profit. Why is this? Because people expect to pay more for the unusual, the unique, the rare. Without much (and in cases, any) competition, you can set your price at what the market is willing to pay. Here are a few good examples:

Instructional kits marketed by my company, IWS, Inc., are unique because they cover topics in greater depth than most books, offer personal consultation with me—either by phone, fax, or in person—and are updated regularly to reflect the latest information. These kits sell for $99.50 and $100 each—a good price for the buyer and the seller.

Fund-raising by mail delivers 75% of the money raised to you; 25% to the organization for which the money is raised. Thus, your expenses, and profit, come from the money raised, not from your pocket! And the more money you raise, the larger your earnings.

Consulting by mail pays you for each question you answer, or each problem you solve. And your fee for consulting can be higher if the questions take research or other work to answer.

Loan services you render to clients pay you a fee based on the amount of the loan. So as the size of the loan increases, so does your fee income. (On large loans your fee is typically 5% for the first million dollars [= $50,000], 4% for the next million, etc.). For smaller loans your percentage will be higher. Thus, on a $10,000 loan you would probably charge 8%, or $800, to your client for the work you do.

Rare items—like autographs, unusual products, etc. can be priced higher because there are not many others available to compete with your offering.

Price your unusual product so you bring in at least five times your cost. Thus, if your cost is $10, price the item or service at $5 \times \$10 = \$50$ (you might have a final price of $49.95 to make your offer more attractive). And if your cost is $150 your price might be $5 \times \$150 = \$750$. Such a price would probably not be rounded downwards to $749.95 because the nickel difference would have little motivational value for the buyer.

The whole key to pricing unusual products or services is not to be afraid of overpricing. You can always reduce your price. But if you underprice you cannot go after your buyer and ask for more money once a sale is made! It's better to err on the high side than on the low side. And with an unusual product or service you will usually get your asking price!

How to Promote, and Sell, Your Unusual Offer

You've heard, I'm sure, the famous remark: "Nothing happens until a sale is made!" This is so true for the unusual product or service. You can have the best product or service around. But if you can't sell it, nothing happens!

For example, in my mail-order/direct-marketing business we started promoting our small-business books and kits in Japan. The results astounded us. We had returns of between 5% and 10% from our catalogs. This is excellent for any catalog marketer making sales in an overseas country.

We couldn't explain our excellent results until I read a publication named *Market: Asia/Pacific.* This publication stated that the average catalog response rate in Japan can be as high as 4% to 9%. Since our products are unusual, we beat the averages, selling more than the typical catalog company.

To promote, and sell, your unusual offers you can use a number of methods. Here they are for your choice and use:

1. **Mail flyers or catalogs** to carefully selected lists of prospective buyers.
2. **Use classified and/or space ads** in suitable publications to generate either inquiries or sales.
3. **Run radio or TV commercials** to generate inquiries or direct sales of your products or services.
4. **Pass out flyers to large groups of people** via stands, personal distribution, or bulletin boards in areas of large population concentrations like shopping malls, train stations, airports, parking lots, campuses, etc.
5. **Cultivate word-of-mouth advertising** by having customers praise your products or services to friends and business associates.

6. **Get free publicity** with news releases in magazines, news-papers, newsletters, and other publications. Free publicity will often produce direct sales for little cost.

For best results, use all of these outlets in one form or another. As the saying goes, "You can never be too young or too rich." Or, "You can never have too many sales of your product or service!" So, never be afraid of over-promoting or over-advertising. Either method can only get you "too many" sales! A good business person recognizes that he, or she, can never have too many sales.

If you're puzzled as to where to start promoting or advertising, take these easy steps to guide you to profitable outlets:

1. **Look to see where your competition is promoting** and advertising. If their ads have been running for years you know these ads are making money in one way or another.
2. **Write, call, or fax the competition.** Ask for free information on their products or services. Analyze what is offered. See how you can offer better service, faster delivery, or other benefits for the same—or a lower—price.
3. **Practice "innovative imitation"**—that is imitate the competition but innovate—get, and use, new ideas, new approaches to promote, and sell, your products or services. Be careful—when imitating—not to violate copyright, patent, or other legal boundaries.
4. **Test, test, test** your mailings, ads, and news releases. Tests will quickly show which mailing, ad, or release pulls the most responses or generates the largest sales. Without testing you're operating in the dark!

Let me share with you a few of the promotion and advertising methods I've used—and still use—that have generated many millions in mail-order/direct-marketing sales for my firm, International Wealth Success, Inc. These methods are:

1. IMITATION

Early in the life of our newsletter, *International Wealth Success,* a mail-order marketer came to us and asked if we would sell his course on loan brokering. We agreed to do so. The first ad in our newsletter pulled in dozens of sales.

We sent the required payment to the marketer and expected instant shipment because our checks were good. Instead, the marketer gave all sorts of excuses for delays—he was out-of-stock, he had an auto accident, his warehouse burned down, etc. A few weeks of this was enough to show us that we had to get our own course, which we could ship instantly via any method the customer wanted. So we developed our own "Financial Broker/Finder/Business Broker/ Business Consultant Kit" (K-1 at the back of this book), which was (and is) written by experts in the field. Many thousands of the kit have been sold at $99.50. (What happened to the original mail-order marketer? He went out of business because he couldn't deliver.)

2. PERSONAL SERVICE

Since our business is worldwide, we early on decided to have longer-than-usual business hours. Thus, you can get me from 8 A.M. to 10 P.M. New York time (Eastern Time) seven days a week on the phone. And our fax line is a 24-hour dedicated one to which you can send messages any time. During winter months in the East our business is open 7 days a week. In the summer we're open 6 days a week. This personal service—and the fact that any customer can reach someone in charge of the business on the first ring—made repeat sales a regular item for us.

3. ADVERTISING

We take both full-page and 1-inch classified ads for our products and services. Based on dollars of sales per dollar spent on ads, our 1-inch ads do better than the usual full-page ad. We have had a few full-page ads that did better than the 1-inch ads. But their pull declined as time went by. The 1-inch ads continue to pull, month after month, and year after year! So test your ads before deciding on which will be best for you!

4. MEETINGS

Many of our readers wanted to meet with me, one-on-one, to discuss their business plans. I meet with them either in their city, when I'm there, or in New York City when the reader is in my city. The reader does NOT have to spend money on travel to see me. If he or she is visiting New York over the holidays, I arrange my schedule to suit their plans. We meet at lunch and I ALWAYS pay for lunch!

5. TESTIMONIALS

When a customer tells you that the product or service that you sold to them really works well, you have a testimonial. And testimonials are powerful selling tools. That's why I use excerpts from letters or conversations in my books and newsletters. People say, after reading a testimonial—"Gee, if that person can overcome adversity and get rich, so can I!" That's why our collection of thousands of testimonials is open to any newsletter subscriber who wants to view them. All we ask is a few days' notice so we can get the testimonials out of the safe-deposit box for your viewing.

6. SEMINARS

Some people prefer public seminars where they can see, listen to, and meet the speaker. So for years I've been conducting seminars all over the world. I've spent more time on the supersonic Concorde airplane traveling to and from Europe than I can remember. On one trip we crossed the Atlantic Ocean in two hours and 59 minutes! As a boy, working as a wiper in the engine room of a slow freighter, it took me 23 days to cross the same ocean! At the public seminars we sell our books and kits at the back of the room. This generates additional income and gets lots of good free publicity for our products. We give the public what they want and this helps sales!

7. SALES TO MAIL-ORDER COMPANIES

There are more than 12,000 mail-order companies constantly seeking new products they can sell to their customers. You can sell your products to these companies and get quick cash flow. We do this—selling to a number of firms that resell our books and kits to their customers. Why do we like this method of selling? For a number of reasons: (1) We're paid up front because the firms order in quantity—20 or 30 books at a time. (2) The check is as good as a money order—it does not bounce. (3) Repeat orders come in every few months with no effort on our part—i.e. no ads, no promotion. (4) Customers who buy from the mail-order companies often buy more books or kits directly from us—at full list price. If you'd like to get more information on more than 12,000 mail-order companies seeking new and unusual products order the *Mail Order Business Directory* from IWS, Inc., POB 186, Merrick, NY 11566. It is priced at $85 and lists over 12,000 mail-order companies using direct mail and/or catalogs to sell their products. Divided into 34 product categories, the directory gives the name, address, phone, fax, contact person, products or services sold, and the annual sales volume. The book has 500 pages. If you have an unusual product or service you may find your first few markets among the companies in this directory. Selling through mail-order houses is a quick way to get started in this great business while testing the demand for your new and unusual items!

8. EXPORTING

The market in the United States for unusual products is enormous. That's why many mail-order/direct-marketing firms never try to sell outside U.S. borders. But when I named my company, International Wealth Success, I was doing lots of international travel. I saw the enormous opportunities for unusual American products in Europe, the Far East, Australia, and elsewhere. So—in thinking of a suitable name—I picked the word "International" as the first word. Next I played around with "Money," "Funds," and similar words. Then the word "Wealth" popped into my mind because it's (in my view) a nice way of saying "money and all the joys brought to people by money. So "Wealth" became the second word in the company name. Then, since most people seek success, achievement, and other accomplishments, I chose "Success" as the third word in the company name. For short, it's IWS. And—incidentally—the name of my beautiful motor yacht is—you guessed it—"Success"!

The very name of our company brought us instant orders from overseas when we started—in 1966. Exporting became one of our main sources of revenue. And it still is. Our books, kits, and newsletters sell all over the world. And—fortunately—postal systems worldwide favor education. So printed materials (books, kits, newsletters) can be shipped at lower cost without customs hassles to every country in the world.

What we find in exporting our unusual products and services is: (1) Overseas customers spend liberally for items they can't buy locally. (2) With international credit cards (Mastercard, VISA, American Express) your customer can order quickly and easily by mail, fax, or phone without any foreign exchange hassles. You get the money in dollars (or whatever currency you deal in if you're outside the United States) and it goes directly into your bank when the charge is approved. (3) Overseas customers are honest, most cooperative, and fun to sell to. (4) Exporting is easy; so we don't overlook this important source of business just because the customer is 10,000 miles away!

So look at your unusual products. Do they have export potential? Would people overseas use them? Do they "travel" easily—that is, apply equally well to people overseas and to customers in your own country? For example, New Age books, health products and devices travel well. Why? Because the human mind and body are about the same everywhere. So books and products on these topics can be used equally well anywhere in the world!

9. MULTI-PRODUCT PROMOTION

Every year dozens of people come to us to promote, and sell, their products. Some of these products compete with our own. But if we think the product is good and can help our customers, we will promote and sell it. Such a policy broadens our offerings to our customers, making our company "the place to shop for reliable financial information for small businesses of all kinds." Result? We sell more, show a higher profit, and provide more jobs for workers. (Some of our part-time workers have put two children through college on the money they earned from their work for us. This makes me feel good.) You can build the scope of your mail-order/direct-marketing offerings by promoting other people's unusual products or services along with your own. Just be certain (1) the product or service meets your standards; (2) that the supplier has a large enough inventory to fill your orders promptly; (3) that the supplier will make refunds in the event a customer returns the product; and (4) that the supplier will be in business for as long as you plan to offer the product or service.

Yes, unusual products or services *can* make *you* a mail-order/direct-marketing millionaire. And *you can* make it big in this business—starting with little money of your own. And I'm here—day and night—to help you. Visit me in person, call me on the phone, fax me—I'll be there to answer your questions, guide you to reliable suppliers, help you get financing—if you're a subscriber to one of my newsletters or a buyer of one of my success kits. Try me and see!

CHAPTER 8

USE CATALOGS TO
SELL YEAR-ROUND

THIS IS THE age of catalog sales! Why do I say this? Because today catalogs are the "in-home store" that people—more and more—shop in, and from. Try to operate your mail-order/direct-marketing business without a catalog and it's like trying to walk on one leg.

If your home is like most others in America, you get dozens of catalogs each year. Many are four-color—some are black-and-white. You may even buy from these catalogs—I know I do—fairly regularly. So does my wife.

When you buy from the catalogs you receive you know that buying is easy. Just pick what you want, call a toll-free 800 number, tell the operator what you want, give your credit card number, and the product or service is on its way to you. And if you want next-day delivery you can have it—provided you're willing to pay the extra cost. Catalog buying is easy; it's fun; it's the way of the world today!

Now don't let this picture of the 800 number, banks of order-takers, credit-card merchant account, and courier delivery from a four-color catalog frighten you. You *can* get started with a simple black-and-white catalog, *without* an 800 number, *without* even a telephone! Your orders will come to you by mail, instead of phone. And—good friend of mine—an order by mail is just as good as an order by phone. This great business got along and made millions for its operators for some 200 years using just the mail! Table 8-1 gives 10 reasons for having a catalog today.

Table 8-1. Ten Reasons for Having a Catalog for Your Business

1. **Catalogs are "the way of the world" today**—you really need one to make it big.
2. **Catalogs can increase your sales** quickly and easily with little hassle to you.
3. **Customers keep catalogs longer** than any other type of mailing you may send to them—a catalog is an investment, instead of an expense!
4. **A catalog helps your company grow faster** than any other type of mailing piece you may use.
5. **A catalog improves your firm's prestige**—you're now "one of the heavy hitters" in mail order.
6. **Customers love the convenience** of catalog shopping. So most of them will buy more from you.
7. **You make your business an "in-home store"** for your customers, giving them a wide choice of what they can buy from you.
8. **Your average order amount will probably be larger** because people buy more when ordering from a catalog—so your income rises.
9. **A low-cost catalog can get you started** with a very small money investment on your part.
10. **Your catalog can sell from anywhere**—your home, your apartment, your motor home, your boat, etc. Customers don't care where you do business from, as long as your product or service is good and reaches them quickly.

Catalogs Can Make Millions for You

We use a 48-page black-and-white catalog in our business, International Wealth Success, Inc., to sell our two newsletters, 30 success kits, and some 80 business books. This catalog costs us about 50 cents a copy to have printed and three first-class stamps to mail.

Using a 1-inch display ad in the opportunity magazines costs $140 per month. We sell a significant number of these catalogs each month at $3 each. We make a small profit on the sale of the catalog from the 1-inch ad. But on what mail-order people call the "back-end"—that is, sales from the catalog that people paid $3 for—we can make as much as $2,000+ on large orders!

In between—of course—are many smaller orders for $25, $50, $100, etc. These orders make our catalog highly profitable. And you *can* do the same with a catalog of your own! Why do I say this? Because if *you* produce a good catalog:

1. **Potential customers will save your catalog;** they won't throw it away. Why? Because a good catalog has an inherent value for future reference. So your catalog stays on the shelf and isn't thrown out.
2. **Good catalogs entice people to buy**—especially if the the products or services offered appeal to the person receiving the catalog. A good catalog sent to the right people will sell for you year-round.
3. **Offering advice to buyers** (as we do on business matters) will make your catalog a "must use" document leading your customer to order what he or she wants, needs, or think they need!

In my hobby—boating—West Marine Inc., a supplier of boating products, has an 860-page, four-color catalog that is one of the best I've ever seen—anywhere. Each section of this great catalog has one or more editorial pages explaining the products in that section. For instance, in the section on inflatable boats, the various types available are discussed with the pros and cons of different types of construction. The reader is given a comprehensive overview so he or she can pick out the right inflatable for the type of boating they do.

More and more catalogs offer editorial material today. Why? Because it makes the catalog more useful and more valuable to the prospective buyer. You can set your catalog apart by giving ideas about the items the catalog sells. Your prospective buyers will appreciate your thoughts and will be more willing to buy what your catalog offers. Here's a great example of this technique at work.

WOMEN'S CLOTHING CATALOG RESCUES FIRED EMPLOYEE

As many of my readers know, I've helped thousands of BWBs find financial freedom in their own business. And we have thousands of letters in our files telling what these BWBs did. But the most moving story of any BWB I've known is that told to me by a woman in her late fifties. She visited me in New York City and at lunch in a famous French restaurant told me:

> At the age of 25 she joined an expensive department store's ladies apparel department. She quickly learned that the store was one of the most exclusive in the New York area. Customers included the wives of judges, politicians, Fortune 500 executives, baseball players, basketball stars, hockey goal tenders, etc. Society matrons spent long hours in the shop picking out their clothes for formal evening wear, summer vacations, and European tours. Within a few months this young woman became a confidant to some of New York's most prominent women. And—she told me— to some of their most secret secrets—such as *their real dress size, their real age, etc.*

> As the years passed, Donna (not her real name) gained more skill in selecting hot clothing designers, working with garment makers, and advising her wealthy customers. Some society women wouldn't buy even a sweater without Donna's advice on color, cut, size, etc. Donna was soon made manager of the apparel department because her followers were so faithful to her and spent so lavishly in the store. Within 10 years, Donna was made a vice-president of the store.

> By picking the most modern designs, the best fabrics, and custom-fitting, Donna built her store into the "place to buy, and be seen" for wealthy women in New York, Connecticut, New Jersey, and Florida. She had hundreds of European women who visited her store, and bought expensive clothing, jetting to New York just to shop!

> Twenty-seven years after starting at the store, Donna was called into the president's office at 3:45 P.M. and told that she was fired and that she should be out of the store within 15 minutes, by 4 P.M.

Donna went into shock and wound up in a hospital that night. It took her six months to "come back to earth," as she said to me. When we met she presented an idea to me. She had designed an 8-page, black-and-white, 5" × 8" catalog featuring designer clothes that she planned to sell by mail to wealthy women. Would it work, she asked?

I told her I thought it would, especially since she provided a short write up (editorial) for each dress, skirt, jacket, and blouse she featured in her catalog. While as a man I'm not a women's style expert (I just pay the bills!), her small catalog was most interesting and intriguing. "Go for it," I said. Donna was worried that the lack of four colors in the catalog would limit sales. "Not so," I said. "You do describe the colors available; women will pick the ones they want, especially since your descriptions of clothes are so good.

Donna made a mailing of 5,000 catalogs to wealthy women in the area at a cost of just under $5,000. The response was enormous. She brought in some $100,000 in business. Today she has a 32-page, four-color catalog that makes money on every mailing. And—by the way—the store that fired her has asked if they could buy from her catalog because the designs are so good!

So what does this real-life incident show you? It shows you a number of important items about mail-order/direct-marketing catalogs, namely:

1. **You CAN start with a short, simple black-and-white catalog,** which is easy and low in cost to produce.
2. **Editorial material CAN help sell more** of the items or services you advertise in your catalog.
3. **A small mailing CAN quickly show you** if your catalog will make a profit and whether you should extend your mailing.

Selling Fragrances from Home Gives Steady Work and Education

Another favorite example of making a success of a home mail-order/direct-marketing business came to me in a letter saying:

> Fifteen years ago my husband and I took advantage of an opportunity to sell designer fragrances for women and men from our home. Because of low overhead, we were able to sell these items at well below the cost a customer would pay at a department store. I've also been able to take the business with us as we moved to three other cities. The business also helped my husband maintain steady employment and I returned to school and earned my medical degree.

Just think of that! This BWB was able to earn her medical degree while selling discount fragrances from her home. Meanwhile, her husband had a steady job in the business, even while they moved from one city to another! Can you ask anything better of a business?

This couple used a simple catalog for their fragrance sales. And they included detailed descriptions of each fragrance as their editorial content. You—too—can do the same. If you get into this business be sure to avoid the "knockoff" fragrances, which supposedly duplicate the well-known ones at just 10% of the genuine fragrance's price. Knockoffs can be illegal and you may run into trouble when you say the knockoff duplicates the fragrance of the original after which it is named.

How to Start Your Mail-Order/ Direct-Marketing Catalog

You can start your own mail-order/direct-marketing catalog and make money from it! To be successful with your own catalog you should keep the following facts in mind:

1. **You need several products or services to start** a successful catalog. While it's true that some catalogs are (and have been) started with just one product or service, your chances of success are much greater with more than one. How many more? I'd say you should have at least four products for a 4- to 8-page catalog. If you can offer six or eight products in 4 to 8 pages, great! The more you offer, the more—in general—you'll sell.

2. **The products or services you offer should be related.** Thus, if you're selling automotive products, all should be auto-type items. Likewise with catalogs of convenience items, clothing, boating products, etc. This way your catalog has a greater impact on the prospects you send or give it to.

3. **Use photos or drawings—illustrations—to liven your catalog.** Plain type can be deadly dull, except for the diehard enthusiast. With so much visual competition today in TV, movies, and computer CDs, you need photos or drawings to catch the prospect's interest and attention.

4. **Decide what types of write ups you'll use for your catalog.** There are two basic types of write ups—serious and humorous. Use a serious tone for catalogs dealing with important products or services—health, safety, pollution, etc. A light, humorous touch can be good for hobby or recreational-type catalogs. Thus, a pet food catalog can give humorous descriptions of a dog's or cat's reaction to a new food product. Such descriptions can amuse your prospect and produce a sale—which is your goal.

5. **Write the product descriptions, or have someone do it for you.** There are plenty of freelance copywriters who do catalog copy at low cost. Be sure to tell a writer which approach you want to use—serious or humorous.

6. **Once your catalog is written, pick your advertising outlets.** For most BWBs their first ad outlet is by mail. Unless you have prospect lists (which most BWBs do not have), you'll have to rent prospect lists from mailing-list brokers. You'll find a selected list of highly reputable mailing-list brokers at the end of this chapter. The names on the list are current as of this writing. If one or two of these brokers should go out of business between now and the time you contact them, please don't blame me. I have no control over what other business firms do! (As a subscriber to the IWS Newsletter you can get a free updated mailing-list broker list by just writing, faxing, or calling for it.) When you contact a list broker, ask for the free rate card for each list. This card will give you valuable information about how the list was generated—from ads or mailings—average order amount, average buyer age, gender, etc. Study this information until you find one or more lists of prospects that fit your potential customers.

7. **Print your catalog.** If you're making just a small mailing—say under 1,000 copies of the catalog, you can photocopy the catalog instead of printing it. As soon as you start getting a profitable response to your catalog you can make arrangements to have it printed.

Distribute Your Catalog and Make Sales

The only reason you prepare a catalog is to make sales. So you must get your catalog into the hands of people who might want to buy your products or services. These people are your *prospects—not suspects!* To reach your prospects you can get your catalog into their hands in several ways, namely:

1. **By mailing your catalog** to (a) names on lists you rent; (b) to people who inquire directly to you about your products or services—called *inquirers;* (c) to people who respond to ads you run for your catalog, product, or services.
2. **By giving away your catalog** at trade shows, hobby events, exhibits, museums, and other places where interested people gather in large numbers.
3. **By placing your catalog in high-traffic areas**—shopping malls, drugstores, specialty shops, etc.
4. **By advertising your catalog,** products, and services on TV and/or radio and sending (by mail or fax) your catalog to inquirers.
5. **By listing your catalog on the various computer online services** available today. You really must get online—sooner or later. Why? Because that's where much of future mail order will be!

All these methods will produce sales—if your catalog has attractive, needed, or valuable products or services. After years of catalog selling I'm convinced that getting a catalog "out there will get you sales!" Here's a real-life example of this at work:

A mail-order BWB I know of is a flight-simulator buff. That is, he loves to "fly" simulated flights on his home computer.

These flights may be routine airline trips from—say—New York to Chicago, or the "red eye" special from Los Angeles to New York (a night flight where you sleep your way across our great country). Or the "flight" may be a simulated dogfight from World War I or World War II, "flying" aircraft with characteristics of the planes flown in those wars.

Early in his flight career this BWB found there was hardly any good flight-simulator software for home computers around. He collected what little was available and prepared a list of it, giving the price, flight details, and the supplier's name, address, and telephone number.

When he told other flight-simulator buffs about his list they begged him for a copy, offering him $5, $10, even $25 for it. This gave him an idea—why not prepare a simple catalog of the software and become a sales agent for the software? Within days he had his small catalog prepared. Then he discovered a small, beginning flight-simulator magazine. The magazine was happy to rent its list of subscribers to him because it needed cash. And it gave him a cut-rate price on small classified ads in the magazine.

Today this BWB's flight-simulator mail-order catalog offers software, control sticks, rudder pedals, and even complete cockpits to flight-simulation buffs around the world. Prices range from a low of about $15 for software to a high of about $700 for a cockpit.

And how's business? It's booming! As more PCs become part of the home, fledgling "pilots" discover simulation and "buy in"—i.e., spend money by mail to acquire software and equipment. And, by the way, if you haven't "flown" your own 747 or Concorde you should try it. You'll get a thrill like no other you've had in your life!

Get into the Business-to-Business Market

While most of our comments so far are on selling to individuals, there's another big market for catalog sales. This market? It's called "Business to Business"—i.e. selling to other businesses. Your business sells business-related items to other businesses. Typical items you might sell by mail order/direct marketing to other businesses include:

Office supplies of all kinds—paper, pencils, pens, tape, etc.

Maintenance equipment and supplies—tools, ladders, safety nets, etc.

Printed items—letterheads, envelopes, forms, shipping labels, etc.

Computer accessories and supplies for both Apple and PCs

Selling "B to B," as it's called in mail-order lingo, can be highly profitable for you. Why is this? Because:

Businesses often buy in larger quantities, making your sales amount higher than with an individual

Business checks rarely bounce—so you don't have to worry about being ripped off by a business

Businesses will buy from you again and again when they're satisfied with your products and service

So if B to B is appealing to you because of the products you like, give some thought to preparing a catalog for this market. There are millions of business names available for you to rent. So your market is almost unlimited!

Expand Your Catalog Coverage and Distribution

Every catalog BWB I know—and I know many—wants to expand his or her catalog as time passes. These BWBs:

1. **Want more pages in their catalog**—they want to go from 8 pages to 16 pages; from 16 pages to 32 pages, etc.
2. **Want to get wider—and larger—distribution of their catalog.** Thus, if they mail only in the United States now, they want to expand to Europe, Asia, etc.
3. **Want to go to color** if their present catalog is printed only in black-and-white

All these desires—and drives—are good—and positive. But you should be careful not to destroy any neat balance you now have between your costs and your profit. Here's a good, real-life example:

1. **Say that your catalog costs you 50 cents per copy** to print. You bring in—we'll say—an average of $300 per order per catalog sale.
2. **You print 10,000 catalogs and mail all of them.** You get orders from 200 catalogs, or 2% of your mailing—this is your response rate.
3. **Your income is** therefore 200 orders × $300 per order = $60,000 from your catalog mailing.
4. **You want to expand your mailing** to 20,000 catalogs, or double your first mailing. While your printing cost may go down somewhat—say to 45 cents per catalog, your postage cost will double. And your cost of goods or services per order will be about the same, or slightly less because you'll be buying larger quantities of what you sell.
5. **You should expand** to a 20,000—or 40,000 or 60,000 mailing—IF your average sale and response rate remain at about $300 and 2%. Why? Because you'll double—or better—your income! The whole key is whether your average order amount and response rate will hold up, and if there are enough new names to mail your catalog to. (If you started with a list of only 12,000 names in a specialized market you cannot double or triple your mailing because there aren't that many names available.)

So, the whole key here is: Expand your catalog mailing if (1) there are enough new names available for you to mail to; (2) your average order amount and the response rate will hold to about their initial level. Some catalog marketers get as high as a 12% response rate when they mail to a specialized list. These same catalog houses get a 10% response rate when mailing to carefully selected rented lists. So you see, there IS money to be made with mail-order catalogs!

Suppose, however, you're not sure that the two conditions noted above will remain. What can you do to expand your mailing safely, and at lower cost to yourself? Here are two methods we see used frequently with great success:

1. **Where you're constrained by the number of names available,** use sales agents in other countries where more names are likely to be available.
2. **Use a catalog distributor** to get your catalog into more hands at low cost to you.

Let's take a close look at each of these methods to see how you can use it to earn more money in your mail-order/direct-marketing business today. You'll get some good ideas from each.

Use Overseas Sales Agents for Your Catalog

If your market is restricted by a lack of names—such as only 6,852 brass doorknob suppliers—you might want to try overseas agents to get a larger market for your catalog products or services. We've done this at my company, IWS, Inc., with great success. Here are profitable steps you can take to greater catalog success:

1. **Decide to explore overseas distribution** of your catalog, or portions of it.
2. **Look for agents overseas** by placing ads in international papers such as the *Herald Tribune, Financial Times,* etc. Your ad might say:

   AGENTS SOUGHT for successful mail-order catalog. Write ABC, Box 123, Anytown USA.

3. **Have each agent give you a short business plan** as to how he or she would promote your products or services.
4. **Review each plan** and pick the agents who seem best equipped to sell your products or services.
5. **Give each agent a short written agreement** covering the commission he or she will be paid for sales from your catalog—you can start your agents at a 40% commission and raise this to 50% after a certain dollar amount in sales of your products or services. Having this "stepped" arrangement gives your agents an incentive to work hard to make big sales for you!

Our overseas agents really expand our business each year. They bring to us many advantages, such as:

1. **New ideas for marketing** our products and services are introduced by people who see the world from a different perspective than we do.

2. **New enthusiasm** for our BWB-approach to success brings in customers who might never have heard of us from our usual ads.

3. **New money comes into our business** for inventory because overseas agents like to have a few of each of our products on hand for quick sales. We do NOT require that an agent have inventory on hand—this is a decision each agent makes on his or her own.

4. **New customers generate more sales.** This makes the agent—and us—happy. Because—after all—the purpose of a business is to make sales that earn money for the owners or corporate shareholders!

The sales that overseas agents make can be significant. Thus, we have agents who send us $2,000 for inventory. Others send $500 a week when they're promoting our products along with others they sell. A good agent can generate sizable sales for you by using either your entire catalog or just selected items from it.

So if you want to expand your catalog sales—and almost every BWB catalog salesperson seeks expansion—consider overseas sales agents. They can turn a sleepy, lackluster business into a booming success which puts enormous money into your bank account!

Use a Catalog Distributor to Get Wider Circulation of Your Catalog

As we said earlier, a catalog stays around much longer than a single-page flyer or any other form of ad. So it has a longer selling life. This means it works much harder for you. And the more catalogs you can get into the hands of your prospects, the greater your chances of increasing the sales of your mail-order/direct-marketing business.

One excellent way to get wider circulation of your catalog is to use a catalog distributor. Here's how this will work for your catalog:

1. **The catalog distributor sends** a short description of your catalog along with an illustration of it to a large number of prospects—often in the millions.

2. **Other interesting catalogs are promoted** along with your catalog in the distributor's mailing.
3. **A nominal fee—$2 or $3— is charged for your catalog.** The catalog distributor keeps this fee and sends you the name and address of the person requesting your catalog. You send your catalog to the prospect.
4. **You save ad costs, and mailing costs,** looking for prospects to whom you can send your catalog. Meanwhile, you're getting your catalog into the hands of people who really want, or need it, because they've paid for your catalog.

The only danger with using a catalog distributor is that you may be swamped with orders. This could strain your printing and mailing budgets. A number of my mail-order friends have told me stories of getting requests for 15,000 or 20,000 copies of a their catalog when they printed just 3,000 copies! They had to run to catch up with the demand.

But their sales boomed out within a few weeks after they mailed the catalog. So a little pain resulted in much stronger health for their business! To avoid this situation, ask the catalog distributor how many copies he or she thinks will be requested by prospects. Most distributors can give you a fairly accurate answer. Then you'll be ready when the requests come flooding in.

If a catalog distributor interests you, contact me by mail, phone, or fax. If you're a subscriber to one of my newsletters I'll be glad to give you—free of charge—full details on three catalog distributors you might work with. But just remember what I said—you may be "blown away" by the number of requests for your catalog and the amount of business it generates. As the man said—"Happiness is a positive cash flow!" That's exactly what a catalog distributor will give your company if your catalog is taken on.

Believe Me When I Say:
Catalogs Can Make You Rich!

I wish you could spend one day—about 7 hours—with me in my business opening the mail that comes in, reading the fax orders pouring through the machine, and answering our 800 number to take the credit-card orders people place from our catalog. Just get this:

Our 48-page, 8.5" × 11" catalog costs us about 50 cents a copy to print in black and white. Yet this 50-cent catalog generates orders of $200, $400, $800, etc. The largest order we ever had from one copy of the catalog was $2,486.50! Just imagine that—a 50-cent black-and-white catalog brought in 5,000 times its cost! This is business efficiency at its best. You must keep in mind—of course—that our average order from our catalog is less—it's about $257.

Other catalog houses do very well also. Here are a few I picked at random to show you what you might do using catalogs to promote your mail-order/direct-marketing products: (1) A small specialty-food catalog does $1.6 million in business with its 36-page, 7" × 10" catalog; (2) A reading-and-writing tools catalog (lamps, pens, engraved letter paper, etc.) does $40 million in sales annually from its 56-page, 6" × 11" catalog; (3) A ski equipment catalog (pants, jackets, suits, plus accessories) will do $1.4 million in annual sales in its fifth year from its 56-page, 8.5" × 11" catalog; average order is $325.

What You Can Sell in Your Catalog

There's almost NO LIMIT to what you can sell in your catalog. If something is a product or service, it is almost certain that it can be sold in a catalog. Of course, there are certain items you cannot—and would not—sell in a catalog. Thus, you would not try to sell a medical diagnosis by catalog! The patient must be present in a doctor's office for a diagnosis to be made. But you could sell a book on making medical diagnoses to people who do this work! Keeping this in mind, here are just a few items you can sell by catalog—selected at random:

Seeds of all types for home and professional gardens

Clothing for many purposes—regular wear, sports, safety

Marine products for pleasure and commercial boaters

Automotive products for hot rodders and just plain drivers

Business products of many types—machines, supplies, maintenance

Hobby supplies—model airplanes, boats, soldiers, sailors

Computers—hardware, software, desks, paper, labels

Tools for hobbyists and professionals

Sporting goods—fishing rods, skis, tennis racquets

Food—cheeses, meats, fruits, candies

There you have 10 types of products you can sell in your catalog. You—I'm sure— can come up with at least 10—or 100 more! The main point to keep in mind is that catalog selling is the way of the world today. If you want to be part of the world you MUST have a catalog!

Once you have your catalog you'll want to get it around. Here—as promised—are a number of active mailing-list brokers. Contact them for free data on the lists they have available for rent. Just remember—if one or more these brokers goes out of business—you can get a new list from me free of charge, if you're a subscriber to one of my newsletters:

The Coolidge Co., Inc., 25 W. 43 St., New York, NY 10036 (212) 642-0300

Alan Drey Co., Inc., 333 N. Michigan Ave., Chicago, IL 60601 (312) 346-7453

Fairfield Marketing Group, Inc., 830 Sport Hill Rd., Easton, CT 06612 (203) 261-5585

IC Direct List Brokers, 17 Paul Dr., Ste. 202, San Rafael, CA 94904 (415) 472-3332

Market Share, 5726 Cortez Rd. W., Ste. 303, Bradenton, FL 34210 (813) 794-6059

You—I believe—can do as well in your own mail-order/direct-marketing catalog business! To get started just use the ideas in this chapter. *They really do work!* If the ideas don't work for you, just give me a call, write me a letter, or fax me. I'll be glad to guide you—if you're a subscriber to one of my newsletters. Remember—you have a good friend in your author!

CHAPTER 9

MAKE SERVICES MAKE YOUR MAIL-ORDER WEALTH

As YOU NOW know, in mail order/direct marketing you can sell either products or services. Examples of products you might sell include books, auto license-plate holders, garden seeds, etc. Services you might sell include consulting, income-tax preparation, correspondence clubs, etc. A service may include a product but the assistance you give your customers as part of your service is usually more important than the product.

Pick Your Moneymaking Service

You *must like* the service you sell by mail order/direct marketing. Why? Because in a service business:

1. **You usually deal with your customers** on a direct basis—supplying personal or business help of some kind.
2. **Your income depends on results** you produce for your customer.
3. **You may talk to your customer** on the telephone, receive a fax message from him or her, or may meet your customer personally.

If you don't like the service you're providing you may find the three aspects above unattractive. Then you'll be unhappy and won't do as good a job as when you like—and enjoy—what you're doing.

So you *must* know yourself; *must* know what you like, and *must* know what you dislike if you're to succeed in your own mail-order/direct-marketing service business. To pick your service business, answer these five easy questions:

1. **Do you enjoy talking** to people
   on the telephone?   ___Yes___No

2. **Do you enjoy meeting** people and
   talking to them face-to-face?   ___Yes___No

3. **Would you prefer** to deal with people
   only by mail or fax?   ___Yes___No

4. **Do you enjoy trying** to help people solve
   their problems?   ___Yes___No

5. **Can you "get out of yourself"** to
   concentrate on other people's
   interests and problems?   ___Yes___No

If you answer YES to three or more of these questions you'll probably enjoy a service mail-order/direct-marketing business. And if you answer YES to all five questions, a service business *is* for you!

You may have already picked your mail-order/direct-marketing service business. If you haven't, here are a number of mail-order/direct-marketing businesses that can make money for you.

Good Moneymaking Mail-Order/ Direct-Marketing Service Businesses

In a mail-order/direct-marketing service business you help people or businesses. Typical ways you can help people or businesses:

1. **Get loans for individuals or businesses.** You act as a financial consultant, assisting people or businesses in obtaining

loans for a variety of purposes—to buy a business, expand a business, purchase equipment, promote products by advertising or publicity, buy income-producing real estate, etc. Most of your contacts with your customers are by mail, telephone, or fax. You are paid a retainer for your work, plus a percentage of the loan after the funding money is obtained by the borrower.

2. **Obtain grants for people or companies** seeking money to help others by improving their lives in some way—such as better health, improved roads for transportation, more effective education, etc. A grant never need be repaid, as contrasted to a loan, which *must* be repaid. Most of your contacts with your customers will be by mail, telephone, or fax. You will be paid a retainer for your work, plus a fee based on the the amount of the grant, once the person or firm seeking the grant gets the funding money.

3. **Franchise business** ideas or methods that will help others earn more money in their own business. You guide your franchise clients into writing a business plan for their franchisees (the people who buy the franchise), suggest prices to charge, ways to advertise their franchise, etc. Most of your contacts will be by mail, phone, or fax.

4. **Teach a subject to people via mail.** Your subjects can range from raising house plants to home appraisals, to small-boat navigation, to—you name it. You can use previously published materials (the easiest way) or you can write your own materials. You sell your course by mail-order ads, direct-mail, or telephone. Almost all your contacts will be by mail, with a few by fax or phone.

5. **Help people get credit cards for themselves or their business.** Millions of people in this world are trying to get their first credit card. You can help them and earn a fee for your work. Your fee can come from either the person you help get the credit card, or from the bank issuing the card. Many banks—when seeking more cardholders—will pay you a commission for each person you direct to them who gets a credit card by qualifying for it through the bank.

6. **Be a mortgage cashout consultant** to help people get money for mortgages they hold. Thus, when people sell a house they will often "take back" a mortgage in place of cash because the buyer does not have enough liquid

funds for the down payment. After a few years, the seller may decide that he or she wants to get cash out (i.e. obtain a cashout) of the mortgage instead of receiving a monthly payment on the mortgage. Why does the person want cash? For a number of good reasons—to buy a new car, to pay college tuition for children, to take a round-the-world cruise, etc. You find a buyer for the mortgage by mail and bring the seller and buyer together to earn a 4% (typically) commission on the sale. You find the seller by mail, also.

7. **Help businesses export their products or services.** You guide businesses—by mail or phone—into the correct ways to find overseas customers for their products or services. You are paid a commission on each sale and a similar commission on future sales to that overseas firm by your client. You do not have to be able to speak a foreign language to earn money this way. The "official" language of exporting and importing is English. If you can speak English—even haltingly— you can become successful in exporting or importing.

8. **Settle business debts by mail.** Suppose Company A owes Firm B $250,000. The debt is almost a year old and Firm B never expects to be repaid. You find Company A by mailing a letter to it telling the owner(s) that you negotiate debt reductions—also called commercial-debt mediation. You ask the owner—by mail or phone—how much they can afford to pay Firm B to wipe out the debt. Company A tells you they can afford half the debt, or $125,000. You write Firm B and offer to settle the debt for $125,000. Firm B—never expecting to get a penny of what's it's owed even if they went to court—gladly accepts your offer. Company A pays the $125,000, wiping out its debt. Firm B gets $125,000 more than it ever expected to take in. You collect 10% of the amount of money saved, or $0.1 \times \$125,000 = \$12,500$. And all this can be done by mail! It's a great business that can earn you as much as $100,000 a year.

9. **Offer investment advice by mail.** Do you know anything about pork bellies, hogs, feeder cattle, copper, palladium, sugar, cotton, or any other commodity traded on the various exchanges? If you do, you can make big money providing investment advice by mail. You can

even do this for stocks and bonds—if they're your specialty. Plenty of people charge high prices for giving all types of investment advice by mail. Some even offer a hotline telephone service their client can call to get the latest information. Others offer fax online help to their clients. The big feature you should offer is KNOWLEDGE OF THE INVESTMENT YOU RECOMMEND. People will be happy to pay you thousands of dollars for your investment-advice service.

How to Make Big Money in Your Service Business

Now that you know more about yourself (from the question-and-answer quiz above) and nine types of service businesses, you're ready to make big money in your mail-order/direct-marketing service business. So let's put *you* into a service business of *your* choice.

As some of my millions of readers know, I've been in the mail-order/direct-marketing business a "few" years—more than 30 years to be precise! People who work with and for me often say—laughingly—"Ty, you've created an enormous moneymaking machine. The money just pours into your business every day. How can I do the same?"

You can do the same! All it takes is a few simple steps. And you don't have to be a college graduate; you don't even need a high school diploma. All you need do is take these simple steps:

1. **Find, or develop, a needed service** you can sell by mail order/direct marketing to a specific market.
2. **Figure out how, where, and to whom,** you'll sell your service by mail order/direct marketing.
3. **Set up a marketing plan** for your mail-order/direct-marketing service; make estimates of the cost of your sales.
4. **Estimate how many sales you can make** of your service in one year, two years, and three years in units and dollars.
5. **Compute your total cost of doing business;** compare this to the income you'll earn from the sales you estimated in Step 4. If you show a profit, which = (Sales \$ — Cost \$)/ Sales \$ = 20%, or more, go ahead with your business. Your

income taxes will be paid out of your profit. After-tax profit will probably be 10%, or higher.

Now these steps may seem like a lot of work. But they really aren't! To show you that this is so, let's put *you* into your own mail-order/direct-marketing service business using each of the five steps above.

Find, or Develop, a Needed Service—Step 1

There are thousands of services you can deliver by mail. Let's say that the types of services you feel comfortable with are:

- Finding money for people
- Finding significant partners for people
- Finding business opportunities for people

The types of services you like clearly show you enjoy helping people. But you want to do it by mail instead of in person. Looking at these three services you decide that the first—finding money for people—would be best for you. Your decision is based on these thoughts:

- **Money—not water—is the universal solvent**—at least that's what Ty Hicks said in one of his books!
- **You like money**—and you've always liked it! Working with money will be fun for you.
- **Almost everyone**—and every company—needs, or wants, money at sometime during their life.

Thinking about your choice of a service business, you're happy with your decision. You feel you have an enormous potential for helping people—and yourself!

Figure Out How, Where, and To Whom You'll Sell Your Service—Step 2

You can have the best service in the world. But if you can't sell it, the service is worthless to you. As someone once said:

"Nothing happens until a sale is made." So, figuring out *how, where,* and *to whom* you'll sell your service is very important for your future success.

Your service business will be that of finding money for people and businesses. You remember having seen *Money Available* ads in the past. To refresh your memory you review a number of large newspapers and magazines to see what kinds of ads are run under the *Money Available* category. After reviewing the *New York Times, Wall Street Journal, Los Angeles Times, Business Week, Forbes,* and *Fortune,* you find that:

- **Small classified ads** are popular for most *Money Available* offers being made today.
- **A few accounts receivable (factors) lenders** use 1- or 2-inch pace ads.
- **Large lenders**—banks, mortgage companies—use full-page space ads.

Counting the ads for two weeks, you find that 97% are classifieds. And all these ads just ask the potential customer to either write, or call, for more information. You decide to run similar ads—imitating what the competition does but doing it better than they do. (This is called *innovative imitation,* where you imitate your competitors but introduce new, innovative ideas that set you apart from other firms in the field.) Your decision answers the *HOW* part of Step 2.

The *WHERE* part of Step 2 is also answered—you'll advertise in newspapers and magazines read by people seeking money for personal or business needs. As part of your innovation you decide to also advertise in the *Opportunity Magazines*—such as *Moneymaking Opportunities, Spare Time, Income Opportunities,* etc. to promote your service to people in smaller businesses.

The *TO WHOM* part of Step 2 is likewise answered by your market research. You'll be offering money sources to individuals needing loans or grants. And—at the start—to small businesses. As time passes and your business grows you will offer your services to medium-size and large corporations.

You have now answered all the questions which are part of Step 2. You're ready to move ahead to Step 3.

Set Up Your Marketing Plan—Step 3

You may not want to go to the trouble of setting up a marketing plan. But let me tell you this. Preparing a marketing plan is highly valuable to you because such a plan:

- **Helps you see where** you'll advertise and promote your new business
- **Gives you a precise idea** of the cost of your ads and promotion
- **Allows you to evaluate** the relative productivity of each type of advertising outlet you use—newspaper, magazine, local giveaways, etc.

To prepare your marketing plan, use a form like that in Table 9-1. Fill in the various columns as you develop your marketing plan. You can get ad costs from the various publications by writing, faxing, or calling them for their rates. Choose the type of ad to use based on Step 2. Since you're offering more than just accounts receivable financing, you decide to start only with classified ads.

Estimate the number of responses you'll get by assuming a certain percentage of the publication's circulation: 1% is a good starting number.

Table 9-1. Advertising Cost and Response Estimates

Ad Outlet	Type of Ad	Cost	Expected Number of Inquiries per Mo.
Opportunity Magazine No. 1	Classified	$185/mo.	2,000
Opportunity Magazine No. 2	Classified	$210/mo.	2,300
Newspaper No. 1	Classified Wed. & Sun.	$130/wk.	1,000
Newspaper No. 2	Classified Sun.	$48/day	1,200

Once you know the number of inquiries you'll get you can estimate how many of these you can convert to sales.

You use what mail-order pros call the *conversion rate*—which is the percentage of inquiries to whom you make sales. Thus, if you convert 25% of 1,000 inquiries, you'll make sales to 0.25 × 1,000 = 250 people or companies, or a combination of them.

Conversion rates can vary from 1% for high-priced items to 25% for competitively priced products or services. With good, convincing sales materials, you can expect to convert 25% of your inquiries. In my business we regularly convert 24.8% of our inquiries to sales.

Knowing (1) the number of inquiries you'll probably get, (2) the estimated number you'll convert to sales, and (3) your average sales price, you can easily figure your income from: Income Per Day, $ = Number of Inquiries per Day × Conversion Rate, Expressed as a Decimal × Average Price, $ per Sale.

Let's take two typical examples, presented in Table 9-2, to figure your daily income:

Table 9-2. How to Figure Your Daily Income

	INQUIRIES PER DAY	CONVERSION RATE	AVERAGE $ PER SALE
(A)	140	25%	139
(B)	250	30%	88

(A) Income per day = 140 × 0.25 × 139 = $4,865
(B) Income per day = 250 × 0.3 × 88 = $6,600

Do these numbers impress you? They *do* impress me! Even if the numbers were for one week they would impress many people. I even know some people who would be impressed with monthly sales numbers like these!

From these sales numbers you must—of course—subtract your sales costs, made up of:

Advertising

Service cost—see below for details

Postage, shipping, or communications (phone/fax)

Labor

Overhead

At the start you can keep these costs small. Also, at the start, your sales will probably be small! The second week I was in business my sales were $7. But the third week they were $600. And they kept increasing every week after that. Remember—it takes any business time to get "on a roll"— that is, get started bringing in large amounts of money. And your service mail-order/direct-marketing business will probably be the same as any other business, or:

Small income—Small costs; Large income—Larger costs

This is good because when your business is small you really don't have much money to spend on ads, promotion, or other methods of bringing in new customers. As your business grows you have more money you can spend on getting new customers.

Some companies spend 5% of their total sales dollars on advertising and promotion—after they're established and known to their customers. At the start you should consider spending 10%, 20%, even 30% of your total sales dollars on advertising and promotion.

To see how this works, let's assume you have different levels of income and various ad and promotion percentages. Table 9-3 presents your income and cost at each level:

Table 9-3. Your Possible Income and Ad Expense

Total Sales, $	Percent Spent on Ads and Promotion	Cost of Ads and Promotion, $
100,000	5	5,000
100,000	10	10,000
100,000	20	20,000
150,000	5	7,500
150,000	10	15,000
150,000	20	30,000

Now these ad and promotion costs may seem high. But they really aren't—if they bring back sales dollars. You should aim at bringing back at least $3 for every $1 you spend on ads and promotion. Many small mail-order/direct-marketing service firms bring back $10 per $1 spent! I'd like to see *you* do the same—starting right now.

Estimate How Many Sales You Can Make—Step 4

Are you afraid to make sales guesses? You are? Let me tell you something—almost all BWBs (Beginning Wealth Builders) ARE afraid to make sales estimates. Why? Because you're "going out on a limb" when you make a sales estimate. You're "flying in unknown skies" because no one—not even YOU—knows if the estimates are correct.

But if you don't make the sales estimates, who will? Does anyone know more about your business than you? No? Then only YOU can make the sales estimates! So you're stuck with the job. But really it isn't that bad a job—instead it's fun! And the more sales estimates you make, the easier it is to make them—and the more accurate they will be.

To make any sales estimate you need certain information. In a service mail-order/direct-marketing business the information you need is:

1. **The size of your market**—i.e. the number of people or companies that might be interested in the service you're offering.
2. **Your market penetration**—i.e. the number of people or firms to whom you can sell your service—in some markets a 1% penetration (sales) is considered good; in other markets a 10% penetration may be possible. You have to decide what penetration level you can reach with the service you're offering.

Your service business—as you recall—is finding money for people and small companies. So you ask yourself: "How many people seek money?" Once you answer this question you ask: "How many small companies seek money?"

As we all know, millions of people and companies seek money. But not all these people read the magazines and newspapers in which you plan to advertise. Going back to the marketing plan in Step 3, we see that if we advertised in the two monthly magazines and the two daily newspapers we could have inquiries amounting to:

2 Monthly magazines	4,300 inquiries per month
2 Daily newspapers	@ 2,200 inquiries per week and 4 weeks per month 8,800 inquiries per month
Total inquiries per month	13,100

If you can convert 10% of these to sales you'll make $0.1 \times 13,100 = 1,310$ sales per month. Your monthly sales income, if your service is priced at—say—$149 would be $1,310 \times \$149 = \$195,190$. And if you could convert only 1% of your inquiries to sales, your monthly sales income would be $0.01 \times 1,310 \times \$149 = \$19,519$.

As you get more experience selling your service your sales will almost certainly increase.

Thus, if you convert 1% of your sales your first year in business, you'll probably convert 1.5% to 2% in your second year, and 2.5% to 2.75% in your third year in business. With these numbers in mind you make your 1-year, 2-year, and 3-year sales projections as in Table 9-4.

Table 9-4. Sales Projections for 1, 2, and 3 Years

	1st Year	2nd Year	3rd Year
No. of Inquiries (= 12 × 13,100/mo.)	157,200	157,200	157,200
Conversion Rate (expressed as a decimal)	0.01	0.015	0.025
Unit sales (= conversion rate × inquiries)	1,572	2,358	3,930
Total Sales $ (= Unit Sales × $149 List Price)	**$234,228**	**$351,342**	**$585,570**

There you have your sales estimates—in both units and dollars. It really wasn't hard, was it? And the more sales estimates you make, the easier it will be for you!

To find out if you can make any money with sales such as these you must now figure your total cost of doing business—Step 5. Let's see how you can do this and if you'll be able to make any money from the business—that is, a profit.

Compute Your Total Cost of Doing Business—Step 5

Your cost of doing business is—as we said earlier—comprised of Advertising, Cost of the Service (either as a product or someone's time, or—usually—a combination of product and time cost), Shipping (postage, telephone, or fax), Labor (which may be included in the Cost of the Service), and Overhead—your rent, light, heat, etc. for your place of business. If you operate from your home at the start—as most BWBs do—your overhead will be close to zero. But we'll include a charge for overhead because every business needs a place to operate from.

Your cost of advertising in the two monthly magazines and the two daily newspapers will be: 12 months × $185/mo. for Magazine 1 = $2,220; for Magazine 2: 12 × $210 = $2,520. For the two newspapers it will be: Newspaper 1: 52 weeks × $130/wk = $6,760; Newspaper 2: 52 × $48 = $2,496. Adding these costs gives you a total of $13,996. You figure that your ad cost will rise 20% per year after the first year—either from increased advertising or inflation, or a combination of both.

The Cost of the Service, including Shipping and Labor is $90 per sale. You get this by adding all your costs for products and/or labor that are part of the Service you're selling. Your suppliers will gladly give you cost estimates (free) when you have a product as part of your Service.

You figure your overhead as 15% of your sales the first year, and 20% in the second and third years. This reflects the increased cost of overhead to support the larger sales in your second and third years of business. Now let's see, using Table 9-5, if you can make any money at this business.

Table 9-5. Profit Projections for 1, 2 and 3 Years

	1ST YEAR	2ND YEAR	3RD YEAR
TOTAL SALES, $	234,228	351,342	585,570
AD COST, $	13,996	16,795	20,154
PRODUCT COST @ $90/SALE, $	141,480	212,220	353,700
OVERHEAD @ 15%, 20%, AND 20%	35,134	70,268	117,114
TOTAL COST, $	190,610	299,283	490,968
PROFIT (= Total Sales, $ – Total Cost, $)	43,618	52,059	94,602
PROFIT PERCENTAGE (= Profit, $/Total Sales, $) × 100	18.6	14.8	16.2

Your study shows you earn $43,618 your first year in business. That's excellent. Especially if you figure that in your overhead at 15% and 20% there may be some salary for you. So your total take on which you may pay income taxes could be more than the $43,618 shown! That's great news for you.

And your profit at 18.6% is typical for this type of business. So your sales, and costs, are right on target. If you were showing a much higher percentage profit I'd be suspicious of your sales or cost estimates.

Between your first and second years in business your profit percentage declines—from 18.6% to 14.8% This is not unusual. Why? Because as your sales increase from year to year, so—too—may your costs. This means that your profit percentage may fall off. But your profit dollars rise—

from \$43,618 to \$52,059. And, in your third year, your profit percentage starts to rise again. This means your business is following the typical pattern such mail-order/direct-marketing service businesses do. You're right on target!

And if you wonder why your business shows a profit in the first year, instead of taking two or three years to break even, let me say this:

> A well-run mail-order/direct-marketing service business can easily break even—or show a profit in its first year—because most such new businesses serve niche markets with unusual products or services dreamt up by their owners to serve a need they perceive. The public "beats a path to their door," allowing the firm to show a good profit quickly!

Push Ahead to Your Service Business Success

You now have the tools you need to pick, start, and succeed in, your own mail-order/direct-marketing service business. Also, you know how to "work the numbers" for your future business. With these skills as part of your business tool kit it should be easy for you to get started.

To help *you* get started in *your* mail-order/direct-marketing service business, I developed Table 9-6. This is a form you can fill out (after making a copy of it or using the entries as shown) and send to me. I'll get back to you by phone, fax, or mail, telling you if your business—in my opinion—has a chance to succeed. There is NO charge of any kind for this service, if you're a subscriber of one of my newsletters—see the back of this book.

To prevent any thoughts of my "borrowing" your ideas I will not evaluate any service business that's primarily directed at publishing a book, kit, manual, or other document. Why? Because I'm in the publishing business myself. So I don't want any reader saying they came to me with an idea for a publication and I ran away with it! While I certainly would never borrow your idea(s), it's hard to predict what some people might think.

So DO NOT SUBMIT ANY PUBLISHING IDEAS TO ME. I'll just bounce them back to you with a "no comment."

Table 9-6. Proposed Mail-Order Service Business

1. Service business I want to start _____

2. Customers who'll buy my service_____

3. Ways I'll use to reach my prospects:

   (a)_____

   (b)_____

   (c)_____

   (d)_____

4. Average estimated sales price, $_____

5 Estimated service unit sales, $

   1st year_____

   2nd year_____

   3rd year_____

6. Estimated service unit cost, $

   1st year_____

   2nd year_____

   3rd year_____

7. Features that will set my service apart from the competition:

   (1)_____

   (2)_____

   (3)_____

   (4)_____

8. Additional information that may help you judge my new
   business:

   _____

   _____

9. Your name_____

   Your address_____

   Your phone/fax
   numbers_____

10. Send to: Tyler G. Hicks, IWS, Inc., PO Box 186, Merrick,
    NY 11566-0186.

Now you can have the help you need. Just fill out the form and send it to me. I'll give you all the help I can. Just remember this: Do NOT send me data on any type of publishing business! I'll bounce it back to you—pronto. Publishing is my business and I don't want any ideas for it but my own!

More Service Businesses for You to Consider

Since I want YOU to succeed in your own mail-order/direct-marketing service business, here are a number of highly successful businesses you might want to consider—almost all can be started in—and run from—your own home, right now:

1. **Mortgage reduction specialist**—you show people, by mail, how to save money on their home or business mortgage—there are millions of clients for you!
2. **Low-cost telephone services** people can get by mail, phone, or fax. You earn a sales commission, plus—with firms—a commission on all calls made.
3. **Help foreign investors make money in your country**—do it all by mail, phone, or fax. Put them into business, real estate, products they need. Your payment comes from finder fees you're paid on completion of each deal.
4. **Be a disability consultant** showing—by mail, phone, or fax—disabled people how—and where—they can get disability benefits, take legal action to recover damages, or obtain other reimbursement to which they're entitled.
5. **Audit utility bills**—electric, gas, phone, etc. by mail, phone, or fax. Receive a percentage of the savings you produce for your clients.
6. **Introduce people by mail, phone, fax, CD-ROM,** or a special videotape you prepare. You will earn a fee for each introduction you do. Specialize in professionals, firefighters, police officers, pilots, etc. It's a great business for those who like people!
7. **Supply small directories of local businesses** for free distribution in stores, amusement parks, places of religious

worship, etc. in your area. Contact merchants by mail to advertise at low cost in your directory. Some people report earnings of $10,000 a month, from home, from a directory with just 200 listings in it!

8. **Find, and place, child-care providers** for working parents. Do this by mail or phone and earn a fee for each "nanny" you find. People are desperate for good, responsible childcare during the working day. Provide the right people and you have a lifetime mail-order business you can run from your home part- or full-time.

9. **Run a professional billing service from your home** for small businesses of many types. Find your customers by mail from your home. All you do is send out bills regularly for work done by your customers for their customers. You can do this by hand, on a typewriter, or by computer. Take your choice as to how you want, and prefer, to work. Earnings range from $500 to $5,000 a month, depending on the number of clients you have.

10. **Check on older people** to see that they're healthy and safe. Use the mail to find customers among younger people who are responsible for aging parents. Regularly monitor their parents and report any problems to whomever they designate—a doctor, hospital, police, etc. Your income expands as the population ages—which it is doing now!

11. **Help professionals** build their medical, dental, legal, accounting, engineering, etc. practice. What you do is contact the professionals by mail, telling them that you can get more "customers" into their office. You receive a monthly payment based on the work you do. You associate with the best people in town—via mail!

12. **Analyze handwriting by mail.** Run this from your home in your spare time. All of us wonder what our handwriting reveals about ourselves. Cash in on this human trait and do it all by mail! Your income could be in the $1,000 to $5,000 a month range—if you work at getting lots of customers!

There you have 12 profitable mail-order/direct-marketing service businesses. One of them might be for you. Or one of these businesses might suggest another, related business that turns you on. The point to keep in mind is this:

Find a mail-order/direct-marketing service business YOU like and get it going. Your income may be much more than you ever dreamed was possible!

And if you need help, your author is always ready, if you're a subscriber to one of my newsletters. Just give me a call. I'm ready to help no matter what your age, no matter what your gender, no matter where you're located! I've helped thousands. You might as well be next!

CHAPTER 10

OFFBEAT SERVICES CAN BRING IN BIG CASH

IN OUR LAST chapter we talked about you selling services by mail order/direct marketing. The services we suggested there were what you might call "standard." They're services most of us see fairly regularly in the mail we receive and the magazines we read. In this chapter we'll show you some off-beat services you can sell by mail and profit enormously.

What Are Offbeat Services?

An offbeat service is one that you don't see offered regularly by regular mail-order dealers. Offbeat services are often niche—i.e. specialized—services. Most offbeat services are those the BWB developed himself or herself. Some of the offbeat services we mention in this chapter might not appeal to you. And in mentioning these services we're not recommending them. Instead, we're just reporting to you on the various offerings available in the mail today.

Offbeat services that are providing good incomes for BWBs of all types today include these:

1. **New Age**—spiritual, sacred, soul—services are the rage today for stressed-out people in all walks of life. And New Age is so diverse these days you can define your version of it with yoga, meditation, spiritual awareness, energy sources for success, angels, psychic events, the

153

occult, mind-body-soul relationships, etc. You name it and you can probably sell it by mail order/direct marketing.

2. **Weaving, knitting, crocheting, cross-stitching, etc.** are popular with women today. Thus, mailing-list brokers offer 100,000 names of women who sew who bought needlework products during the last 12 months; 93,000 buyers of crochet books; 53,000 buyers of a magazine on cross-stitching. So if you have a service for these enthusiasts you can do well. You should know your field well—or get a service from someone who does because these people love their hobby!

3. **Irish-Celtic music** is loved by millions of people around the world. With a catalog listing the Irish-Celtic music you have available you can see sales of 20,000 to 30,000 copies of a CD or tape album. While this isn't a "golden" album it sure can bring in lots of bucks—especially at $15, or more, per album, depending on its size. And you can take this basic idea and work it for many other types of music—Polish, German, Italian, French, English, Japanese, etc. Music lovers will love you if you provide them with the music they enjoy hearing.

4. **Golfers everywhere want to better their game!** Why? Because most golfers are duffers—they can't hit the ball straight. Give any golfer a better way to play his or her game and you're almost assured of making a good profit. Thus, one firm that markets a special golf club via a TV infomercial expects to sell between 150,000 and 200,000 of the clubs at $15 each in one year. That's sales of $2,250,000 to $3,000,000 in one year! Again—provide an offbeat service—in this case the possibility of playing a better game—and you can rake in the big profits. Another dealer has a golf-ball retriever—a device that will extend 12 feet into a pond and find a golf ball on the bottom! Big sales are expected to duffers.

5. **Fishing enthusiasts—both saltwater and freshwater—**love their hobby. They spend millions of dollars every year on information services telling them where the big fish are, how to catch them, who set new records for weight and length, and what equipment can help land the most unusual fish. You can cash in by supplying useful information, techniques, records data, etc.—if you know fishing,

or can hire someone who does know fish and how and where to catch them!

6. **Alternative health** is another rage today. This is the approach to health that uses diet, herbs, mental images, prayer, and a variety of other ways to improve one's physical well-being. People today turn to alternatives to find ways to improve their health that are not in the regimen of conventional medicine. If you can give them ways to do this they'll pay you—over and over. But you must have reliable information—either from yourself or from someone who knows!

7. **Sell offbeat electronic services** via mail order/direct marketing. The whole world is going electronic. And the interest in electronics—computers, VCRs, TV, cellular phones, satellite-dish transmission, etc.—seems never-ending. You can cash in on the hunger for information and products in this field by providing a unique service that few others offer. What service is that? Only you can give an answer to that question because you're the one to come up with the offbeat, the unique. But it can make millions for you—*that I do know!*

8. **Find, and sell, collectibles of all types** to people who want to have them in their possession. And what's a collectible, you ask? It could be a coin from an early shipwreck, a watch worn by a well-known sports figure, autographed musical instruments from pop music stars, jewelry from the estates of movie and TV actors and actresses. Prices for collectibles can be high—ranging from $200 to $30,000. Your service consists of finding the collectibles and then offering them to an interested audience. The usual way to sell high-priced collectibles is via TV—especially satellite dish owners, of which—at this writing—there were some 5 million in the United States, with the number increasing every day. Sales are made when customers call in to order by credit card or with a check debit account. This service is booming and you might want to consider getting in on it—now!

9. **Psychic services**—where the caller talks to someone who will help solve their problems—are raking in the big bucks these days. A person calls an 800 number and for $2.99 a minute can have his or her problems "solved."

The charge is put on the person's credit card. Or for $3.99 a minute the same person can call a 900 number and get the help he or she needs. You advertise such services in the occult magazines, using 1-inch display ads. Radio and TV ads can also pull in the calls. At this writing the highest price charged for calls is $4.99 per minute. Business is booming. And you can get in on it—if the occult interests you!

There you have nine offbeat services that are making big money for BWBs today. And these offbeat services can make money for you, too! But none of these services interests you? Here are a few more, in Table 10-1, you might want to consider:

Table 10-1. More Offbeat Services You Might Offer

Family education—for parents, children, grandparents

Home hobby help and information for men, women, and children

Data for international investors seeking to earn more

Video "jukebox" providing unusual and rare videotapes for sale or rent

Fingernail beauty tips, procedures, and supplies for women worldwide

Business startup help for all kinds of beginners in different countries

Hi-tech entertainment supplies and equipment information

Stamp and coin collector data for beginners and/or experienced collectors

Lottery-ticket buyers schedules and info for more winning opportunities

Female clothing buyers sources for unusual garments and designs

"Cyber fighter" virtual reality data and suppliers information

---

Profitable Offbeat Services for All BWBs

Sell U.S.-type services to Asian, European, Australian, etc. consumers. Mailing-list houses have millions of names of such consumers you can rent for selling your services. And since many of these people receive little direct mail offering them unique services, your response rate can be "through the roof"—i.e. 10% or higher! Many a fortune is being made in overseas direct marketing and mail order today.

Provide folk music services to people who love this kind of entertainment. Services you can sell include recordings of popular stars on disk or tape, or biographies.

Introduce, by mail, people of the same culture residing in foreign lands. Thus, a woman runs a highly profitable dating service introducing Japanese people residing in America, where they find it hard to meet other Japanese.

Supply information on the sources of and prices for rare wines people can buy. Plenty of wine lovers will be glad to pay you hefty fees to locate the source of their favorite vintage. You can send them a helpful newsletter every other month—for which they'll be happy to pay anywhere from $48 to $350 a year.

Cater to medical specialists—of which there are many dozens—providing a service they need. Thus, one BWB supplies clinical nurses with up-to-date information on the latest advancements in their field. There are—of course—dozens of other medical and health-care specialties in which you—or a person you hire—can provide useful information for a price. Since purchase of such information is tax deductible to the specialist, the sale is easy to make.

To be salable, your service should be unique, should answer a specific need your customers have, and should be priced at a level they can afford. The more often you provide the service, the higher the price you can charge. Here are two examples of this:

- **A weekly newsletter** serving the AIDS field is issued 52 times a year and is priced at $1,895 per year for the domestic market, $2,095 per year for the international market.

- **Two other weekly newsletters,** one on hepatitis, the other on malaria, are each priced at $1,095 and $1,295 per year for the domestic and international markets.

Why the difference in pricing? It could be because the first newsletter serves a field in which there is a greater urgency for information than the second two. The diseases covered by the second two newsletters have been known by medical specialists for much longer than the disease covered by the first newsletter. While the reason given here is pure speculation on my part, it does indicate a possible approach to the pricing of information services.

And—as you can see—these newsletters meet the criteria we mentioned above, namely, each newsletter:

- **Is unique**—that is, it gives useful ideas that the reader would have difficulty finding easily elsewhere
- **Meets the needs** of its readership by giving helpful information that can be used in daily practice
- **Is priced at a level** that people in the field can afford to pay for data they can use every day in their important work

There are hundreds of other services you can develop. That's what's so nice about earning money in this great field. You can put your own "stamp of approval" on an idea by developing it yourself. And since all of us are different in the way we approach a problem or situation, each of us can come up with a unique answer that meets the needs of the market—and might make us a millionaire! So let's see how *you* can hit it big in today's mail-order/direct-marketing business offering unusual services.

Develop Your Idea for an Offbeat Service

We all know people who have great ideas but no follow through. These people will grab you by the sleeve and—with shining eyes—tell you what a wonderful idea they have and how many millions they'll make from the idea.

But run into the same person a month later and they won't say a word about the grand idea they pushed on you. They've either forgotten it or they're on to another idea—which they'll eventually drop also. What's happening here, you wonder.

It's a simple case of *no follow through*. If you get a good idea you *must* develop it. Without development, most ideas wither and fade away. To develop any idea for an offbeat service to be sold by mail order/direct marketing, take these easy steps:

1. **Ask yourself: Is this a unique idea?** Are there other services offering what I have in mind? Is my proposed service better in some way than others available now? Do I offer speed, ease of use, greater frequency, etc.? What makes my idea unique, compared to others that might be available? Would I buy my own idea's offer if I were in the field it serves?

2. **Does this unique idea serve my customer's needs?** Is there a *real need* for the service I plan to offer? Do my customers want what I will offer? Can I reach prospects at a reasonable cost with this unique idea? When I reach prospects can I show them how this unique idea serves their needs? When shown will prospects buy into the unusual service being offered to them? Can the prospect afford the unusual service I'm offering—i.e., does the prospect have the money to pay for the service?

A good example of proper development of a unique idea is that for a service that provides medical doctors around the world with updates of medical developments on audio- and videotapes. Physicians in 103 countries around the world receive two tapes a month, paying more than $200 per year for the tapes. These tapes provide the doctors with valuable continuing education, allowing them to keep up to date on the latest developments in their field. The tapes are sent via airmail using the U.S. Postal Service's WORLDPOST. These tapes are also promoted to doctors via airmail. Testing this service with the two questions above shows: **(1) Is this a unique idea?** Yes, it is—physicians the world over need regular updates; audio- and videotapes provide an easy and quick way to update oneself. **(2) Does this unique idea serve my customer's needs?** Yes, it does. Physicians are busy at their regular work. Having an audiotape allows them to listen while they drive, relax, or have other spare moments during jogging or exercising. And a video gives them graphic details they need to get a better idea of new methods in their field. All they have to do is pop it into their VCR and they have a four-color view of new methods.

Decide How, and Where, You'll Sell Your Offbeat Service

You can have the best and most offbeat service in the world. But if you can't sell it your service is worthless to you, and to your customers. So you must decide how, and where, you'll sell your offbeat service.

One advantage of an offbeat service is that it is developed for a specific group of potential customers. Thus, the audio- and videotape service mentioned above was developed for physicians seeking continuing education. This market can easily be identified because all graduate physicians in practice need continuing education.

With the market identified you can then figure out how to sell to that market. For the physician market, mail order/direct marketing is an excellent way to get to them. Why? Because busy people do read their mail. Most of them set aside a few minutes each day to look over their mail. So if you're selling to them you can get their attention with a well-prepared mailing piece.

Further, if you plan to sell throughout the world—as many offbeat services do—mail order/direct marketing is the way to go!

Working through this actual example of a successful offbeat service allows us to come up with useful guidelines for your offbeat service. To decide how, and where, you'll sell your offbeat service:

1. **Identify your market**—this grows out of the concept of your offbeat service. Why? Because you don't develop an offbeat service unless you perceive a need among a group you want to serve.

2. **Choose the way(s) you'll reach your market** with your sales materials and service. If the way you'll sell and deliver your service are the same—such as the mails— you're in a good position. Why? Because your customer feels comfortable when both are delivered the same way. And your entire business operation is easier because you're using the same services for all facets.

3. **See if you can offer other services to your market** in the same, or a related way. Thus, if you sell by mail, you'll find that many of your customers will also welcome fast delivery by fax of timely information. For instance, in my newsletter publishing business, which concentrates on financing for all types of small businesses, we often fax to our subscribers lists of lenders for specific types of loans—such as for churches, golf courses, etc. This enhances our services and serves our customers better—you can do the same with your offbeat service! The official term for these other services is *ancillary services*—but you don't have to use it. Just think of "related services."

4. **Seek offbeat ways to market your service(s).** Thus, people who sell our books, kits, and newsletters often start by selling directly to friends in their business, church or synagogue, lodge, social club, etc. This gets them off to a fast start with no investment other than time and energy. Other reps will include all, or some, of our promotional material (with their name and address on it) in other mailings they're doing. This is called a *ride-along* and can often generate significant sales for just the extra cost of printing because the postage cost has already been agreed to for the other services being promoted. Some of our reps use *package stuffers or bill stuffers* to promote one or more services. These are ads inserted with packages or bills being mailed by other companies to customers. Again, there's just the cost of the printing, plus a small stuffing charge. For wider distribution, some of our reps use the Internet to promote our products to a market expected to reach 100 million in the United States alone. Outside the U.S., a market of 30 million people in 75

countries is expected. This global interconnected computer network promises to expand markets beyond anything dreamed of just a few years ago! And you—too—can easily get on the Internet with your offbeat services—quickly and easily.

5. **Expand all marketing efforts that work!** You must keep marketing. Once you stop, your business will gradually decline, until the income from it is hardly worth the time you put in. So keep pushing ahead at all times!

Become the Leader in Your Field

You can make millions in mail order/direct marketing in niche markets. These are specialized markets in which you provide a service, or services, that few others have available. Thus, at IWS, my company, we provide unique services such as these:

An export-import kit, which—for just $99.50—can get a person started in this great business, working out of his or her home. Most other courses on this topic require class attendance and often don't give practical, day-to-day answers to questions on making money in this great field, which is growing every year. A number of users of the kit have made sales in the export market, earning significant fees doing so. See Figure 2-3 in Chapter 2 for details of this kit.

A financial broker/financial consultant kit, which helps people get started getting loans for needy companies and/or individuals—or even for their own needs. This kit gives more lenders, more forms, more prewritten releases than any other course I know of. Users of the kit report excellent results getting business and personal loans.

A real estate loan getters kit, which shows people how—and where—to get loans for all types of income real estate. In years of dealing with real estate BWBs my experience shows that most of them can easily find good properties. What they have trouble finding is the financing for the great

*Figure 10-1. Full-page ad for real estate
self-study course.*

income properties they find. This kit shows them exactly where to find the financing they need. Again, a number of kit users have obtained the real estate money they need, using the kit. Figure 10-1 gives details of this kit.

As these and our other services show, we have a niche in the small business financial market. During the 30 years we've served this market our revenues have grown, as has our customer list and base. And many millions of dollars have flowed into our mailbox during these years. To help you come up with niche services of your own, use Table 10-1 (page 156) to trigger your mind into new ideas. All the services listed are being offered somewhere in the world today via mail order/direct marketing.

You—too—can offer an offbeat service which will stuff your mailbox with big checks and money orders. And—if you do it right—your phone will "ring off the hook" with credit-card orders from your customers. To help you "do it right" I'm here—day and night—to help you with advice, possible funding, and sources of help—if you're a subscriber to one of my newsletters or a buyer of one of my kits. Others succeed in mail order/direct marketing every day—why shouldn't you?

CHAPTER 11

MAIL-ORDER MARKETING SUCCESS METHODS FOR MAKING YOU RICH

YOU CAN HAVE the best product or service in the world. But if you can't sell it, your product or service isn't worth anything to you. This is why marketing is so important to you in this business.

If you can't sell what you have you might as well go on vacation and forget about business!

If you were to give me a choice of a great product or service with no marketing or a mediocre product with great marketing, I'd always take the second choice. Why? Because a mediocre product can always be improved. But it's much more difficult to improve marketing to the point where profitable sales can be made. For this reason I want you to pay careful attention to everything in this chapter!

As you might imagine, thousands of people call me every year with questions about their mail-order/direct-marketing business. Since the questions these people ask are fairly similar, I decided to answer these questions in this chapter. So you'll find that the chapter is in question-and-answer form. Let's start—with your questions.

Q. What's the best way to sell my product or service when I first start up?
A.   The "quick" answer is: The way you sell the largest dollar amount of your product or service. The helpful answer is: Look to see what way firms with products or services like

yours are selling theirs. If they've been around for two years, or more, their methods are working. For many products or services you can start with small classified ads and then move on to small space ads. The 1-inch space ad in Figure 11-1 has brought us large chunks of income. Yet it costs less than $150 a month to run.

You can also start with word-of-mouth advertising. In this form you tell friends and business associates about the product(s) service(s) you're offering. Many will offer to buy from you based on your reputation and knowledge. This puts money into your pocket immediately. We find that word of mouth works best for products or services that lots of people want—such as money or financing. Many of the buyers of our *Financial Broker/Finder/Business Broker/ Business Consultant Kit* (see K-1 at the back of this book) get started just by telling their friends and business associates that they can raise money for them. As some of our kit buyers say, "They're breaking down my door, trying to see me to help them get money for their business."

Once your business is rolling and your income is strong, you can turn to full-page display ads, TV infomercials, computer bulletin boards, the Internet, Prodigy, World Wide Web, and radio ads. Such ads are best for products people can hold in their hand. But you can also promote some services the same way.

To summarize, the best way to advertise your product(s) or service(s) is the way that brings in a strong cash flow at the start at low cost to you, allowing you to expand quickly to more extensive advertising methods giving you

Figure 11-1. Highly profitable one-inch display ad.

national coverage. Where your cash is really short at the start you can try some Internet P.I. (Per Inquiry) ads where you pay only for an inquiry or a sale after it is delivered to you by the agency running your ad. You can get a free list of such agencies by writing me and asking for it—if you're a subscriber of one of my newsletters listed at the back of this book.

Q. Which is better—a display ad or a classified ad?
A. Classified ads cost much less than display ads. Yet in some publications the classified ads get as much—or more—readership as the display ads. If your product or service lends itself to such high readership, then a classified ad might be best for you. Offers which pull strongly through classified ads include: Money Available; Pen Pals for You; Computer Supplies; Astrological Services; Special Recipes; Health Secrets, etc.

Display ads can pull well for Books; Gadgets; Convenience Products; Foods; Newsletters; Emergency Services (towing, security, etc.); Repair Specialties (auto, boat, home, etc.); plus many others. But since a display ad costs several times that of a classified ad, you must be careful to see that you're getting a suitable return on the money you spend. Thus, if a full-page display ad costs you \$2,000 to run, you should sell at least three times its cost, or $3 \times \$2,000 = \$6,000$ in products or services. While some mail-order people are happy with a 2-to-1 return, or $2 \times \$2,000 = \$4,000$, you should aim for the higher return. Why? Because it will make you much richer—much sooner!

Classified ads should bring you in at least the same 3-for-1 return. But since classifieds cost less your total cash income may be lower. What should you do to raise your cash income—which is the whole idea behind going into business? Run more classified ads to bring in more money!

You can run classified ads on the Internet. And with CD-ROM presentations you can run full-page display ads in four colors that people can access on their home computers. So your range for reaching prospects (not suspects!) is larger than ever before in history. If you make wise use of the ad outlets available to you, a million-dollar mail-order fortune is easily within your grasp!

Q. How, and where, can I get the ad rates for various ad outlets?

A. Make a list of the publications, radio stations, and TV networks in which you'd like to advertise. Go to your local public library and look for *Standard Rate and Data* publications. These are thick magazine-like reference guides giving the name, address, telephone number, staff personnel names, and ad guidelines for a variety of magazines (industrial and consumer), radio stations, and TV networks. Many have toll-free numbers.

Call the advertising manager and ask for their media kit. This free kit will give you the ad rates currently being charged. If you don't like using the phone, you can write or fax the ad manager, asking for the same information.

For computer bulletin boards, the Internet and similar Cyberspace ad outlets, check various computer magazines—*Byte, PC Magazine, PC World, Windows,* etc.—for ads for online ad services. Some charge as little as $20 per month for you to advertise, along with thousands of other businesses, on the Internet. You will be given a subject category for your products or services so that potential customers can easily find you.

For example, one service charges a one-time setup fee of $50 for one full-page ad promoting your products or services. A full-page ad is defined as 50 lines of text with each line having a maximum of 60 characters. Each full page can contain one image with a maximum size of 20 KB. With this service you can run as many full pages as you wish. There is the one-time setup fee of $50 per page, plus the monthly charge of $20 per page.

Currently available category listings for online ads include: Business; Consumer Products; Industry Products; Art/Jewelry; Books; Music & Video; Clothing; Entertainment; Electronics; Gifts; Health Products & Cosmetics; Restaurants; Travel; etc.

Also, as mentioned above, there are P.I. ads you can run. These don't cost you anything until you receive an inquiry or an order. See the first question, page 165, for more details.

Q. **What unusual sales methods can I use?**
A. There are a number of unusual sales methods you can use to put big dollars into your bank every day of the week. Here are a few that work well for smart mail-order/direct-marketing professionals:

1. **Pick a company name that sells for you.** Thus, the name of my company, International Wealth Success, brings us business from around the world because of the word "International." And people seeking money come to us because of the word "Wealth." Lastly, people seeking success buy from us because of that word in our company name. The advent of the Internet, the electronic superhighway, has caused our business to boom out because people around the world are attracted by our name. With world population soaring to the 7-billion mark, being in the international market can almost guarantee your success!

2. **Cross-sell with every product or service you have.** When you cross-sell you use one product or service to sell another. Thus, the vacuum-cleaner manufacturer sells disposable paper bags to people who buy the vacuum. A computer manufacturer might sell software along with a computer. Cross-selling is one of the best-kept secrets in this business. When you cross-sell you're trading on your customer's good feelings towards you for a product or service he or she already paid for. So—in effect—your ads for the item you cross-sell are free! Just think of the last time you paid to go to a seminar and wound up buying a book or course at the back of the room. That's pure cross-selling!

3. **Build a line of related products or services for your market.** Thus, we have basic books and kits on real estate. Then we have books and kits on financing real estate— the natural followup when a person goes to acquire properties after learning the basics of income real estate. With a line of related products you help your customer "coming and going"—i.e. every step of the way to his, or her,

success. Building a line of related products or services will keep you busy "all the days of your life!"

4. **Use word-of-mouth and other low-cost advertising methods.** Ads need not break you! Instead, low-cost ads can often pay off handsomely. Many of our Executive Representatives—people who sell our books, kits, and newsletters—start by using such low-cost ad methods. Some sell $2,000 a week of our products using such low-cost unusual methods.

5. **Sell every time you contact your customer.** Thus, you should include your catalog or other sales material when you ship or deliver your product or service. We include our 48-page, 8.5" × 11" catalog with every book and kit we ship. This catalog just keeps selling and selling. Why? Because customers—when pleased with what they get from you—will order, again and again. And that's exactly what you want to happen! So sell with every contact. But don't oversell. By that I mean this: Only sell your customer a product or service you believe will genuinely help him or her. Don't sell just to make a sale! Sell to help your customer. Many times when a customer calls me and asks about buying an expensive product of ours I will advise him or her to buy another, lower-cost product, if I believe it will be more helpful to the customer. People remember this and buy more. Or they'll recommend your products or services to friends!

6. **Give personal service to your customers** via the phone or fax. Thus, if you're a customer of my company, IWS, Inc., you can call me at (516) 766-5850 day or night and I'll answer your questions clearly and quickly. Or you can fax me at (516) 766-5919 and I'll call you back with answers to any questions you may have. I don't answer questions in writing because when I'm writing letters I "ain't" writing books or my newsletters. And since I see my mission in life as a book and newsletter writer, I'll answer your questions by voice—if that's OK by you!

7. **Go beyond just shipping a product or giving a service.** Offer your customers more than just the routine business does. Thus, at IWS, Inc., my firm, we offer people who subscribe to our newsletter for 2 years or longer the ability to request loans or grants from us. These loans or grants are available at the start of the person's sub-

scription—that is, when they send in for their 2-year, or longer, subscription to *International Wealth Success,* ($48 for 2 years) or for 1 year to the *Money Watch Bulletin* ($95 for 1 year). Send your check or money order to IWS, Inc., POB 186, Merrick, NY 11566. Or call or fax the above number to order by credit card. Just be sure to ask for your business or income real estate loan application.

8. **Get free publicity for your business whenever you can.** Keep the name of your company in front of the public. Get as much free publicity for your product (s) or service(s) as you can. You are given details in the next question in this chapter on mail-order marketing.

Q. **What kind of publicity works best for products and services?**

A. There are three kinds of publicity available to you: (1) magazines; (2) newspapers; (3) electronic. Let's look at each so you can use it in your business:

Magazines run free New Product and/or New Service announcements. These can bring you strong sales for little more than the cost of preparing a New Product or New Service release, plus the postage cost to get the item to the magazine. To write such a release, just describe your product or service, tell who can benefit from it, list important features, and give the price and where the product or service can be purchased. If you can include a photo or drawing of the product, do so because it will get your news release more space in the magazine. When you write a release for a new book, send it to the Book Review Editor. Include a photo or drawing of the book. Figure 11-2 is an example of a well-written book review, including a drawing of the book. As a service to subscribers to my IWS Newsletter, I'll be glad to review—free of charge—any product or service News Release you want to send me. I'll even rewrite it for you—free—if it needs it!

Newspapers also run New Product and New Service announcements free of charge. But with a newspaper you can get better coverage if you can tie your New Product or New Service announcement into a news story of some kind. You'll get more space and more illustrations with a news story. Such

HOW TO GET RICH ON OTHER PEOPLE'S MONEY	**HOW TO BORROW YOUR WAY TO REAL ESTATE RICHES**	**MAIL ORDER SUCCESS SECRETS**	**199 GREAT HOME BUSINESSES YOU CAN START (AND SUCCEED IN) FOR UNDER $1,000**
Tyler G. Hicks	*Tyler G. Hicks*	How to Create a $1,000,000-a-Year Business Starting from Scratch *Tyler G. Hicks*	*Tyler G. Hicks*

One of the all-time best-selling authors of books on money, Tyler Hicks knows that people can't make money without money. Here, Hicks offers hundreds of little-known ways to build wealth using OPM (Other People's Money). Every method in the book is practical and easy to do.

TYLER G. HICKS has built his fortune in real estate, publishing, mail order, and other fields, and is the author of a number of bestselling money books. He lives in Rockville Centre, New York.

This 110,000 plus-copy bestseller is the first no-money-down real estate book. The hook, of course, is making money on borrowed money. Financial expert Tyler Hicks knows that low interest rates and real estate prices mean greater opportunities to get rich. This book, updated to include the new federal tax laws, identifies the opportunities and explains all the how-to's.

TYLER G. HICKS has built his fortune in real estate, publishing, mail order, and other fields. He lives in Rockville Centre, New York.

Written by the two-million-copy author of business opportunity books, this is his most accessible and practical book on starting a mail-order business. No other mail order book gives the down-to-earth experience and insider secrets of a long-time businessman who built a mail order future with just pieces of paper and stamp.

TYLER G. HICKS has built his fortune in real estate, publishing, mail order, and other fields. He lives in Rockville Centre, New York.

Tyler Hicks shows readers how to free themselves from the fear of layoffs and mass firings, to acquire an independent source of income, to make more money than will ever be possible in a routine job, to have more free time to spend with their families, to build up a bigger retirement nest egg, and to take their vacations where and when they want!

TYLER G. HICKS lives in Rockville Centre, New York.

🌐 INDONESIAN & CHINESE RIGHTS SOLD
⊠ A SELECTION OF THE BETTER HOMES AND GARDENS BOOK CLUB

1-55958-000-3
$9.95 U.S.
210 pages • Paperback
5½" x 8½" • $13.50 Can.
Index

0-914629-57-3
$12.95 U.S.
324 pages • Paperback
6" x 9" • $17.50 Can.
Index

1-55958-144-1
$12.95 U.S.
320 pages • Paperback
5½" x 8½" • $17.50 Can.
Index

1-55958-224-3
$12.95 U.S.
288 pages • Paperback
5½" x 8½" • $17.50 Can.
Index

Figure 11-2. Short book reviews that can generate book sales.

stories might be: *New Medical Product Saves Lives; New Child-Care Service Helps Working Mothers,* etc. The free space your news release gets is often regarded as better than advertising. Why? Because people tend to read editorial matter more than the ads.

Electronic publicity outlets can include videos of your new product or service, computer bulletin boards, the Internet, etc. You begin with a written description of your new product or service and then add a photo or drawing, if one is available and suitable for your product or service. If a TV station is interested in your offer, or you can build a story around your new product or service, the station may send a crew out to tape your story for broadcast on national TV. Thus, I've been on national TV channels publicizing my money books. The story hook? *How to Make Your Kid a Millionaire!* The free publicity helped sell lots of books to parents wanting to make their kids rich. Just keep in mind at all times this fact of publicity life: Electronic outlets gobble up huge amounts of information. If you can provide some of this information, your mail-order/direct-marketing sales can zoom!

Why seek publicity for your product(s) or service(s)? (1) To get free advertising when your ad budget may be zero. (2) To get information about your product or service out to the world of consumers who may be interested in buying what you offer. (3) To build credibility for your company and your product or service. With the cost of publicity so low, and the results so significant, you should take every step you can to get as much free publicity for your product(s) or service(s) as you can. If you subscribe to my newsletter, *International Wealth Success,* for one year or longer, I'll be glad to send you—free of charge—a helpful booklet I wrote called "How to Write a Profitable News Release for Your Product or Service." Just ask for it when you subscribe.

Q. **Will electronic marketing pay off today?**
A. Yes, it will—if you have the type of product(s) or service(s) that sells well on TV, computer bulletin boards, the Internet, etc. Just think of what you see sold on TV—music

compact disks, videotapes of important events, security devices for home and auto, income-tax preparation services, home-study courses of various types, best-selling books, exercise tapes, etc. If your type of product or service is being advertised on an electronic medium then the chances are excellent that you can make big money in electronic direct marketing.

And even if your product or service isn't now being advertised electronically, it's possible that you can make a big hit with it. Remember: There always has to be a leader—a person or company that believes in itself and takes a risk by spending some money in a new area of marketing. So if you think your product or service will be a hit in the "electronic mall," take a chance and try it. You might come up a big winner!

Q. **Will full-page ads pay off for me?**
A. Yes, they will—if your ad has a good headline, offers a useful product or service that fills a need, and is priced at a level that people believe is fair. Your full-page ad must have all these elements to bring in three times its cost in sales. Thus, if your full-page, black-and-white ad costs you $2,500 to run in a magazine for one month, you should bring in at least $7,500 in sales. Some of our full-page ads have done as much as four times their cost. Others did just twice their cost. Remember Figure 1-3 in Chapter 1? It shows a full-page ad that has pulled very strongly for us—year after year.

Take a look at that full-page ad in Figure 1-3 and note its headline in the famous "how to" form, namely "How to MAKE BIG MONEY as a FINANCIAL BROKER/FINDER/BUSINESS BROKER/BUSINESS CONSULTANT. The headline pushes the "how to" theme—one of the strongest selling motivations known today. Then it shifts to MAKE BIG MONEY—an even stronger theme for people today. Next, it details the four ways you can make big money today.

The body of the ad details a portion of the contents of the product the buyer will get. Notice that the ad lists dozens of specific items—typical business loan application forms, 2,500 sources of business loans, useful agreements and forms (41 of them), fees you can collect, taking a company public, etc. Many of these topics will make a potential buyer salivate at just the thought of them. Then the ad goes on to give testimonials—what buyers say about the product. These testimonials include specific numbers—$463,750; $45,000; $180,000, first year, six months, one merger deal, placed two loans, etc.—that get a potential buyer's mind racing. The physical details of the product are given—12 Speed-Read Books, 500 pages, 4 ready-to-frame membership certificates.

Lastly, the price of $99.50 is reasonable for the amount of information and the free consultation provided. If this product were priced at $395 it wouldn't sell anywhere near its current level. Why? The price would be too high for the average man or woman interested in this business. But at $99.50 the average person wanting to start his or her own business will find the needed money.

This full-page ad has sold thousands of products over the years. And it continues to sell, year after year. Why? Because it has all the elements of a good full-page ad—appealing and eye-stopping headline, strong offer, moderate price. Your full-page ads can bring in thousands of sales dollars to you if the ad combines these three elements. So sit down and start writing your full-page ad right now!

Q. **Are newspaper ads good for my product or service?**
A. BWBs like newspaper ads because the time lag between ordering the ad and its running can be just hours. This compares with weeks (or months) it may take to get an ad into a monthly publication. So BWBs say "I can get the ad in tomorrow's paper—that means I can start making money faster!"

Could be. Or it could be you're wasting your money. Results of ads can never be predicted accurately. But I can tell you this: Large newspaper ads can pay off for you. Classified ads—unless they appeal to lots of people—can be a waste of money.

What do I mean by appealing to lots of people? As a watcher of newspaper classified ads, the only types of offers

I see that appear regularly are for: Loans Available; Make Money Gambling (Craps is the most popular gambling topic); 900 Numbers Available; Ways to Make Money in Real Estate; and Businesses for Sale. Of these topics, Loans Available is the strongest, running day after day, year after year. This means people are making money from newspaper classified ads offering loans of various types.

Full-page newspaper ads pull for books, seminars, and health products of various types. Why? Again—they appeal to lots of people. Books on making money, improving your health, dieting, and personal relations (sex) sell well in full-page newspaper ads. Likewise, ads for seminars on getting rich, building a real-estate empire, and starting your own business pull well with full-page ads in newspapers.

What does all this mean to you? It means that:

Newspaper full-page ads can make you rich if your product or service appeals to large groups of people.

Newspaper classified ads will pull well when you offer needed products or services in areas of key interest to readers—loans, easy income, new ways to make money today.

If your product or service doesn't meet any of the criteria listed above, think carefully before you spend money on newspaper advertising. Newspaper ads can make you rich. Or they can break you! Be sure they don't bankrupt you.

Q. **Should I ask for money in a classified ad?**
A. You can ask for $2, $3, say $5 in a classified ad for a catalog. But it's best not to try to sell your product or service from a classified ad. Why? Because you can't give enough information in a short classified ad to convince a person to buy. So the best procedure is to have the person ask for either a catalog or more information. You can charge for the catalog as mentioned above but your response rate will decline versus offering a free catalog.

If you send a catalog to people who inquire about your offer, your catalog will do the selling. If you don't send a catalog then you will send a follow-up sales letter to your inquiries. Your follow-up sales letter should:

1. **Give full information on your product or service.** Remember the proven adage—"The more you tell, the more you sell!" So give full details on your product or service in your follow-up letter.
2. **Show photos or drawings of your product or service.** Buyers today come from the TV generation. So they're graphics-alert. When they see a photo or drawing of your product or service it immediately grabs their attention.
3. **Sell related products or services** along with your advertised item. This way you have a better chance of making a sale. Why? Because if a customer doesn't need your main offer, he/she may "go for" an additional offer you include in your follow-up sales letter.
4. **Cram your sales letter with interesting and useful information.** Your prospective buyer wants to know as much about the offer as you can provide. Figure 11-3 shows one of the offering sheets we enclose with our follow-up sales letter. It offers nine books that people buy and buy. You can do the same!

Some mail-order advisors (many of whom never made a penny selling a product or service they developed) advise: Offer only one item per sales letter. Then you won't confuse the prospect. In 30 years in this great business, during which time we always earned a profit, our sales letters regularly offer multiple products. And do you know what? People buy and buy—again and again.

What does this tell me? It proves the saying:

The more you tell, the more you sell!

So cram your follow-up letter with as much detail as you can. You can mail five 8.5" × 11" sheets of 17-lb. paper, plus a return No. 6 envelope for one first class stamp. These five sheets will give you 10 sides of paper. Cram them with data on your products or services and you can get rich soon!

Our No. 6 return envelope requires the buyer to use his, or her, own return postage. Why? Because if a person really wants to order they will provide their own postage. If you include a postage-paid BRE (Business Return Envelope) you

*Figure 11-3. Nine books in one full-page ad
can bring in strong sales.*

may generate a lot of questions, or so-called humorous remarks—all at your own expense with NO money enclosed! So save yourself money and use a No. 6 return envelope with no postage on it. If you do a good sales job, your customer will be glad to pay the postage.

Q. **Do I need an advertising agency to place my ads?**
A. No, you don't need an ad agency at the start. When your business is doing $10 million a year you can consider getting an ad agency. At the start, you can place your own ads. And if you get a letterhead with an ad agency name on it you can take the 15% agency discount on your space ads. This is a big saving for you!

Another advantage of placing your own ads is that you'll learn a lot talking to the ad managers of the magazines and other publications in which you plan to run ads. Ad managers talk to all the major advertisers in their publication. During these conversations they learn:

1. **The state of business today**—good, mediocre, poor, improving, steady, declining
2. **What's pulling for advertisers**—"hard offers"—i.e. payment with the order; "soft offers"—payment on a bill after delivery
3. **Who's doing well in the business today**—and what they're selling at various prices
4. **Which company "came back";** which one "went belly up"; who's being investigated by the postal inspectors, FBI, attorney general, etc.

This is the kind of information that is valuable to you as a mail-order/direct-marketing wealth builder. You'll even learn which types of ads are pulling best today. Such insider information won't be relayed to you by an ad agency. So you lose out when you don't place your own ads at the start of your business. Once your company grows to the point where you can hire an ad manager, you can stop placing ads yourself.

Q. **What percentage return can I expect from various types of ads?**

A. This is the most frequently asked question in mail order today. Typically, a BWB will be considering taking an ad in a publication having a circulation of—say—1 million. The question then is: How many inquiries and sales can I expect from my ad in this 1-million circulation publication?

Typically, the BWB will say: "If I make sales to 10% of the circulation I'll sell $0.10 \times 1,000,000 = 100,000$ people. At 1%, my sales will be 10,000 units. Which number can I expect to reach with this ad? Or the BWB may ask, "If I make a mailing if 1,000 flyers or letters, how many sales might I expect?"

I wish I could answer these questions. But without seeing your offer, your price, and ad copy, there's little I can tell you. But I can say this: We "convert"—that is, sell to—24.8% of our inquiries. This means that if 100 people write us asking for information, nearly 25 of those 100 people will order from us after we send them our 10-page flyer for one first class stamp.

The 24.8% has held steady—year after year. Sometimes it rises to 25.9%; sometimes it falls to 23.8%. But it stays at an average of 24.8%. Other mail-order/direct-mail operators I know tell me that their returns follow a similar pattern. By that they mean that they reach a certain return rate that holds fairly steady while they continue offering the same line of products or services.

So, to find your percentage return you must test each type of ad or mailing you plan to do. Run your ad; make your mailing. Key—with a number or letter—each ad and each mailing. Then keep accurate records of the inquiries you receive and the sales you make. As time passes you'll build a history of percentage return for each type of ad and each type of mailing you make. I hope you reach the levels we do!

Some mail-order/direct-mail BWBs say they can make money with a one-tenth of one-percent return from large-circulation—one-million or more—publications. Typical of such publications are *Parade* Magazine, *National Enquirer,* *Globe,* Sunday *New York Times,* Sunday *Los Angeles Times,* etc. Just do the numbers and you'll see why their percentage return might work. Thus:

Publication's Circulation	Number of Returns @ 0.1%
1,000,000	1,000
3,000,000	3,000
6,000,000	6,000

With a product priced at $25, your income would be $25,000, $75,000, or $150,000 per ad. And if you control your costs carefully you'll probably make money on each of these sales. Further, the more ads you run in a publication, the lower the cost of each ad. If your ad pays off, keep running it! You make more money each time it runs.

Q. **How, and where, can I find a good printer for my mailing pieces and ads?**
A. Look in your local *Yellow Pages* under *Printers* for a listing of those near you. Contact each printer by phone or mail and ask them to send you a sample of their recent work, plus a typical price list. Most printers will be glad to get you as a customer—especially if the work you offer them is new and different, as it probably will be.

Ask each printer you like to give you a price and time bid on some of your work. Such work could be your promotion letter, your catalog, and special flyers you're planning to use. Compare the prices you're given, and the time schedule.

Keep in mind several important facts about printers *before* you give them any work. These facts are based on some 30 years' experience with all kinds of printers around the world:

1. **Printers have more excuses for being late** than any other class of trades people.
2. **"Beat" printers at their own game** by giving them your work early and setting a deadline ahead of the actual time you'll need the finished job.

3. **Pay only 50% of the price of the job** when you deliver it to the printer if they demand advance payment—as they will at the start; pay the balance when you get a satisfactory job.

4. **Never be afraid to reject inferior work.** Your printer must do a good job if your business is to succeed.

5. **Be ready for excuses—never trust a printer** who says: "The press broke down; The truck had a flat; My head guy's wife had a baby; The electric power failed"; etc.

6. **Arrange your life to work around printers**—you need them but you don't need the aggravation they can give you if you're unprepared for their excuses, stories, and other concoctions.

7. **Treat printers well—pay them on time**—pay them what you owe them. But demand top-quality service for your marketing materials because well-produced letters and flyers can make your business a success!

8. **Get comfortable with one or more printers** and stay with them. You'll get better and faster service than if you try to switch printers every few weeks or months!

Follow the above rules and you'll have a happy life with printers. Ignore these rules and you'll be sorry!

Q. **Should I produce my own ad materials?**
A. Yes, you should! Why do I say this? For a number of good reasons, based on long experience in this great business. When you produce your own ad materials—that is, write your own ads and letters:

1. **You save enormous amounts of time** because you don't have to explain your product or service to a copywriter who will probably botch up the ad which you'll then have to rewrite to make right!

2. **You'll learn a lot about your product or service** when you write your ads and letters. There's no better way to learn about a product or service than to describe it in an ad.

3. **You can put your own "personality stamp" on the ad** by bringing your reader into your product or service in your unique way. This separates you from all the others who may be selling a similar product or service. For ex-

ample, in the ads I write for IWS products I point out—again and again—that I'm a friend of every customer. I've never met a customer I disliked! People welcome this attitude and call me for advice and to place orders. Talking to customers every day helps me keep in touch with what people want. Using this information we develop targeted products to suit customers' needs.

4. **You have full control of your business.** This means you don't have "creative types" telling you your ads aren't any good—even when you have so many orders your banker welcomes you with a big smile and hello every day!

Plenty of people who know nothing about your business are ready to tell you to get an ad agency. When your company reaches $5 million a year in business you can get an ad agency. Before that, stick to doing your own letters and ads. You'll get them done sooner and they'll be more suitable for your business!

Q. **Will "package inserts" work for my product or service?**
A. A package insert is an ad flyer you pay to have inserted in another firm's package shipped to its customer. Thus, if you're selling laptop computers by mail order, you might have a one-page flyer inserted in the packages containing software ordered from another company.

The logic here is this:

1. **Your computers do not compete** with the software seller's product; hence, sales won't be lost.
2. **Your computers will use the software seller's product**. Hence, the seller might get more sales from users of your computers.
3. **Your payment for the insertion of the one-page flyer helps** pay the shipping cost of the item sent. This increases the seller's cash flow.
4. **If your flyer is successful in the seller's packages,** you might be willing do the same in your packages for the seller.

Package inserts are extremely low cost. You pay for the printing of the insert. Size of your insert can range from a

3" × 5" card to a full 8.5" × 11" page. The charge for the insertion is much less than for a first class stamp. Thus, the charge can range from a low of about 5 cents to a high of about 10 cents, depending on the number of flyers being inserted, and the demand for the particular package.

To use package inserts, contact an agency specializing in this form of mail-order marketing. If such promotion interests you, contact me and I'll give you the name, address, and telephone number of an outstanding package-insert agency. It is not being listed in this book because I want to give you the newest information when you call, fax, or write me—as a subscriber to one of my newsletters.

Q. **Will postcard mailings work for me?**

A. Postcard mailings DO work for some products. Thus, you'll find that newsletters, books, software, and similar products work well with postcard mailings. Your postcard can sell a low-priced product—typically $10, or less. Or you can use the postcard to generate inquiries. With this approach you send a more comprehensive mailing to people who respond to your postcard mailing.

You can use postcards in two ways. These ways are:

1. **Direct-mailed to lists of prospects for your product**—these prospects may be from rented lists, lists which you "swap" with other mail-order operators who use your list while you use theirs to promote products to, or lists you compile of people with certain interests. (For example, you could mail information on a boating product to yacht club members.)

2. **In a "deck" mailing in which 50 to 100 postcards are mailed** as a deck or pack to interested people or businesses. The typical cost of a 100,000 deck mailing for one black-and-white postcard is $2,400. You can use both sides of the postcard to promote if you have an 800 number from which people can order.

Postcard mailings are designed to save postage costs. If you can design a postcard that pulls strongly—say 1% or better—you can get rich in mail order/direct marketing using postcards. To show you how effective postcards can be here's a real-life example:

> An entrepreneur who publishes newsletters and books on small-business success mails a postcard to prospects in which he asks for $5.00 as a starter fee for people who want to market his $99 per year newsletter. This mailing is so successful that he uses a first class stamp on his postcard, instead of the usual postcard stamp which costs about two-thirds of a first class stamp!

Postcard direct-mail marketing takes time to develop. But if you work on your postcard, writing the ad copy yourself, you have a good chance of hitting it big! Try it and see for yourself. And if you're strapped for cash at the start of your mailings, you can mail your postcards at bulk rate, thereby reducing your postage costs. While it will take a little longer for your postcard to reach your prospect, its selling message will not be reduced by the lower postage cost!

Q. **When should I stop marketing my product or service?**
A. Never! The whole key to great success in this business is continual marketing. You must market when business is strong—and when it's weak. Every new customer you bring in is a potential goldmine for you. Why? Because you can:

1. **"Cross-sell" another product or service** once a customer buys your first service. Cross-selling is easier than "cold" selling because your customer already likes you because he/she has bought something from you that's useful or helpful. Thus, a customer whose first purchase is worth $24, as our newsletter is, may wind up buying $3,000 of materials from you—as some of our customers have from us. Yet if we hadn't promoted the first sale we might never have made the second one!

2. **Rent out your customer's name** to other mail-order houses for a good profit. Many mail-order/direct-marketing firms earn more from their list rentals than from their regular business! Further, a dollar from a list rental is a "clean" dollar because you don't have to ship a product or render a service for it.

3. **Market on the Internet to reach new prospects,** if you know your product or service is of interest to them. At this writing some 30 million prospects are online, with 100 million predicted soon. This is one of the biggest markets in the history of the world!

4. **Never go to bed at night** without having done some marketing during the day. If you want cash flow—and who doesn't?—market—day, night, Saturdays, Sundays, holidays, summer, winter, spring, fall. Marketing is your key to success—make sure you NEVER lose your key—ever!

At my company, IWS, Inc., which has been outstandingly successful (the name of my yacht is SUCCESS), we market every day of the year. Our regular mailing is a 5-sheet 8.5" × 11" piece that effectively gives us 10 pages of copy. Along with a No. 6 return envelope this piece goes into a standard No. 10 envelope. Postage cost? One first class stamp.

When we ship a product we enclose our 48-page catalog. This generates additional sales when people study it. So everything we do is "marketing"—you might say. And it pays off. It should also pay off for you!

Q. Should I try to market to overseas customers?
A. Yes—some of your best customers will be overseas. We regularly market to them and we find it highly profitable. Our products—books and kits—are heavy. Yet our overseas customers are happy to pay large airmail costs to get their items sooner.

Why is this? There are a number of reasons which you will find apply to your business—just as they do to ours. These reasons are:

1. **Most businesses ignore requests for information from overseas** prospects. So if you answer an overseas request by sending your catalog or brochure, there's a good chance you'll get an order.

2. **Many overseas countries don't have advanced products** or services. So they're happy to buy from a company (and country) that does offer such wares.

3. **Credit cards make it easy for an overseas customer to order** from you without the hassle of the exchange rate,

getting an overseas money order, etc. Your overseas customer can call, fax, or write you with his or her order, credit card number, expiration date, and telephone number and have the product shipped the same day the order is placed. We get thousands of orders from around the world this way.

4. **Rapid courier services**—Express Mail, FedEx, UPS, Airborne, TNT, etc.—offer fast delivery around the world. Your customer can have his/her product in just a few days. The day of "Allow 4 to 6 weeks for delivery" is gone forever. Customers want—and demand—fast service. You can give it to them—provided they are willing to pay for it. To show you how important speed is, two of the major courier services now have SAME DAY DELIVERY—airport to airport. It costs, but some people are so anxious they're willing to pay the typical $100+ charge!

5. **By being accessible to customers you can beat out** local overseas companies. Why? Because many overseas firms are stuffy and pompous. They think they and God sit in the same seat. So they rarely talk to customers. And even more rarely do they answer questions or give guidance. By being accessible you can make a bundle in your mail-order/direct-marketing business!

So look for—and cultivate overseas business. When you get checks for $2,000 and $3,000 from overseas customers, as we do, you'll be glad you listened to your friend, Ty Hicks!

Q. **What parts of the world are good for international marketing?**
A. Certain parts of the world seem to be more mail-order/direct-marketing oriented than others. Here are a number of areas we've found highly productive for both mailings and sales:

England—particularly the London area; Scotland and Ireland respond, but not as strongly as England.

Singapore, Kuala Lumpur and surrounding areas buy lots of items by mail from the United States.

Papua, New Guinea is a hotbed of entrepreneurship; these people buy and buy.

Australia and New Zealand are full of people who want to imitate the success of U.S. business people.

South Africa is another hotbed of entrepreneurship. These people are highly motivated to improve their situation in life.

Nigeria and some of the other West Coast of Africa republics house very ambitious people.

Canada is almost a second United States in its interest in small business and success.

Now you may find other parts of the world are partial to your product or service. Fine! But most mail-order pros I know agree that the above list confirms their experience. So if you gets lots of orders from one or more of these areas, remember that I told you so.

Having been told about the active mail-order areas around the world, you might wish to consider advertising in publications, on the radio and TV, in those areas. You'll find that:

1. **Ad rates tend to be lower** in countries outside the United States for print ads, radio and TV time.
2. **Response rates may be higher** than those you experience in the United States—many people get better returns overseas.
3. **Prices people are willing to pay may be higher** than in the United States because the competition is less. But don't raise your prices just because people are willing to pay more. Overseas—this can give your business a bad reputation when people learn they can buy the same product for less in the United States.
4. **People are often willing to spend more** when ordering from overseas. Thus, we often receive $400, $600, and $1,000 orders from overseas. Some mail-order BWBs find this difficult to believe. But we have our bank deposit tickets to show this is so. And I'll be glad to let you go through these tickets to verify what I say. All I ask is that you give me a few moments to get them ready for you!

So if your product or service "travels well," as we say in the business, consider trying overseas markets in the areas noted above. Just ask for payment by money order, cashier's check, or credit card. You may laugh all the way to the bank!

You now have lots of ideas for marketing your mail-order products and services. You're really ready to start making money—right now. And I'm here to help you EVERY step of the way, if you're a subscriber of one of my newsletters. So try me, and see!

Meanwhile, let's give you profitable tips for running any mail-order/direct-marketing business. These tips will help you keep more of the dollars that flow into your company every business day of the week!

CHAPTER 12

PROFITABLE TIPS FOR RUNNING YOUR MAIL-ORDER BUSINESS

*T*HE BUSINESS THAT you like—mail order/direct marketing—is a BIG business! Thus, in the year of this writing, mail-order/direct-marketing sales were $253 billion. That's 8% higher than in the previous year.

In that total, consumer mail-order sales were $130 billion, or 51% of the total; business-to-business (where you're selling to another business) was $71 billion, or 28% of the total. Charitable fund raising accounted for $52 billion, or 21%. On a per-capita basis, each person spent $497 on mail-order sales!

With such a large amount of money in the business, you must run your business properly to earn the maximum profit possible. This chapter shows you exactly how to run your business so you bring home the largest number of dollars every day!

See How Simple This Great Business Is

Many people make life a lot more complicated than it need be. We want your life to be simple and profitable! See mail order/direct marketing as it really is and your life will be much simpler. Here's the inside scoop on mail order:

1. **You advertise a product or service**—either by mail, print, radio, TV, computer network, word-of-mouth, or other means. You may use just one—or many—of these methods.
2. **Sales result from your advertising and orders arrive** in your mailbox, by telephone, or by fax.
3. **You deposit the money you receive,** either at the bank in person, or electronically via your credit card merchant account.
4. **You ship the product or deliver the service** that was paid for. You keep a record of your shipping date and the method of shipping or delivery.
5. **You push ahead to more sales** to new customers and re-peat sales to your existing customers. Your income rises, day by day!

Start Your Records at the Beginning

Every step in your business is easy to track and record. Thus, at the start, you get word out to people that you have a great product or service available for them. You get the word out in the form of publication ads, direct-mail letters, radio ads, TV commercials, computer online notices, word-of-mouth, etc. To earn the maximum profit from your business you keep accurate records of each form of advertising you use. Figure 12-1 shows an example of a publication ad record sheet which can be kept on a piece of paper or a computer spreadsheet.

You can use a similar record sheet for ads you run on electronic media—radio, TV, computer online network. See Figure 12-2 for an example of such a record sheet.

At the start all you need is a simple loose-leaf book with record sheets for each type of ad you use. When you make mailings you will use a key code on your return envelope (usually a No. 6—i.e. about a 6"-long—envelope) to iden-tify the list from which you obtained the name. Your key code is nothing more than a letter, or number, or a combi-nation of them, that identifies, for you, the ad from which

PUBLICATION AD RECORD SHEET AND DATA

Publication Name _____

Date Ad Ran _____

Cost of Ad _____

Number of Responses to Ad _____

Cost per Response =
Cost of Ad/No. of Responses _____

Number of Sales from the Ad _____

Income from Sales, $_____

Ad Cost per Sale, $ =
Cost of Ad/ No. of Sales _____

Sales $/Ad $ =
Sales, $/Cost of Ad, $_____

Product or Service Cost per Sale, $_____

Gross Profit per Sale =
$ per Sale – Cost per Sale, $_____

Figure 12-1. Typical Record Sheet for
Publication Ad Cost and Profit.

the item or service was ordered. Typical key codes you might use are:

For publication ads—Initials of publication name, plus date
Example: *Income Opportunities* magazine 12/—
ad = *IO*/12—

For electronic media ads—Use department or desk name
Example: Dept. 22; or Desk EM

For direct-mail promotions—Mailing list source by number
Example: On back of return envelope #19 identifies your house list of responses from publication ad No. 19 which appeared in—we'll say—*Spare Time* magazine in a stated month

---

ELECTRONIC MEDIA AD
RECORD SHEET AND DATA

Media Used _____

Date(s) Ad Ran _____

Cost of Ad _____

Number of Responses _____

Cost per Response =
Cost of Ad/No. of Responses _____

Number of Sales from the Ad _____

Income from Sales, $_____

Ad Cost per Sale, $ =
Cost of Ad/ No. of Sales _____

Sales $/Ad $ =
Sales, $/Cost of Ad, $_____

Product or Service Cost per Sale, $_____

Gross Profit per Sale =
$ per Sale – Cost per Sale, $_____

---

*Figure 12-2. Typical Record Sheet for Electronic
Media Ad Cost and Profit.*

Don't let key codes frighten you! Whatever key code
you choose that works for you is the right one. The main
points to keep in mind with respect to key codes are these:

1. **Pick a key code that means something to you.** Why? Because you're the one who will use the key code when sales
   come into your business.
2. **Be certain to use a key code** on *every* ad, *every* mailing,
   every promotion you make.
3. **Keep a careful record of all your key codes.** If you don't
   have a good record of your key codes, I guarantee that
   you'll have trouble remembering which letters, or numbers, or combinations you used for various ads and
   mailings!

With an accurate record of all your ads you'll have good control of your business. You'll know what your costs—and your profits—are. And, at the end of the year, when your accountant does your business tax return, you'll have the records you need to prepare an accurate return.

Keep Careful Track of Your Income

At the start, most of your orders will probably arrive by mail. Why is this? Because your ads—whether classified or display—will ask for orders by mail. You won't—usually—have a credit card merchant account where you can accept credit-card orders. That will come later. And we show you—later in this chapter—how, and where, to get your credit card merchant account. For now let's deal with the hundreds of checks that will flow into your business every week via the mail. Follow this procedure:

1. **Mark each incoming envelope with the amount of money** it contains, the form of the payment—i.e. check or money order—the date the order was received, the name of the product or service ordered, and the source of the order—an ad, a radio commercial, TV infomercial, etc. With what we call a "regular" check—personal or business—mark the date of its deposit. When you receive a money order payment, just mark it as M.O. on the outside of the envelope. So, one of your order marks on an envelope might read thus:

   6/8/— rec'd. $99.50 M.O./MOK/dep 6-9; ship 6-10—; 19A.

   This means you received $99.50 for the "Mail Order Riches Success Kit" in the form of a money order on 6/8/—. The money order was deposited in the bank on 6-9—; the kit was shipped to the customer on June 10, —. The source of the order was your ad No. 19A.

2. **Save your order envelopes for at least two years** after you ship the product or deliver the service. We save our order envelopes for 5 years. Why? Because with the envelope on hand we can reconstruct the entire order from the information on it, namely:

Date of mailing to us: From the postmark;

Date received: From our date stamp;

Date deposited: From the date stamp;

Date shipped: From the date stamp.

This is valuable information because if your customer complains that he/she never received your shipment you can go back to your envelope and tell him/her the date the order was mailed to you by your customer, when it was received, and when it was shipped. This is useful information, which will impress your customer and any authorities who might come in on you to check your business procedures.

As a last resort, you can always refer to your bank deposit ticket which will show you the amount you deposited on the date marked on your envelope. Thus, if the check or money order was for $99.50, you can see if a deposit of this amount was made on 6/9/—, as you listed on your envelope.

3. **Report ALL your income—don't play games with the tax laws!** There are enough legal, legitimate deductions available to you to shelter most of your income in this business. If you begin trying to avoid taxes by not reporting some of your income you will become confused and full of guilt. Further, you may not be able to figure out how much you're really earning. You may not even know if you're making or losing money! So—be honest with yourself and the tax authorities. You'll earn more and you'll sleep lots better!

4. **Establish a strong relationship with a commercial bank—** that is, a business bank. Such a bank has N.A. (National Association) after its name. Open a business checking account. And if you have excess funds, open a money market or other type of savings account. The interest you earn may not be the highest but the accounts will make you a favorite with your banker. As they say—it's never bad to have a friend at the bank!

5. **Make full use of the offers your bank makes to businesses.** Banks are always looking for ways to increase their profits. So they will often offer lines of credit, corporate

credit cards, low-cost safe deposit boxes, etc. to their business account holders. Snap these up! Why? Because it will improve your relations with your bank and enable you to get more services from the bank when you need them.

6. **Get to know an officer at your bank.** Talk to him/her now and then. Tell the officer about your business, what it does, how your profits compare with last month, last year, etc. Such a friendship can really pay off when you need some kind of help from the bank—such as a loan, a letter of credit, etc. Keep in mind that many bankers are closet BWBs—they just don't have the courage you have to go out on their own and try to hit it big!

7. **Keep careful records of your income.** In our mail-order business we use weekly records to tell us where we stand. You might wish to use daily records, comparing today with the same day last year, and the year before. The reason we use weekly records is because it fits our working and shipping procedures best. Figure 12-3 shows how we keep our income records.

A mail-order joke service, which sells jokes on audio cassettes, videos, CDs, T-shirts, mugs, and in books, keeps daily records of its sales. Why? Because after going online via World Wide Web sales boomed out. To keep track of its income this firm decided that daily records are best. Selling online works seven days a week in over 200 countries with

Week No.	Income, $	Average week's income YTD*	Total income, YTD, $	Total income, YTD vs last year YTD, $	Week's income vs last year week's income	Total income, YTD vs 2 years ago YTD
25	5,802	6,082	152,100	+12,189	−406	+18,195

* YTD = Year To Date

Figure 12-3. Weekly Income Record Sheet.

an audience of over 30 million people. If you like jokes you might want to consider marketing to niche groups—ethnic, occupational, geographic, etc.

Or you might want to keep your sales records by the month—as some specialty advertisers do. They run shopping pages on the Internet for niche products aimed at boaters, pilots, midget race car drivers, art collectors, etc. Sales tend to be a few per day. With this type of activity, monthly sales records are suitable. Your accountant will even approve of them!

Ship Your Product or Deliver Your Service Quickly

This is the age of "instant" delivery. People can't wait to get what they order. So if you want to stay in business you must take either of two steps:

1. **Ship same-day or next-day when people ask for such service,** being certain to charge them for the extra cost—which can be two, three, or four times the usual cost of parcel post, book rate, etc.
2. **Ship on a stated day of the week;** tell ALL your customers that you ship—let's say, on Friday. No matter how fast the customer wants your product or service, tell him or her that you ship once a week—on Friday. Do you know what will happen? Almost 100 percent of your customers will say: "That sounds good to me; I'll look for my order to be delivered next week."

The whole key here is to level with your customer. Tell him/her exactly how—and when—you will ship. Don't disappoint your customer by saying you'll ship tomorrow and then delay a week or so. If your customer knows when you'll ship, he or she will be willing to wait. It's not knowing that "kills" them and destroys you in the customer's eyes.

Get evidence of delivery for every item you ship to your customer. Do this by any of the following methods:

1. **Use insured U.S. mail**—the customer must sign for the item delivered and you have evidence of delivery that will

stand up in any court of law and will be acceptable to any regulators or other groups that come in on you—such as the postal inspectors, Federal Trade Commission, Better Business Bureau, attorney general, etc. Your insurance receipt clearly shows when, how, and to whom you shipped your product or service (see Figure 12-4).

2. **Use Certificate of Mailing furnished** from the U.S. post office. While a Certificate of Mailing does not provide any insurance coverage, it does give you evidence of mailing acceptable to the regulators and other groups mentioned in 1, above. Figure 12-5 shows a Certificate of Mailing form available free at your post office.

3. **Use Recorded Delivery for overseas shipment** sent by U.S. mail. This is a numbered yellow ticket you can get free at any U.S. post office, as shown in Figure 12-6. The overseas post office keeps a record of the delivery and the

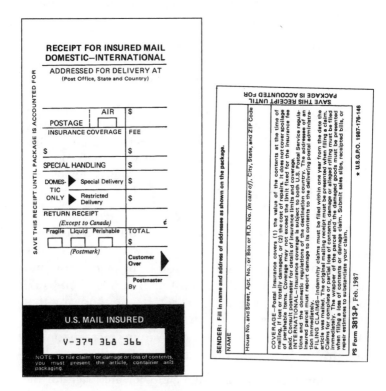

Figure 12-4. U.S. Postal Service Receipt for Insured Mail.

U.S. POSTAL SERVICE

CERTIFICATE OF MAILING

Affix postage and postmark. Inquire of Postmaster for postage

Received From:

One piece of ordinary mail addressed to:

MAY BE USED FOR DOMESTIC AND INTERNATIONAL MAIL, DOES NOT PROVIDE FOR INSURANCE — POSTMASTER

PS FORM MAY 1976 3817 ☆ U.S. GOVERNMENT PRINTING OFFICE: 1980-750-240

Figure 12-5. U.S. Postal Service Certificate of Mailing Receipt.

A 007 379 022

UNITED STATES POSTAL SERVICE

Receipt for Recorded Delivery

For International Mail

No Insurance Coverage Provided

Sent to	
Street and No.	
City	
PO, Country of Destination	
Postage	$
Recorded Delivery Fee	
Return Receipt	
Restricted Delivery	
TOTAL Postage & Fees	$
Postmark or Date	

PS Form 8099, November 1990

RECORDED

A 007 379 022

DELIVERY

AFFIX POSTAGE STAMPS TO ARTICLE TO COVER APPROPRIATE POSTAGE AND FEES, RECORDED DELIVERY SERVICE, AND CHARGES FOR ANY SELECTED OPTIONAL SERVICES (see front).

1. If you want this receipt postmarked, stick the gummed stub to the right of the return address leaving the receipt attached and present the article at a post office service window or hand it to your rural carrier (no extra charge).

2. If you do not want this receipt postmarked, stick the gummed stub to the right of the return address of the article, date, detach and retain the receipt, and mail the article.

3. If you want a return receipt, write the recorded delivery number and your name and address on a return receipt card, Form 2865, and attach it to the front of the article by means of the gummed ends if space permits. Otherwise, affix to back of article. Endorse front of article RETURN RECEIPT REQUESTED adjacent to the number.

4. If you want delivery restricted to the addressee, or to an authorized agent of the addressee, endorse RESTRICTED DELIVERY on the front of the article.

5. Enter fees for the services requested in the appropriate spaces on the front of this receipt. If return receipt is requested, check the applicable blocks on Form 2865.

6. Save this receipt and present it if you make inquiry.

☆ U.S. GPO: 1991—287-984

Figure 12-6. U.S. Postal Service Receipt for Recorded Delivery.

person receiving your item must sign for it. Again, you have evidence of delivery.

4. **Use Certified Mail, Return Receipt Requested** from the post office. Here you have a numbered parcel and evidence of delivery in the form of a returned postcard signed by the recipient, Figure 12-7.

5. **Use Express Mail** for next-day or second-day delivery of your package. Express Mail gives you $500 insurance coverage for each item you ship, as part of the standard fee you pay. It's well worth the cost. Further, Express Mail requires that the recipient sign for the item he/she receives. This gives you firm evidence of delivery. Figure 12-8 shows the form you use for Express Mail.

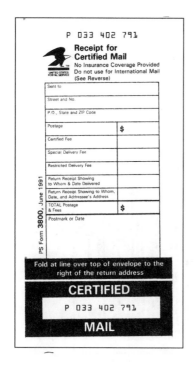
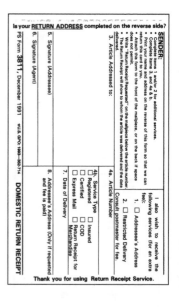

Figure 12-7. Certified Mail and Return Receipt Requested forms of the U.S. Postal Service.

Figure 12-8. U.S. Postal Service Express Mail Receipt.

6. **Use any of the courier services**—FedEx, UPS, TNT, Airborne, etc. Each includes a minimum insurance coverage plus requires a signature of the recipient, unless you, as the shipper, elect not to require a signature by the recipient. Take my advice—ALWAYS get a signed receipt showing the item was received by the addressee. This helps you avoid fights over whether your customer did—or did not—receive the item you sent.

7. **Get a signed receipt when the package is delivered** by hand. This will prove that the recipient received what you delivered to him or her.

Why all this emphasis on evidence of delivery, you ask? For several excellent reasons that will become plain to you, namely:

1. **Evidence of delivery shows that you gave the customer** what he or she paid for. This is important when a customer claims they never received what they ordered from

you. As your sales increase you'll find that some customers are difficult to deal with because they have problems in their lives which they project onto you and your company. Having evidence of delivery quickly "converts" these customers from enemies to friends. Why? Because your official receipt has a ring of authority to it. Many of these troubled customers are seeking guidance of some sort and your receipt is welcomed by them!

2. **Evidence of delivery proves what date you sent the item** to your customer. This shows that you complied with the FTC (Federal Trade Commission) "30-Day Rule," which states that you must ship within 30 days after receiving payment in good funds from your customer. Since almost all reputable mail-order dealers ship within 30 days, you will probably do the same. In today's environment if you take 30 days to ship, your phone will "ring off the wall" because people will bug you with demands for the exact shipping date.

3. **Evidence of mailing creates a good impression** among any regulators who may come in on you. Such regulators might be the U.S. postal inspectors, the FBI, the attorney general of your state, the Better Business Bureau, etc. When you can provide evidence of mailing and delivery these regulators will be most favorably impressed. Why? Because by showing evidence of mailing (or shipping) and delivery you tell them that you're a careful business person who respects, and cares for, his or her customers. You "take the steam out" of any complaints they may have about you and your company. I've seen regulators change from adversaries to friends when they saw the care taken to ensure quick, accurate delivery of items to customers.

4. **Evidence of mailing (or shipping) and delivery is valuable** when a credit-card customer claims he or she never received what you sent. Customers sometimes forget what they sent for. Or they don't recognize the name of your company when they get their regular monthly credit-card bill. Calling them and telling them that you have a receipt showing that you sent an item to them on June 10 will quickly improve their memory of you, what they bought, and what they owe!

5. **Evidence of shipping is extremely important** when you're dealing with wholesalers or other resellers. These

are often large organizations and they "lose" their inventory. If you can send them a copy of your shipping receipt they quickly "find" what you sent! We've also found that evidence of shipping is helpful in getting large firms to pay their bills faster. When you send them a shipping receipt they seem to find—more quickly—the check to pay your bill!

Many customers new to mail-order/direct-marketing are suspicious of all firms marketing their products this way. So you must overcome their basic distrust of you and your products. By shipping with some form that gives you evidence of mailing you transmit a message to your customer. That message? *This company really cares about my getting this item. They must be legit!*

Further, the very fact that you care enough about your customers to exert this degree of attention to their orders, makes the customer less likely to ask for a refund. So you have fewer items "bouncing back" to you with a request for a refund.

But before you ship you should be careful to take care of some "housekeeping" details. These details will increase your profit and make you a happier, more satisfied mail-order/direct-marketing BWB. Let's take a quick look at them now.

Get Paid BEFORE You Ship

This may seem like a basic truth. But some mail-order/direct-marketing BWBs overlook it. And lots of these BWBs lecture me about the silliness of this advice. They say: *"Don't you know that very few checks bounce? So why wait for a check to clear before shipping your item? The amount of money you'll lose is small compared to the goodwill you generate."*

Having received, and deposited, many millions of dollars in mail-order/direct-marketing checks, I'm an expert on bouncing checks. And—yes, bouncing money orders! It is a bitter experience for the mail-order BWB when a check bounces after the item is shipped. To avoid the losses (product/service cost, shipping, labor, postage cost, bank charge, etc.) from bounced checks and money orders take these easy steps:

1. **Wait for each deposited item to "clear"**—i.e. be paid by the bank or other entity on which it is drawn.
2. **Tell each customer you're waiting** for their check to clear "because not all checks clear," they all will understand because they've been victims of bounced checks themselves.
3. **Ship only when the check or money order clears.** And don't automatically assume that money orders never bounce. We've received counterfeit money orders that bounced worse than a golf ball. Yet the person who sent these counterfeit money orders kept calling us asking if we'd shipped yet. Somehow we were suspicious and didn't ship. It saved us more than $600 in lost costs.
4. **Process each credit-card charge BEFORE you ship!** Just because someone has a credit card does NOT mean that the charge will automatically go through. The person may be "maxed out" on his or her card—meaning that no new charges will be allowed until a payment is made by the cardholder to the bank. We've had people give us four different card numbers, asking us to keep trying to put the charge through until it went. Sometimes all four cards were maxed out!

By following these hints you will bring in more money with fewer hassles. And that—after all—is one reason you're in business—to make money with the least possible worry. If business isn't fun then it really isn't worth your time and effort!

Use Credit Cards to Speed Your Sales

This is the age of the credit-card sale made via an 800 number or faxed order with the product shipped via a courier service for delivery by 10 a.m. the following day. Most customers today never heard of the word patience. THEY WANT IT NOW!

Unless you cater to this instant-delivery urge you'll lose business. (You can still, however, do business without taking credit cards. Plenty of people do. But if you want to speed your cash income, you should accept credit cards.)

To accept credit-card charges you must get a merchant account. Until recently it was extremely difficult for mail-order and home-businesses to get a merchant account. Banks were afraid of being ripped off by shady merchants who would run up big charges and then disappear.

Many banks now actively seek mail-order/direct-marketing merchant accounts because they realize that they can make money from them. So it's much easier for you to get a merchant account today than in the past. We've helped dozens of mail-order BWBs get their merchant account. And we have a helpful kit, Figure 6-2 on page 97, that gives you six different ways to get your merchant account.

To ensure that your merchant account is not plagued by charge backs—where the bank deducts from your account a charge you've made against a customer's credit card—take these easy steps:

1. **Get full data from the customer**—name, address, home phone number, credit-card number, and expiration date.
2. **Train your staff to detect possible fraud on the phone.** Typical indicators of possible fraud are:
   - Shipment to a post office box requested
   - No home address available
   - Hesitation when asked to give phone number or home address
   - Charging a purchase to another person's card—you MUST get authorization from the cardholder before you make any charge to a card
   - Loud noises in the background when a phone-in order is called in—this may indicate the call is being made from a prison
   - A careless attitude towards a large dollar charge—thus, if a person doesn't seem to care whether an item costs $300 or $600, he or she may be ordering via a stolen credit card
3. **Don't process any credit-card charge you're suspicious about.** Instead, send the person a letter such as that in Figure 12-9 to explain why you did not make the charge, and asking that a check or money order be sent to you.

We find that about 95% of the people will send payment to you.

4. **Send two copies of the charge ticket to your customer,** along with the item ordered. Ask the customer to sign the credit-card receipt and return it in the stamped self-addressed envelope (SASE) you provide with the receipt. You now have several valuable bits of useful business information:

INTERNATIONAL WEALTH SUCCESS INC.

P. O. Box 186, Merrick, N. Y. 11566

OFFICE: 24 Canterbury Rd, Rockville Centre NY 11570-1310   Ph: 516-766-5850
                                                            Fx: 516-766-5919

Dear Associate:

Thank you for your order which you placed with us. You were most kind to do so and we greatly appreciate it.

To process your order faster, we suggest you send us a check or money order in the amount shown in the space below. Once we receive your payment we will ship your order. When paid by money order, the item is shipped the same day the order is received. For orders paid by check, we wait for the check to clear before shipping.

Again, thank you for your order. Please send a check or money order for the amount shown below.

Cordially yours,

Tyler G. Hicks, President

TGH:st

Kindly send a check or money order for: $_____

For Priority Mail (Air Mail) shipment,
              please add: _____

Total enclosed $_____

Name of book, Kit, or Newsletter ordered_____

Thank you, again.

PS: For fastest shipping, send your order to: IWS, Inc.
                                               24 Canterbury Rd
                                               Rockville Centre NY 11570-1310

---

*Figure 12-9. Letter written to cardholder when
card issuer declines a charge.*

- The customer's name/address/telephone number
- Your shipping receipt (see above) showing shipment date and method of shipment
- Your signed credit-card receipt, which—since it was with the shipment—indicates the customer did receive what you sent. With these items in hand, plus your telephone record of the order (see below) you have a full history of the sale. Using any one of the many mail-order records programs available for your computer, you can build a valuable data base of your sales. Or—at the start—you can keep these records in paper form and get much the same value and information from them.
- Save your credit-card receipts for at least 3 years; some banks recommend 7 years. If your bank prefers the 7-year holding period, be sure to follow their guides.

Now all of these procedures may sound silly to you. Some people tell me that the way we run our business is ultra-conservative. Yet we keep growing each year and our customers are happy with what they buy from us. And I might add that the people who tell me this are guests on *my* beautiful 56-foot yacht. I'm not a guest on theirs because they cannot afford one. Yet they're ready to tell me what mistakes I make in running my business!

As your business grows you'll find that credit-card orders increase in both numbers and dollar amount. It can become a real chore trying to keep track of these orders. Here's the way we control our credit-card orders:

1. **The telephone operator(s) have** what we term their *Order Book* into which they enter each order they get by phone. They enter the data mentioned above.
2. **On weekends and during the evening** when we in the company (including myself) get telephoned credit-card orders we enter the same information in a book we call the *Telephone Log.*
3. **Orders received by mail** are put into what we call our *Order Envelope.*
4. **When the orders are processed** through our merchant account terminal, Figure 12-10, a record of each order is entered on a *Merchant Batch Header Ticket,* Figure 12-11. Each

Figure 12-10. Typical Merchant Account Terminal for
transmitting credit-card charges.

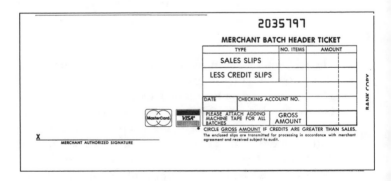

Figure 12-11. Typical Merchant Account
Batch Header Ticket.

line on this form carries the following: Customer's Last Name; Amount of Order, $; Approval Code; Location of the original order identified by *OB* for Order Book, *TL* for Telephone Log, *OE* for Order Envelope. Then, if it's ever necessary to find the original order we just go back to the *Day's Work Sheet,* as we call the Header Ticket, and this tells where the order is located. With this information in hand we can reconstruct the entire order.

5. **When the order is shipped** we check it off on the Header Ticket to show that the work has been done. At the same time we enter in the Order Book, Telephone Log, or Order Envelope the date of shipment and how shipped— U.S. Mail, UPS, Fed Ex, etc. If the customer calls and wants to know when his or her order was shipped, we have the key data readily available.

6. **Prior to shipping any item,** each credit-card receipt printed out by the merchant account printer, Figure 12-10, is photocopied and filed with that day's Header Ticket in a letter-size accordion envelope which holds the month's credit-card charges.

7. **As the last step in this process the order data** (customer's name, address, telephone number, what was ordered, price paid, etc.) are all entered in a database in our computer. Thus, we have full information on each customer. This can be used for future mailings (to send the customer data on related products), for list-rental purposes (what the customer bought, how much was paid, how paid, etc.), and similar uses. Some mail-order/direct-marketing firms earn as much from renting their mailing list as they do from their product or service sales.

Now you may ask: "Why do you go to all this trouble with these records? Why not just ship what's ordered and forget about it?" You CAN do that—plenty of mail-order operators do. But if an item or service doesn't arrive, your customer can start screaming. Or the customer may refuse to pay the credit-card charge. If your records are well organized and you can put your finger on an order within minutes after a customer calls, your life will be much easier. And your profits will be higher! So think about using our methods. They really do work—for you!

Never Be Afraid of Overseas Sales

If your product or service has international use you will get lots of overseas orders by credit card. Why is this? For a number of good reasons:

1. **It's much easier to order by credit card** than by using an international money order, cash, or other forms of payment available to overseas customers.
2. **Exchange-rate problems are avoided** when a credit-card order is placed by mail, phone, or fax.
3. **Greater speed is obtained in ordering and in delivery** of the product or service when a credit card is used.

When an order is placed by credit card you must always be alert to the possibility of fraud. Some BWBs get nervous when they receive a credit-card order from overseas. Don't worry! Our experience—and that of many other mail-order merchandisers who accept overseas orders is:

1. **Overseas customers** are honest and reliable. There is much less fraud with overseas orders than with domestic orders paid for by credit card.
2. **Overseas customers** will often place larger orders than domestic customers because they want as much of a product or service as they can get at once.
3. **Overseas customers** will be precise in signing their credit-card receipt and returning it to you.
4. **Overseas customers** will often fax you their order and sign it. This means you have a signed order which is most valuable in the event it is ever questioned.
5. **Overseas customers** are much less likely to return items they order because it's a real hassle to do so. Further, these customers seem to be more easily satisfied than others.

Many mail-order companies find their overseas sales rival their domestic sales in both units sold and dollars of income. Thus, today:

- **Japanese consumers** buy millions of dollars of U.S. products by mail order every year.
- **Products popular** with Japanese consumers include books, clothing, music CDs, videos of various types—popular

movies, how-tos, recreation, travel, etc.—even small heli-copters are sold via mail order!

- **Most sales are made using a credit card** to pay for the purchase—you receive your money within 24 hours.
- **The courier services**—FedEx, UPS, Express Mail—have convenient low-cost airmail from all countries into Japan. Thus, packages can be shipped from the U.S. to Japan in 10 days, or less, via airmail.
- **Other countries in which mail-order sales are strong** include England, Germany, Sweden, Denmark, Spain, Italy, Indonesia, Nigeria, South Africa, Brazil, Argentina, Canada, Mexico, Panama.
- **Unusual products** sold by mail order to such countries include powerboats, kayaks, canoes, musical instruments of many types—guitars, harps, flutes, banjoes, etc.

Thus, you can make big money in mail order selling to overseas customers. Your business will be more profitable and it will grow faster. Just be sure to:

1. **Accept credit cards** for the purchases your overseas customers make. Without credit cards your sales will be much less.
2. **Offer airmail delivery,** paid for by the customer. You cannot make money if you have to pay for the product or service and airmail delivery when you're shipping heavy items. Products or services that can be sent by letter-weight airmail—i.e. one or two ounces—can be sent at your cost because the charge is relatively low and will not reduce your profit on high-priced products or services.
3. **Be certain** your products or services are top quality. Overseas customers expect—and demand—the best in quality and service.
4. **Be ready to point out differences** in sizes, electrical current, procedures, etc., so your customers will know what to expect when they buy from you.

Twenty-Three Profit-Making Tips for Your Mail-Order Business

Here—in quick, easy-to-use form—are valuable tips to help you earn more in any mail-order/direct-marketing business you choose to run:

1. **Sell helpful products or services.** You'll earn more and get greater satisfaction from your work when you know that the items you sell really help people enjoy life more, do their business more efficiently, or earn more money from their work.

2. **Shun scams of all types**—pyramid schemes, chain letters, lotteries, advance-fee swindles, etc.—they're not worth your time or energy. Running a business that helps people do positive things in life will reward you in many ways—financially and mentally. Never engage in a rip-off—it's dishonest and hurts people. And eventually it will hurt you, and your family. So, shun scams of all types!

3. **Learn the postal and courier rules.** The United States Postal Service is the best in the world. In our business we mail millions of items all over the world. And—good friend—the mail DOES go through! You can tell me all the horror stories you want to—I'll tell you one good story for each of your bad ones. When you get to know the postal and courier rules you'll see that they are written to speed the handling of millions of pieces of mail or packages a day. So: (A) Address your mail correctly, according to the rules; (B) Apply the correct postage; (C) Do not use hand-written labels—use either a typewriter or a computer to address each label; (D) Check the name and address to see that it agrees with the one you were given; (E) Deposit your mail or shipments in accordance with the rules of the post office or courier—UPS, FedEx, TNT, etc.

4. **Get to know people at the post office and courier service.** You'll find that they're friendly and cooperative. They want to help you! When a problem arises your friends will stand up for you, saying: "Oh, Box 123—he's a real nice person." Or, "Box 168, she's a hard-working business person. She never gives us a problem!" When regulators or others who might be looking at your business hear such remarks they change their opinion of you—from possibly bad to probably good!

5. **Look for cooperation amongst all people you deal with**—the post office, the courier service, your suppliers, your staff, etc. Remember: Honey gets a lot more smiles than vinegar.

6. **Make fast refunds—but get your due.** You MUST make refunds to dissatisfied customers—if you want to stay in business. But there are a number of points about refunds that favor you—the hardworking business person. These points are: (A) The item or service MUST be returned to you in resalable condition if you are to make a full refund; (B) Where you supply a portion of a service—such as a monthly magazine—and a person asks for a refund after receiving 6 issues out of the 12 they paid for—they should get only HALF the annual subscription fee—i.e. a proportional refund. Some publishers even deduct the cost of an extra issue to reimburse themselves for the time and labor needed to put the subscription up on computer; (C) You are also entitled to a "restocking fee" when a person returns a product you must put back into inventory. Such a fee could be $5, $10, etc., depending on how much work you or your staff must do to return the item to inventory. What does all this mean to you? It means that even though you MUST make refunds, you can still come away from the transaction with a few pennies in your pocket!

7. **Join the Better Business Bureau** and support its work. The BBB is an excellent organization and your company will have greater credibility when you're a member. People can call your BBB and get a free report on your business. When they get a good report it helps the person overcome any fear they may have of ordering from you. Your annual membership cost isn't too high. And it can pay off over and over again!

8. **Be available to your customers and prospects** to answer questions they may have. Being able to talk to the "top honcho" makes people feel good. And it also makes them more likely to buy. Remember: The whole idea of this business is to make the sale! So be available—you'll take more money to the bank every day if you are.

9. **Keep good records at all times.** You need good records to run your business properly—and profitably. Further, you need good records so you pay only the exact tax due—not a penny more. Without good records you may overpay your income taxes. I'm sure you don't want to do that!

10. **Use a competent certified public accountant (CPA)** and attorney to guide your business. Pay them on a per-hour

basis. This means you'll pay only for the work they do. They will not be on a permanent payroll with your firm.

11. **Be honest with your customers at all times.** Tell them if a product is suitable or unsuitable for them. Don't sell a customer an item that is unsuitable for him or her. You may make a sale. But you'll have an unhappy customer. Better to not make a sale than to cause a person to hate you and your firm!

12. **Computerize your business**—it's ideal for mail order/direct marketing. You'll do your work faster and profits will show up in your bank sooner. With PCs so low-cost today you really don't have an excuse for going computer-less. What's more—people will think more of you and your business when they see you're computerized! You'll make more money—faster.

13. **Get online—it will help your sales and image.** Online selling of products will boom out. The earlier you get in on this great new "electronic mail-order/direct-marketing business" the sooner you'll enjoy another way to make money that's fast, in keeping with the way today's consumer thinks, and sets you apart from those BWBs who think in terms of the past.

14. **Be able to deliver your catalog by fax**. More and more customers want your catalog NOW—not tomorrow or next week. Prepare a simple, pared-down catalog for easy faxing to people who inquire about your products or services. Follow up your faxed catalog with your full catalog, sending it by mail. This way you'll convert more inquiries to sales—and faster. This means your cash flow will zoom!

15. **Don't be too impressed with yourself—sell all the time!** Remember—the idea of this business is to make money. You're a merchant selling a product or service. If you get inflated ideas about yourself you'll probably stop making as many sales. So get down to business and bring the money in. When you do that you can get whatever you need—big house, luxury car, private jet, sparkling white yacht, etc., to impress yourself with your success!

16. **Be an expert in your business**—you'll make more money at it and you'll have more fun. Further, your customers will come back to you—again and again—happily to put money into your outstretched hand! Can you ask for a better deal?

17. **Know mail-order/direct marketing regulations—and obey them!** The regulations are really simple. Don't rip people off! Never promote a lottery, chain letter, pyramid scheme, fake "cures," miracle sex products, etc. by mail. Give a refund quickly, no questions asked. Treat your customers exactly how you'd like to be treated if you sent your money through the mail or ordered a product or service by phone or fax.

18. **Be attentive to any regulators who may contact you.** Regulators—such as postal inspectors, attorney generals, FBI, SEC, etc.—are busy people. If they write or call you they're doing so for a specific purpose. Pay attention to what they say. Answer them immediately and politely. Don't think that if you ignore the question or contact that it will go away. It won't—until you've given a suitable answer. But don't worry—if you're honest, don't rip people off, make refunds quickly, and refuse to engage in any scams—the regulators will soon leave you alone. They have more important cases to handle!

19. **Think—use your head—when dealing with all regulators.** Thus, one mail-order BWB got off to a poor start when he answered a postal inspector's simple question by using a courier service's overnight delivery instead of Express Mail. The postal inspector—who represents the U.S. Postal Service—thought the BWB should have used Express Mail instead of the private competing courier service. The two eventually settled their differences but it took a lot longer than it should have. Think before you act! Always get evidence of delivery when responding to any regulator in writing. How? Send your response via Certified Mail, Return Receipt Requested. If you fax a response to a regulator, save your fax machine printout which gives the date, time, addressee's fax number, and number of pages sent. Send a photocopy of this printout, plus signed copies of your response to the regulator again, via Certified Mail, Return Receipt Requested. Then you have complete records of your timely response to the regulator. Further, the regulator will be impressed with your sincerity and promptness.

20. **Handle customer complaints fast**—don't let the person stew and fret over the poor treatment you've given them. Take immediate action to correct the problem. Tell the

customer what you plan to do—and when he/she can expect the matter to be corrected. Never let a complaint "hang"—get on it and do something to correct the situation—fast! Take charge and let your customer know you've done so.

21. **Give your customers a break—treat them well.** For example, if we ship the wrong item to a customer —as occasionally happens—we take these steps immediately on learning of the error: (1) We apologize to the customer; (2) The customer is told that he/she can keep the item shipped—there's no need to return it to us. This saves the customer the chore of wrapping the item, taking it to the post office, paying for return postage, etc. If the customer says he/she doesn't need the item we tell them to give it to a relative or friend who can use it; (3) The correct item is immediately shipped to the customer via a fast method; (4) As a token of our regret that we made an error we offer the customer the right to receive any of our products up to a certain dollar limit ($25, $50, etc.) FREE, just by calling us on our FREE 800 number and telling us what they want. This approach to customer relations has made us a number of friends and lets the customer know we care about him or her. Try it and see!

22. **Work with customers to make a sale.** Arrange partial payments for expensive items—say those costing over $1,000. Just be sure the customer isn't trying to rip you off by paying only part of the total price for your product or service. Learn to distinguish between "real" people and those looking for a bargain at your expense.

23. **Use testimonials to spark your sales**. When a customer writes you a letter, faxes a compliment, or otherwise tells you you're doing a good job, use his or her statement—with written permission—in your sales literature. Where you can't get written permission to use the statement, use it without the person's name. Instead, give the state where the customer resides. Or give the person's occupation after the quoted material. Just be certain to save the actual written statement in case any regulator comes in on you and demands to see the original. That way "you're covered!"

Get Started Making Your Mailbox Millions Today

You have a great mail-order/direct-marketing career ahead of you. This book gives you 101 great mail-order businesses you can start—and succeed in—using little cash. What's more, as your author and best friend, I'm here to:

1. **Answer your questions—day and night**—on the first ring of my telephone, if you're a subscriber to one of my two newsletters—see the back of this book.
2. **Help you get financing for your business**—without seeking, asking for, or accepting one penny in fees of any kind. Though I've helped BWBs raise millions, I've never taken one penny for the work I did.
3. **Give you frank opinions about ideas you may have** for your business—without you revealing to me the exact nature of your idea, product, or service. If you worry about your idea being stolen, don't bother to call me. I'm much too busy with my own ideas and businesses to even think about borrowing your idea! So keep it to yourself and get advice from someone you "trust."
4. **Possibly finance (through a business loan) your idea** or company. Again, if you're worried about your idea "getting legs," keep it to yourself. Or use a nondisclosure agreement to protect your rights. See your attorney for the wording of the agreement.
5. **Meet with you** in New York City (where we have Wall Street and the Statue of Liberty, among other great attractions) or in your city when I'm on a business or seminar trip to discuss your business. All I ask is that you give me some advance notice of your arrival so we can adjust our schedules to match.

Lastly, your author—who is your good friend—can be reached by subscribers to his newsletter, *International Wealth Success,* at his business telephone number, which is (516) 766-5850, from 8 A.M. 10 P.M. New York time. My dedicated 24-hour fax number is (516) 766-5919. Good luck—I'm here to help *YOU!*

YOUR LIST OF MORE THAN 101 MAIL-ORDER WEALTH OPPORTUNITIES

HERE'S YOUR LIST of more than 101 great mail-order businesses you can start and succeed in on small cash. This list is broken into two parts—Products and Services. In each category the businesses are listed at random, instead of alphabetically. Why did I do this?

Because I find that random lists are stronger at suggesting new, creative ideas to your mind than are alphabetical lists. So look over this list now. I'm sure that the businesses listed will either grab you or suggest other businesses that will!

PRODUCTS YOU CAN SELL BY MAIL ORDER/DIRECT MARKETING:

1. **Books of all types**—education, entertainment, how-to, poetry, drama, etc.
2. **Newsletters**—business, personal, financial, educational, etc.
3. **Contact lenses** for people who replace their lenses every month or so
4. **Videos of all types**—entertainment and/or educational how-to tapes
5. **Computers**—Apple or PCs, new or used for business or personal use

6. **Software for computers** used in personal or business activities

7. **Collectibles**—coins, stamps, statues, signatures, etc.

8. **Miniature lighthouses** and related items—calendars, photos, books, nameplates, etc.

9. **Electronic equipment**—professional or amateur for business or hobbies

10. **Garden seeds** for well-known or unusual plants, vegetables, etc.

11. **Cheeses**—from the simplest Swiss to the most complex Roquefort

12. **Steaks**—thick or thin, beef or pork, lamb or boar—they all sell

13. **Nuts**—salted or unsalted, cashews, walnuts, peanuts, etc.

14. **Popcorn**—the standard brands of the fluffy ones—colored or uncolored

15. **Beers**—from microbreweries or major breweries, in bottles, cans, or kegs

16. **Wines**—domestic or foreign, white, rose, red, they all have enthusiasts

17. **Educational courses**—correspondence or self-study for self-improvement and work skills

18. **Patterns for clothing** for women, children, men for inner and/or outer wear

19. **Toy patterns** for animals, human figures, play things (houses, boats, trains, etc.)

20. **Clothing of all types**—regular dress wear, work clothes, sports wear

21. **Vitamins** for better health, greater energy, improved athletic performance, etc.

22. **Auto parts** for new and used cars, vans, trucks, etc.

23. **Health foods** to improve a person's well-being with better nutrition

24. **Compact disks** for music, stage shows, education, etc.

25. **Boating supplies** of all types for recreational and professional boaters

26. **Home and garden tools and supplies** for people doing work in their "castle"

27. **Flowers of all types**—cut, imitation, waxed, preserved, etc.
28. **Furniture**—home, garden, cottage, boat, vehicle, etc.
29. **Decorations** for the home, auto, trailer, boat, cottage, etc.
30. **Hunting clothes**—parkas, rain coats, jackets, hats, gloves, etc.
31. **Candies**—hard, chocolates, taffy, dessert, caramels, mints, lollipops, butterscotch, etc.
32. **Guns, rifles,** ammunition for police and security personnel
33. **Hunting supplies**—bow and arrows, rifles, traps, cages, blinds, decoys, etc.
34. **Fishing equipment**—rods and reels, hooks, bait, lures, tackle boxes, etc.
35. **Sleep products**—eye shades, blankets, ear plugs, anti-snoring devices, etc.
36. **Flying clothes for pilots**—helmets, jackets, coveralls, scarves, goggles, etc.
37. **House plans** for people seeking to have a home built or wanting to build it themselves
38. **Model airplanes,** parts, plans, supplies, fuels, paints, etc.
39. **Jogging clothes** and supplies—jackets, shirts, shoes, belts, listening devices, timers, etc.
40. **Aircraft equipment** and supplies for recreational and commercial airplanes
41. **Teddy bears** and other lovable animals for collectors
42. **New and used airplanes** for both recreational and commercial buyers
43. **Pet supplies and foods** for dogs, cats, fish, birds, rabbits, etc.
44. **Model plans** for ships, aircraft, autos, tanks, trucks, etc.
45. **Exercise equipment** for home and gym use by people everywhere
46. **Auto tools** for the do-it-yourselfer and professional mechanic
47. **Pilot supplies** for the recreational flyer—charts, navigation instruments, etc.

48. **Sports equipment** for amateurs and professionals
49. **Gourmet coffees and teas** for enthusiasts who want to brew their own at home
50. **Balloons**—for parties, children's gatherings, and other festive events
51. **Calculators for specialized use**—electrical estimating, building "takeoffs," plumbing, etc.
52. **Magazines** and other niche publications for aficionados in various fields
53. **Military models** for former service people and wargamers
54. **Incense** and its various associated apparatus and devices—this is an enormous market
55. **Travel guides** to well-known and little-known parts of the world
56. **T-shirt design and sales** for geographic locations and special events
57. **Recipes** for special foods and gourmet dishes and meals
58. **Frozen fish**—smoked, unsmoked—for fish lovers worldwide
59. **Cooking utensils**—specialized and regular—for home and professional kitchens
60. **Gadgets** for home, hobby, or business—devices that save time and energy
61. **Artist supplies and instructions** for people wanting to learn a certain type of art
62. **Crime prevention devices** and supplies for both the home and business owner
63. **Ice creams and sherbets** shipped frozen to your customers all over the world
64. **Paints and varnishes** for specialized uses—hobbyists, repair shops, etc.
65. **Telephones** and their supplies and gadgets for home and office
66. **Frozen lobsters** shipped via air in dry-iced containers to customers
67. **Legal guides and kits** for do-it-yourselfers seeking to reduce their legal fees

68. **Wood and coal stoves** for environment-conscious back-to-nature enthusiasts

69. **Candles of all types** for home and commercial uses

70. **Mozzarellas of various kinds** shipped to the customer's home or restaurant

71. **"Spy" devices**—hidden TV cameras, listening and recording equipment for business use

72. **Gambling equipment**—cards, boards, wheels, dice, etc., plus instruction books

73. **Astrological charts,** books, forecasts, etc., for people following their stars

74. **Cyberspace products**—instructions, courses, tips, information, etc.

75. **Home tests for health**—pregnancy, AIDS, diabetes, venereal disease, etc.

76. **Horse- and dog-racing** handicap, schedule, and prediction publications

77. **Diet data**—calories, cholesterol, saturated fats, etc.—for weight-conscious folks

78. **Body flattening,** reducing, and slimming products for people seeking the ideal figure

79. **Privacy products** to shield one's identity for people seeking a low profile

80. **Fax machines,** supplies, services, equipment for most effective use

81. **New Age products**—books, charts, predictions, procedures, etc.

82. **Ostrich raising** tips, procedures, information

SERVICES

83. **Clipping service**—where you watch, clip, and send mentions of people, firms, etc.

84. **Family histories** prepared for specific family names, on request

85. **Dating service** where you bring compatible people together

86. **Merchant account help** for merchants seeking to accept credit cards

87. **Foreclosure avoidance advice** and directions for home owners

88. **Credit repair for people** whose credit needs improvement so they can get loans

89. **Investment advice** for the stock market, commodities market, foreign currency, etc.

90. **Raise money for businesses** and individuals for a fee—the second best business

91. **Mortgage cashout guidance** and consulting for people seeking money from a mortgage

92. **Work-at-home advice** and guidance for people confined to their home

93. **Income tax preparation** for businesses and individuals needing this kind of help

94. **Fiction/nonfiction/poetry writing instruction** via the mail with manuscript placement

95. **Obtaining credit cards**—secured and unsecured—for individuals and businesses

96. **Import/export assistance**—preparing documents and shipping instructions

97. **Resume preparation** for job seekers at all levels and all careers needing a resume

98. **900-number rental** to business people seeking to sell via paid incoming calls

99. **Clothing design** for women and men seeking or needing special sizes/fits

100. **Home mortgage reduction service** to help home owners reduce their mortgage cost

101. **Venture capital raising** for promising and seasoned firms having strong growth potential

102. **Teach locksmithing by mail**—there's a steady market for this course

103. **Instruct people in landscape design** by mail—the market is enormous

104. **Get grants for people and companies** by mail—lots of folks seek this service, year round

105. **Teach real estate financing techniques** by mail—money is the universal solvent!

This list of 105 great mail-order/direct-marketing businesses will probably suggest dozens of others to you. For instance, what about photography by mail, correspondence clubs, software-of-the-month service, mailing-list rentals, debt consolidation services, dispute settlement services, etc.? There are thousands of other great mail-order/direct-marketing businesses you can start—and succeed in—on little cash.

If you have an idea you want to check out—call me. I'll give you a fast response. Just remember—I'm your friend, day and night, seven days a week!

PROFIT-BUILDING TOOLS FROM TYLER HICKS' INTERNATIONAL WEALTH SUCCESS LIBRARY

A*S THE PUBLISHER* of the famous *International Wealth Success* newsletter, Ty Hicks has put together a remarkable library of dynamic books, each geared to help the opportunity-seeking individual—the kind of person who is ready and eager to achieve the financial freedom that comes from being a *successful* entrepreneur. Financial experts agree that only those who own their own businesses or invest their money wisely can truly control their future wealth. And yet, far too many who start a business or an investment program of their own do not have the kind of information that can make the difference between success and failure.

Here, then, is a list of publications hand-picked by Ty Hicks, written especially to give you, the enterprising wealth builder, the critical edge that belongs solely to those who have the *inside* track. So take advantage of this unique opportunity to order this confidential information. (These books are *not* available in bookstores.) Choose the publications that can help you the most and send the coupon page with your remittance. Your order will be processed as quickly as possible to expedite your success. (Please note: If, when placing an order, you prefer not to cut out the coupon, simply photocopy the order page and send in the duplicate.)

IWS-1   ***BUSINESS CAPITAL SOURCES.*** Lists more than 1,500 lenders of various types—banks, insurance companies, commercial finance firms, factors, leasing firms, overseas lenders, venture capital firms, mortgage companies, and others. $15. 150 pgs.

IWS-2   ***SMALL BUSINESS INVESTMENT COMPANY DIRECTORY AND HANDBOOK.*** Lists more than 400 small business investment companies that invest in small businesses to help them prosper. Also gives tips on financial management in businesses. $15. 135 pgs.

IWS-3   ***WORLDWIDE RICHES OPPORTUNITIES,*** Vol. 1. Lists more than 2,500 overseas firms seeking products to import. Gives name of product(s) sought, or service(s) sought, and other important data needed by exporters and importers. $25. 283 pgs.

IWS-4   ***WORLDWIDE RICHES OPPORTUNITIES,*** Vol. 2. Lists more than 2,500 overseas firms seeking products to import. (Does NOT duplicate Volume 1.) Lists loan sources for some exporters in England. $25. 223 pgs.

IWS-5   ***HOW TO PREPARE AND PROCESS EXPORT-IMPORT DOCUMENTS.*** Gives data and documents for exporters and importers, including licenses, declarations, free-trade zones abroad, bills of lading, custom duty rulings. $25. 170 pgs.

IWS-6   ***SUPPLEMENT TO HOW TO BORROW YOUR WAY TO REAL ESTATE RICHES.*** Using government sources compiled by Ty Hicks, lists numerous mortgage loans and guarantees, loan purposes, amounts, terms, financing charge, types of structures financed, loan-value ratio, special factors. $15. 87 pgs.

IWS-7   ***THE RADICAL NEW ROAD TO WEALTH*** by A. David Silver. Covers criteria for success, raising venture capital, steps in conceiving a new firm, the business plan, how much do you have to give up, economic justification. $15. 128 pgs.

IWS-8   ***60-DAY FULLY FINANCED FORTUNE*** is a short BUSINESS KIT covering what the business is, how it works, naming the business, interest amortization tables, state securities agencies, typical flyer used to advertise, typical applications. $29.50. 136 pgs.

IWS-9   ***CREDITS AND COLLECTION BUSINESS KIT*** is a 2-book kit covering fundamentals of credit, businesses using credits and collection methods, applications for credit, setting credit limit. Fair Credit Reporting Act, collection percentages, etc. Gives 10 small businesses in this field. $29.50. 147 pgs.

IWS-10   ***MIDEAST AND NORTH AFRICAN BANKS AND FINANCIAL INSTITUTIONS.*** Lists more than 350 such organizations. Gives name, address, telephone, and telex number for most. $15. 30 pgs.

IWS-11   ***EXPORT MAIL-ORDER.*** Covers deciding on products to export, finding suppliers, locating overseas firms seeking exports, form letters, listing of firms serving as export management companies, shipping orders, and more. $17.50. 50 pgs.

IWS-12   ***PRODUCT EXPORT RICHES OPPORTUNITIES.*** Lists over 1,500 firms offering products for export—including agricultural, auto, aviation, electronic, computers, energy, food, health care, mining, printing, and robotics. $21.50. 219 pgs.

IWS-13   ***DIRECTORY OF HIGH-DISCOUNT MERCHANDISE SOURCES.*** Lists more than 1,000 sources of products with full name, address, and telephone number for items such as auto products, swings, stuffed toys, puzzles, oils and lubricants, CB radios, and belt buckles. $17.50. 97 pgs.

IWS-14   ***HOW TO FINANCE REAL ESTATE INVESTMENTS*** by Roger Johnson. Covers basics, the lending environment, value, maximum financing, rental unit groups, buying mobile home parks, and conversions. $21.50. 265 pgs.

IWS-15   ***DIRECTORY OF FREIGHT FORWARDERS AND CUSTOM HOUSE BROKERS.*** Lists hundreds of these firms throughout the United States which help in the import-export business. $17.50. 106 pgs.

IWS-16   ***CAN YOU AFFORD NOT TO BE A MILLIONAIRE?*** by Marc Schlecter. Covers international trade, base of operations, stationery, worksheet, starting an overseas company, metric measures, profit structure. $10. 202 pgs.

IWS-17   ***HOW TO FIND HIDDEN WEALTH IN LOCAL REAL ESTATE*** by R. H. Jorgensen. Covers financial tips, self-education, how to analyze property for renovation, the successful renovator is a "cheapskate," property management, and getting the rents paid. $17.50. 133 pgs.

IWS-18   ***HOW TO CREATE YOUR OWN REAL-ESTATE FORTUNE*** by Jens Nielsen. Covers investment opportunities in real estate, leveraging, depreciation, remodeling your deal, buy- and lease-back, understanding your financing. $17.50. 117 pgs.

IWS-19   ***REAL-ESTATE SECOND MORTGAGES*** by Ty Hicks. Covers second mortgages, how a second mortgage finder works, naming the business, registering the firm, running ads, expanding the business, and limited partnerships. $17.50. 100 pgs.

IWS-20   ***GUIDE TO BUSINESS AND REAL ESTATE LOAN SOURCES.*** Lists hundreds of business and real estate lenders, giving their lending data in very brief form. $25. 201 pgs.

IWS-21   ***DIRECTORY OF 2,500 ACTIVE REAL-ESTATE LENDERS.*** Lists 2,500 names and addresses of direct lenders or sources of information on possible lenders for real estate. $25. 197 pgs.

IWS-22   ***IDEAS FOR FINDING BUSINESS AND REAL ESTATE CAPITAL TODAY.*** Covers raising public money, real estate financing, borrowing methods, government loan sources, and venture money. $24.50. 62 pgs.

IWS-23   ***HOW TO BECOME WEALTHY PUBLISHING A NEWSLETTER*** by E. J. Mall. Covers who will want your newsletter, planning your newsletter, preparing the first issue, direct mail promotions, keeping the books, building your career. $17.50. 102 pgs.

IWS-24   ***NATIONAL DIRECTORY OF MANUFACTURERS' REPRESENTATIVES.*** Lists 5,000 mfrs.' reps. from all over the United States, both in alphabetical form and state by state; gives markets classifications by SIC. $28.80. 782 pgs., hardcover.

IWS-25   ***BUSINESS PLAN KIT.*** Shows how to prepare a business plan to raise money for any business. Gives several examples of successful business plans. $29.50. 150 pgs.

IWS-26   ***MONEY RAISER'S DIRECTORY OF BANK CREDIT CARD PROGRAMS.*** Shows the requirements of each bank listed for obtaining a credit card from the bank. Nearly 1,000 card programs at 500 of the largest U.S. banks are listed. Gives income requirements, job history, specifications, etc. $19.95. 150 pgs.

IWS-27   ***GLOBAL COSIGNERS AND MONEY FINDERS ASSOCIATION.*** Publicize your need for a cosigner to get a business or real estate loan. Your need is advertised widely under a Code Number so your identity is kept confidential. $50.

IWS-28   ***WALL STREET SYNDICATORS.*** Lists 250 active brokerage houses who might take your company public. Gives numerous examples of actual, recent, new stock offerings of startup companies. $15. 36 pgs.

IWS-29   ***COMPREHENSIVE LOAN SOURCES FOR BUSINESS AND REAL ESTATE LOANS.*** Gives hundreds of lenders' names and addresses and lending guidelines for business and real estate loans of many different types. $25. 136 pgs., $8^1/2 \times 11$ in.

IWS-30   ***DIVERSIFIED LOAN SOURCES FOR BUSINESS AND REAL ESTATE LOANS.*** Gives hundreds of lenders' names and addresses and lending guidelines for business and real estate loans of many different types. Does not duplicate IWS-29. $25. 136 pgs., $8^1/2 \times 11$ in.

IWS-31   ***CREDIT POWER REPORTS***—Five helpful reports to improve your credit rating and credit line. Report No. 1: *How to Get a Visa and/or Mastercard Credit Card.* $19.95. 192 pgs., 5×8 in. Report No. 2: *How to Increase Your Credit Limits, Plus Sophisticated Credit Power Strategies.* $19.95. 208 pgs., 5×8 in. Report No. 3: *How to Repair Your Credit.* $19.95. 256 pgs., 5×8 in. Report No. 4: *How to Reduce Your Monthly Payments.* $19.95. 192 pgs., 5×8 in. Report No. 5: *How to Wipe Out Your Debts Without Bankruptcy.* $19.95. 152 pgs. Each book is also available on a cassette tape which duplicates the entire content of the report. The tapes are priced at $19.95 each and run 60 minutes. Please specify which tape you want when ordering; the tape title duplicates the report title.

IWS-32   ***GOOD MONTHLY INCOME.*** Shows how you can sell the books, newsletters, and kits published by IWS to earn commissions starting at 40% and rising to 50% after you reach a sales level of $2,000. Gives examples of how you can advertise and sell these excellent publications to earn significant commission income for yourself. 50 pgs., 8.5×11-in., paperback, $15.00. First Class Shipping $4 extra.

IWS-33   ***HOW TO BUY A BUSINESS WITH NO MONEY DOWN*** by Jeryn W. Calhoun. Gives Step-by-Step Guidance on How to Figure the Value of a Business; Negotiating with the Seller; No-Money-Down Strategies; Dozens of Sample Forms to Help You Buy Right; Startups vs. Existing Businesses; Rules of Thumb for Pricing a Business; Understanding the P & L Statement; Making an Offer That's Right for You; Financing the Business You Buy; Effective Closes When Buying; Legal Considerations for You; Closing Checklist for Any Business. 110 pgs., 8.5×11-in. paperback, $19.50; First Class Shipping $4 extra.

IWS-34   ***HOW TO MAKE A FORTUNE AS A LICENSING AGENT*** by Tyler G. Hicks. Shows the reader how to earn big fees bringing together one company wanting to license its industrial or entertainment products and another seeking to use these products. Gives examples of typical products licensed, agreements covering the license, plus where to find suitable items to license. 66 pgs., 8.5 × 11-in., paperback, $15.00; First Class Shipping $4 extra.

IWS-35 ***HOW TO RUN A PROFITABLE CHILD CARE REFERRAL SERVICE*** by William Frederick. Covers: Introduction to the Child Care Field; Starting Your Child Care Referral Center; Assessing Your Community's Child Care Needs; Recruiting Child Care Providers; Basic Information for Working with Children; Marketing Your Services; Day-to-Day Operations; Considerations in Starting a Day Care Center; Your Child Care Resource Directory. Other important topics covered include: Choosing a Business Name; Where to Conduct Your Business; Working Part- or Full-Time; Advertising for Caretakers; Sample Letter; Caretaker Profiles and Interviews; Records and Forms; plus much more. 64 pgs., 8.5 × 11-in. paperback, $22.95; First Class Shipping $4 extra.

IWS-36 ***SUCCESSFUL FINANCING TECHNIQUES FOR BUSINESS AND REAL ESTATE*** by Tyler G. Hicks. This comprehensive book covers how, and where, to get loans for any business; getting venture capital today; finding free-money grants; going public to get money that never need be repaid; making big money in your own business; proven money-making results for real estate; mail-order success secrets; building riches in exporting. $24.95. 96 pgs. Includes three bonus items related to the book's topics.

IWS-37 ***HOW TO BE A SECOND MORTGAGE LOAN BROKER*** by Richard Brisky. Shows the reader how to make money as a Second Mortgage Loan Broker. Covers these important topics—Why Second Mortgages; How to Get Started; Starting on a Part-Time Basis; The Money Broker/Finder Business; Glossary of Real Estate and Mortgage Terms; How to Get Clients; How to Handle Loan Inquiries; Advance Fees; Commissions; Loan Presentation; Think Like a Lender; What a Difference a Point Makes; The Truth in Lending Law; The Fair Credit Reporting Act; The Equal Credit Opportunity Act; The Fair Debt Collection Practices Act; How to Help Financially Distressed People When You Can't Get Their Loan Approved; You Will Learn Many Things in Dealing with Lenders; Other Prime Loan Projects; Other Types of Loans; Mortgage Payment Tables; It's Almost Time to Get Started; Second Mortgage Money Sources. 90 pgs., 8.5 × 11-in. paperback. $25; First Class Shipping $4 extra.

NEWSLETTERS

IWSN-1   ***INTERNATIONAL WEALTH SUCCESS,*** Ty Hicks' monthly newsletter published 12 times a year. This 16-page newsletter covers loan and grant sources, real estate opportunities, business opportunities, import-export, mail order, and a variety of other topics on making money in your own business. Every subscriber can run one free classified advertisement of 40 words, or less, each month, covering business or real estate needs or opportunities. The newsletter has a worldwide circulation, giving readers and advertisers very broad coverage. Started in January 1967, the newsletter has been published continuously since that date. $24.00 per year. 16 pgs. plus additional inserts, $8^1/_2 \times 11$ in., monthly.

IWSN-2   ***MONEY WATCH BULLETIN,*** a monthly coverage of 100 or more active lenders for real estate and business purposes. The newsletter gives the lender's name, address, telephone number, lending guidelines, loan ranges, and other helpful information. All lender names were obtained within the last week; the data is therefore right up to date. Lenders' names and addresses are also provided on self-stick labels on an occasional basis. Also covers venture capital and grants. $95.00. 20 pgs., $8^1/_2 \times 11$ in., monthly, 12 times per year.

SUCCESS KITS

K-1   ***FINANCIAL BROKER/FINDER/BUSINESS BROKER/ CONSULTANT SUCCESS KIT*** shows YOU how to start your PRIVATE business as a Financial Broker/Finder/Business Broker/Consultant! As a Financial Broker YOU find money for firms seeking capital and YOU are paid a fee. As a Finder YOU are paid a fee for finding things (real estate, raw materials, money, etc.) for people and firms. As a Business Broker YOU help in the buying or selling of a business—again for a fee. See how to collect BIG fees. Kit includes typical agreement YOU can use, plus four colorful membership cards (each 8 × 10 in.). Only $99.50. 12 Speed-Read books, 485 pgs., $8^1/_2 \times 11$ in., 4 membership cards.

K-2   ***STARTING MILLIONAIRE SUCCESS KIT*** shows YOU how to get started in a number of businesses which might make YOU a millionaire sooner than YOU think! Businesses covered in this big kit include Mail Order, Real Estate, Export-Import, Limited Partnerships, etc. This big kit includes four colorful membership cards (each 8 × 10 in.). These are NOT the same ones as in the Financial Broker kit. So ORDER your START-ING MILLIONAIRE KIT now—only $99.50. 12 Speed-Read books, 361 pgs., 8¹/₂ × 11 in., 4 membership cards.

K-3   ***FRANCHISE RICHES SUCCESS KIT*** is the only one of its kind in the world (we believe). What this big kit does is show YOU how to collect BIG franchise fees for YOUR business ideas which can help others make money! So instead of paying to use ideas, people PAY YOU to use YOUR ideas! Franchising is one of the biggest businesses in the world today. Why don't YOU get in on the BILLIONS of dollars being grossed in this business today? Send $99.50 for your FRANCHISE KIT now. 7 Speed-Read books, 876 pgs., 6 × 9 & 8¹/₂ × 11 in. & 5 × 8 in.

K-4   ***MAIL ORDER RICHES SUCCESS KIT*** shows YOU how YOU can make a million in mail order/direct mail, using the known and proven methods of the experts. This is a kit which is different (we think) from any other—and BETTER than any other! It gives YOU the experience of known ex-perts who've make millions in their own mail order busi-nesses, or who've shown others how to do that. This big kit also includes the Ty Hicks' book *How I Grossed More Than One Million Dollars in Mail Order/Direct Mail Starting with NO CASH and Less Knowhow.* So send $99.50 TODAY for your MAIL ORDER SUCCESS KIT. 9 Speed-Read books, 927 pgs., 6 × 9 & 8¹/₂ × 11 in.

K-5   ***ZERO CASH SUCCESS TECHNIQUES KIT*** shows YOU how to get started in YOUR own going business or real estate ven-ture with NO CASH! Sound impossible? It really IS possi-ble—as thousands of folks have shown. This big kit, which includes a special book by Ty Hicks on *Zero Cash Takeovers of Business and Real Estate,* also includes a 58-minute cassette tape by Ty on "Small Business Financing." On this tape, Ty talks to YOU! See how YOU can get started in YOUR own business without cash and with few credit checks. To get your ZERO CASH SUCCESS KIT, send $99.50 NOW. 7 Speed-Read books, 876 pgs., 8¹/₂ × 11 in. for most, 58-minute cas-sette tape.

K-6   ***REAL ESTATE RICHES SUCCESS KIT*** shows YOU how to make BIG money in real estate as an income property owner, a mortgage broker, mortgage banker, real estate investment trust operator, mortgage money broker, raw land speculator, and industrial property owner. This is a general kit, covering all these aspects of real estate, plus many, many more. Includes many financing sources for YOUR real estate fortune. But this big kit also covers how to buy real estate for the lowest price (down payments of NO CASH can sometimes be set up), and how to run YOUR real estate for biggest profits. Send $99.50 NOW for your REAL ESTATE SUCCESS KIT. 6 Speed-Read books, 466 pgs., $8^1/2 \times 11$ in.

K-7   *BUSINESS BORROWERS COMPLETE SUCCESS KIT* shows YOU how and where to BORROW money for any business which interests YOU. See how to borrow money like the professionals do! Get YOUR loans faster, easier because YOU know YOUR way around the loan world! This big kit includes many practice forms so YOU can become an expert in preparing acceptable loan applications. Also includes hundreds of loan sources YOU might wish to check for YOUR loans. Send $99.50 NOW for your BUSINESS BORROWERS KIT. 7 Speed-Read books, 596 pgs., $8^1/2 \times 11$ in.

K-8   *RAISING MONEY FROM GRANTS AND OTHER SOURCES SUCCESS KIT* shows YOU how to GET MONEY THAT DOES NOT HAVE TO BE REPAID IF YOU do the task for which the money was advanced. This big kit shows YOU how and where to raise money for a skill YOU have which can help others live a better life. And, as an added feature, this big kit shows YOU how to make a fortune as a Fund Raiser—that great business in which YOU get paid for collecting money for others or for yourself! This kit shows YOU how you can collect money to fund deals YOU set up. To get your GRANTS KIT, send $99.50 NOW. 7 Speed-Reading books, 496 pgs., $8^1/2 \times 11$ in. for most.

K-9   *FAST FINANCING OF YOUR REAL ESTATE FORTUNE SUCCESS KIT* shows YOU how to raise money for real estate deals. YOU can move ahead faster if YOU can finance your real estate quickly and easily. This is NOT the same kit as the R.E. RICHES KIT listed above. Instead, the FAST FINANCING KIT concentrates on GETTING THE MONEY YOU NEED for YOUR real estate deals. This big kit gives YOU more than 2,500 sources of real estate money all over the U.S. It also shows YOU how to find deals which return BIG income to YOU but are easier to finance than YOU might think! To get started in FAST FINANCING, send $99.50 today. 7 Speed-Read books, 523 pgs., $8^1/2 \times 11$ in. for most.

K-10   *LOANS BY PHONE KIT* shows YOU how and where to get business, real estate, and personal loans by telephone. With just 32 words and 15 seconds of time YOU can determine if a lender is interested in the loan you seek for yourself or for someone who is your client—if you're working as a loan broker or finder. This kit gives you hundreds of telephone lenders. About half have 800 phone numbers, meaning that your call is free of long-distance charges. Necessary agreement forms are also included. This blockbuster kit has more than 150 pgs. $8^1/_2 \times 11$ in. Send $100 *now* and get started in one hour.

K-11   ***LOANS BY MAIL KIT*** shows YOU how and where to get business, real estate, and personal loans for yourself and others by mail. Lists hundreds of lenders who loan by mail. No need to appear in person—just fill out the loan application and send it in by mail. Many of these lenders give unsecured signature loans to qualified applicants. Use this kit to get a loan by mail yourself. Or become a loan broker and use the kit to get started. Unsecured signature loans by mail can go as high as $50,000 and this kit lists such lenders. The kit has more than 150 pgs. $8^1/_2 \times 11$ in. Send $100 *now* to get started in just a few minutes.

K-12   ***REAL-ESTATE LOAN GETTERS SERVICE KIT*** shows the user how to get real estate loans for either a client or the user. Lists hundreds of active real estate lenders seeking first and junior mortgage loans for a variety of property types. Loan amounts range from a few thousand dollars to many millions, depending on the property, its location, and value. Presents typical application and agreement forms for use in securing real estate loans. *No* license is required to obtain such loans for oneself or others. Kit contains more than 150 pgs., $8^1/_2 \times 11$ in. Send $100 *now* to get started.

K-13   ***CASH CREDIT RICHES SYSTEM KIT*** shows the user three ways to make money from credit cards: (1) as a merchant account, (2) helping others get credit cards of their choice, and (3) getting loans through lines of credit offered credit card holders. Some people handling merchant account orders report an income as high as $10,000 a day. While this kit does not, and will not, guarantee such an income level, it *does* show the user how to get started making money from credit cards easily and quickly. The kit has more than 150 pgs., $8^1/_2 \times 11$ in. Send $100 *now* to get started soon.

K-14   ***PROFESSIONAL PRACTICE BUILDERS KIT*** shows YOU how to make up to $1,000 a week part time, over $5,000 a week full time, according to the author, Dr. Alan Weisman. What YOU do is show professionals—such as doctors, dentists, architects, accountants, lawyers—how to bring more clients into the office and thereby increase their income. Step-by-step procedure gets you started. Provides forms, sample letters, brochures, and flyers YOU can use to get an income flowing into your bank in less than one week. The kit has more than 150 pgs., $8^1/_2 \times 11$ in. Send $100 *now!* Start within just a few hours in your local area.

K-15   ***VENTURE CAPITAL MILLIONS KIT.*** Shows how to raise venture capital for yourself or for others. Gives steps for preparing an Executive Summary, business plan, etc. You can use the kit to earn large fees raising money for new or established firms. $100. 200 pgs.

K-16   ***GUARANTEED LOAN MONEY.*** Shows how to get loans of all types—unsecured signature, business, real estate, etc.—when your credit is not the strongest. Gives full directions on getting cosigners, comakers, and guarantors. $100. 250 pgs.

K-17   ***IMPORT-EXPORT RICHES KIT*** shows you how to get rich in import-export in today's product-hungry world. This big kit takes you from your first day in the business to great success. It gives you 5,000 products wanted by overseas firms, the name and address of each firm, procedures for preparing export-import documents, how to correspond in four different languages with complete sentences and letters, names, and addresses of freight forwarders you can use, plus much more. Includes more than 6 books of over 1,000 pages of useful information. $99.50.

K-18   ***PHONE-IN/MAIL-IN GRANTS KIT.*** This concise kit shows the reader how to jump on the grant bandwagon and get small or large money grants quickly and easily. Gives typical grant proposals and shows how to write each so you win the grant you seek. Takes the reader by the hand and shows how to make telephone calls to grantors to find if they're interested in your grant request. You are given the actual words to use in your call and in your proposal. Also includes a list of foundations that might consider your grant application. $100. 200 pgs., $8^1/_2 \times 11$ in.

K-19   ***MEGA MONEY METHODS*** covers the raising of large amounts of money—multimillions and up—for business and real estate projects of all types. Shows how to prepare loan packages for very large loans, where to get financing for such loans, what fees to charge after the loan is obtained, plus much more. Using this kit, the BWB should be able to prepare effective loan requests for large amounts of money for suitable projects. The kit also gives the user a list of offshore lenders for big projects. $100. 200 pgs., $8^1/_2 \times 11$ in.

K-20   ***FORECLOSURES AND OTHER DISTRESSED PROPERTY SALES*** shows how, and where, to make money from foreclosures, trustee sales, IRS sales, bankruptcies, and sheriff sales of real estate. The kit contains six cassette tapes plus a workbook containing many of the forms you need in foreclosure and trustee sales. Addresses of various agencies handling such sales are also given. $51.95. 80 pgs., and 6 cassette tapes, $8^1/_2 \times 11$ in.

K-21   ***SMALL BUSINESS LOAN PROGRAM*** is designed to obtain loans for small and minority-owned businesses doing work for government agencies, large corporations, hospitals, universities, and similar organizations. The small business loan program pays up to 80 percent on accounts receivable within 48 hours to manufacturers, distributors, janitorial services, building contractors, etc. Startups acceptable. You earn a good commission getting these loans funded, and receive an ongoing payment when the company places future accounts receivable with the lender. $100. 200 pgs., $8^1/_2 \times 11$ in.

K-22   ***PHONE-IN MINI-LEASE PROGRAM*** helps you earn commissions getting leases for a variety of business equipment—personal computers, copy machines, typewriters, laser printers, telephone systems, office furniture, satellite antennas, store fixtures, etc. You earn direct commissions of 3 percent to 10 percent of the cost of the equipment up to $10,000. You get immediate approval of the lease by phone and the lender finances the equipment for the company needing it. Your commission is paid by the lender directly to you. $100. 150 pgs., $8^1/_2 \times 11$ in.

ORDER FORM

Dear Ty: Please rush me the following:

☐	IWS-1	*Business Capital Sources*	$15.00	_____
☐	IWS-2	*Small Business Investment*	15.00	_____
☐	IWS-3	*World-wide Riches Vol. 1*	25.00	_____
☐	IWS-4	*World-wide Riches Vol. 2*	25.00	_____
☐	IWS-5	*How to Prepare Export-Import*	25.00	_____
☐	IWS-6	*Real Estate Riches Supplement*	15.00	_____
☐	IWS-7	*Radical New Road*	15.00	_____
☐	IWS-8	*60-Day Fully Financed*	29.50	_____
☐	IWS-9	*Credits and Collection*	29.50	_____
☐	IWS-10	*Mideast Banks*	15.00	_____
☐	IWS-11	*Export Mail-Order*	17.50	_____
☐	IWS-12	*Product Export Riches*	21.50	_____
☐	IWS-13	*Dir. of High-Discount*	17.50	_____
☐	IWS-14	*How to Finance Real Estate*	21.50	_____
☐	IWS-15	*Dir. of Freight Forwarders*	17.50	_____
☐	IWS-16	*Can You Afford No to Be . . . ?*	10.00	_____
☐	IWS-17	*How to Find Hidden Wealth*	17.50	_____
☐	IWS-18	*How to Create Real Estate Fortune*	17.50	_____
☐	IWS-19	*Real-Estate Second Mortgages*	17.50	_____
☐	IWS-20	*Guide to Business and Real Estate*	25.00	_____
☐	IWS-21	*Dir. of 2,500 Active Real Estate Lenders*	25.00	_____
☐	IWS-22	*Ideas for Finding Capital*	24.50	_____
☐	IWS-23	*How to Become Wealthy Pub.*	17.50	_____
☐	IWS-24	*National Dir. Manufacturers' Reps*	28.80	_____
☐	IWS-25	*Business Plan Kit*	29.50	_____
☐	IWS-26	*Money Raiser's Dir. of Bank Credit Card Programs*	19.95	_____
☐	IWS-27	*Global Cosigners and Money Finders Assoc.*	50.00	_____
☐	IWS-28	*Wall Street Syndicators*	15.00	_____
☐	IWS-29	*Comprehensive Loan Sources for Business and Real Estate Loans*	25.00	_____
☐	IWS-30	*Diversified Loan Sources for Business and Real Estate Loans*	25.00	_____
	IWS-31	*Credit Power Reports*		
☐		*Report No. 1*	19.95	_____
☐		*Report No. 2*	19.95	_____
☐		*Report No. 3*	19.95	_____
☐		*Report No. 4*	19.95	_____
☐		*Report No. 5*	19.95	_____
☐	IWS-32	*Good Monthly Income*	15.00	_____
☐	IWS-33	*How to Buy a Business with No Money Down*	19.50	_____
☐	IWS-34	*How to Make a Fortune as a Licensing Agent*	15.00	_____
☐	IWS-35	*How to Run a Profitable Child Care Referral Service*	22.95	_____
☐	IWS-36	*Successful Financing Techniques for Business and Real Estate*	24.95	_____
☐	IWS-37	*How to Be a Second Mortgage Loan Broker*	25.00	_____
☐	IWSN-1	*International Wealth Success*	24.00	_____
☐	IWSN-2	*Money Watch Bulletin*	95.00	_____
☐	K-1	*Financial Broker*	99.50	_____
☐	K-2	*Starting Millionaire*	99.50	_____
☐	K-3	*Franchise Riches*	99.50	_____
☐	K-4	*Mail Order Riches*	99.50	_____
☐	K-5	*Zero Cash Success*	99.50	_____
☐	K-6	*Real Estate Riches*	99.50	_____

Order form is continued on back of this page

☐ K-7	*Business Borrowers*	$99.50	_____
☐ K-8	*Raising Money from Grants*	99.50	_____
☐ K-9	*Fast Financing of Real Estate*	99.50	_____
☐ K-10	*Loans by Phone Kit*	100.00	_____
☐ K-11	*Loans by Mail Kit*	100.00	_____
☐ K-12	*Real-Estate Loan Getters Service Kit*	100.00	_____
☐ K-13	*Cash Credit Riches System Kit*	100.00	_____
☐ K-14	*Professional Practice Builders Kit*	100.00	_____
☐ K-15	*Venture Capital Millions Kit*	100.00	_____
☐ K-16	*Guaranteed Loan Money*	100.00	_____
☐ K-17	*Import-Export Riches Kit*	99.50	_____
☐ K-18	*Phone-in/Mail-in Grants Kit*	100.00	_____
☐ K-19	*Mega Money Methods*	100.00	_____
☐ K-20	*Foreclosures and Other Distressed Property Sales*	51.95	_____
☐ K-21	*Small Business Loan Program*	100.00	_____
☐ K-22	*Phone-in Mini-Lease Program*	100.00	_____

Total Amount of Order _____

Regular Mail:
$3 first book / $1 each addl.
$6 first kit / $4 each addl.
Priority Mail:
$5 first book / $2 each addl.
$11 each kit / $6 each addl.

I am paying by: ☐ Check ☐ MO/Cashier's Check ☐ Visa/MC

Name: _____

Address: _____

City: _____ State: _____ Zip: _____

Visa/MC#: _____ Exp: _____

Signature: _____

Send all orders to: Tyler Hicks
Prima Publishing
P.O. Box 1260HF
Rocklin CA 95677

Or with Visa/MC, call orders at (916) 632-4400 Mon.–Fri. 9 A.M.–4 P.M. PST

INDEX